France in Revolution 1774–1815

DYLAN REES AND DUNCAN TOWNSEND

FIFTH EDITION

HODDER
EDUCATION
AN HACHETTE UK COMPANY

The Publishers thank OCR for permission to use specimen exam questions on pages 49, 75 and 216, from OCR's A Level History A specification H505 © OCR 2014. OCR have neither seen nor commented upon any model answers or exam guidance related to these questions.

The Publishers would like to thank Robin Bunce, Nicholas Fellows, David Ferriby and Sarah Ward for their contribution to the Study Guide.

The Publishers would like to thank the following for permission to reproduce copyright material:

Photo credits: pp10, 18 Bibliothèque national de France; **p31** Roger-Violet/TopFoto; **pp36, 45** Bettmann/Corbis; **pp59, 61, 69, 70** Bibliothèque national de France; **p79** Library of Congress, LC-USZ62-45308; **p85** Roger-Violett/Topfoto; **p88** Bibliothèque national de France; **p89** Bettmann/Corbis; **p91** Hulton Archive/Getty Images; **p105** Bettmann/Corbis; **p107** Library of Congress, LC-USZC2-3607; **p116** Bibliothèque national de France; **p122** Library of Congress, LC-USZ61-635; **p126** Bibliothèque national de France; **p140** Bettmann/Corbis; **p141** Robert Gray; **p156** Bettmann/Corbis; **pp157, 167, 180** Bibliothèque national de France; **p190** The Gallery Collection/Corbis; **p206** Burstein Collection/Corbis.

Acknowledgements: Abacus, *The Terror: Civil War in the French Revolution* by David Andress, 2006. Arnold, *The French Revolution Sourcebook* by John Hardman, 2002. Batsford, *The First French Republic 1792–1804* by M.J. Sydenham, 1974. Blackwell, *The French Revolution 1770–1814* by François Furet, 1988. Cambridge University Press, *The Social Interpretation of the French Revolution* by Alfred Cobban, 1964. Faber & Faber, *Napoleon: Soldier of Destiny* by Michael Broers, 2014. Fontana, *Revolutionary Europe 1783–1815* by George Rudé, 1964. Libris, *Artisans and Sans-culottes* by Gwyn A. Williams, 1989. Macmillan, *A Documentary Survey of the French Revolution* by J.H. Stewart, 1951. Marxists.org, Jean-Paul Marat Archive. Methuen, *France Before the Revolution* by J.H. Shennan, 1983; *Napoleon* by Jean Tulard, 1986. Oxford University Press, *The French Revolution* by J.M. Roberts, 1978; *The Oxford History of the French Revolution* by William Doyle, 1988; *The Parisian Sans-culottes and the French Revolution 1793–4* by Albert Soboul, 1964. Palgrave, *Napoleon Bonaparte and the Legacy of the French Revolution* by Martyn Lyons, 1994. Peregrine Books, *Napoleon: For and Against* by Pieter Geyl, editor, 1976. Routledge & Kegan Paul, *The Counter Revolution, Doctrine and Action 1789–1804* by Jacques Godechot, 1972; *The Directory* by Georges Lefebvre, 1965. Routledge, *The French Revolution: Recent Debates and New Controversies* by Gary Kates, editor, 1998. Simon & Schuster, *The French Revolutions* by Richard Cobb and Colin James, 1988. Thames & Hudson, *The French Revolution: A Concise History* by Norman Hampson, 1975. University of Queensland Press, *The French Revolution: Introductory Documents* by D.I. Wright, editor, 1980. Unwin, *The French Revolution 1787–1799* by Albert Soboul, 1989. Verso, *In Defence of the Terror: Liberty or Death in the French Revolution* by Sophie Wahnich, 2012. Viking, *Citizens: A Chronicle of the French Revolution* by Simon Schama, 1989. Vintage Books, *The Coming of the French Revolution* by Georges Lefebvre, 1947.

Every effort has been made to trace all copyright holders, but if any have been inadvertently overlooked the Publishers will be pleased to make the necessary arrangements at the first opportunity.

Although every effort has been made to ensure that website addresses are correct at time of going to press, Hodder Education cannot be held responsible for the content of any website mentioned in this book. It is sometimes possible to find a relocated web page by typing in the address of the home page for a website in the URL window of your browser.

Hachette UK's policy is to use papers that are natural, renewable and recyclable products and made from wood grown in sustainable forests. The logging and manufacturing processes are expected to conform to the environmental regulations of the country of origin.

Orders: please contact Bookpoint Ltd, 130 Milton Park, Abingdon, Oxon OX14 4SB. Telephone: +44 (0)1235 827720. Fax: +44 (0)1235 400454. Lines are open 9.00a.m.–5.00p.m., Monday to Saturday, with a 24-hour message answering service. Visit our website at www.hoddereducation.co.uk

© Dylan Rees and Duncan Townsend
Fifth edition © Dylan Rees and Duncan Townsend 2015

First published in 2001 by
Hodder Education
An Hachette UK Company
Carmelite House, 50 Victoria Embankment
London EC4Y 0DZ

CLL21289
944.04 REE
IWK

Impression number	10	9	8	7	6	5		
Year			2019	2018	2017			

Cover photo by © Prisma/UIG/Getty Images
Produced, illustrated and typeset in Palatino LT Std by Gray Publishing, Tunbridge Wells
Printed and bound by CPI Group (UK) Ltd, Croydon CR0 4YY

A catalogue record for this title is available from the British Library

ISBN 978 1471839009

France in Revolution

Contents

Dedication

Keith Randell (1943–2002)

The *Access to History* series was conceived and developed by Keith, who created a series to 'cater for students as they are, not as we might wish them to be'. He leaves a living legacy of a series that for over 20 years has provided a trusted, stimulating and well-loved accompaniment to post-16 study. Our aim with these new editions is to continue to offer students the best possible support for their studies.

CHAPTER 1

The origins of the French Revolution

The storming of the Bastille on 14 July 1789 came to symbolise the start of the French Revolution, one of the most dramatic events in modern European history.

The origins of the Revolution were a combination of political, economic and social factors. This chapter examines these factors as two main themes:

★ Long-term causes of the French Revolution

★ Short-term causes of the French Revolution

The key debate on *page 21* of this chapter asks the question: What are the different ways in which the origins of the French Revolution have been interpreted?

Key dates

1614	Last summoning of the Estates-General before 1789		1781–7		Economic crisis
1756–63	The Seven Years' War		1786		Eden Treaty
1774	Accession of Louis XVI		1787	**Feb.**	The Assembly of Notables met
1778	France entered the American War of Independence		1788		Declaration of bankruptcy

 ## 1 Long-term causes of the French Revolution

▶ *How did long-term causes contribute to the outbreak of the Revolution?*

During the ***ancien régime*** there were a number of deep-rooted problems that affected successive royal governments. These problems influenced:

- the way France was governed, particularly the taxation system
- the carefully ordered, yet deeply divided, structure of French society
- the gradual spread of ideas that started to challenge this structure.

These deep-rooted problems can be seen as long-term causes of the French Revolution. In order to understand them fully, it is necessary to understand the nature of French society before 1789, namely:

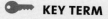 **KEY TERM**

Ancien régime French society and government before the Revolution of 1789.

- the structure of royal government
- the taxation system
- the structure of French society
- the Enlightenment.

Royal government

France before 1789 was an absolute monarchy ruled by the Bourbons. This meant that the authority of the French Crown was not limited by any representative body, such as an elected parliament. The King was responsible only to God and answerable to no one on Earth. This system of government is also known as absolutism. In such a system, the personality and character of the ruler are very important as they set the tone for the style of government.

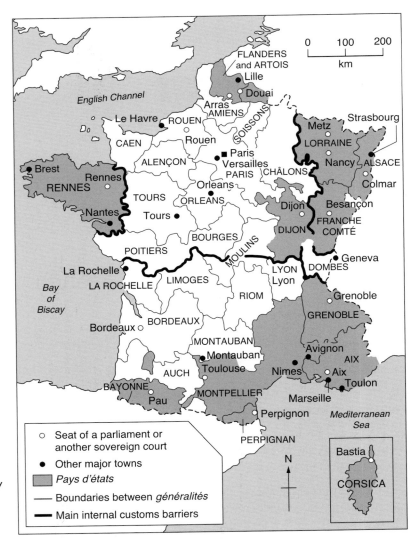

Figure 1.1 Pre-revolutionary France's main administrative, judicial and financial sub-divisions.

In the century before the outbreak of the Revolution there were three French kings: Louis XIV, Louis XV and Louis XVI (see the profile on page 4). Louis XV said in 1766 that 'sovereign power resides in my person alone … the power of legislation belongs to me alone'.

Limitations to power

Although their power was absolute, kings were bound by the laws and customs of their kingdom. For example, there were many independent bodies such as the Assembly of the Clergy which had rights and privileges guaranteed by law. The King could not interfere with these.

The King also had to consult his council of ministers and advisers to make laws. This meant that considerable power was in the hands of a small number of men. The most important of these was the Controller-General, who was in charge of royal finances. Each minister dealt with the King on an individual basis and did not form part of a cabinet system of government.

In the provinces, the King's government was carried out by the *intendants*, who had far-reaching powers in the *généralités*. In 1774 Louis XVI, the grandson of Louis XV, acceded to the French throne. The new King was well intentioned but never came to terms with the State's financial problems. In an absolutist system the monarch needed to be a strong figure with a dominant personality. Louis was rather weak and indecisive.

In 1770 Louis married **Marie Antoinette**, the daughter of the Austrian Empress Maria Theresa. When Louis acceded to the throne in June 1774, the young couple were very popular. Over the following years, however, this popularity dissipated owing to a combination of Marie Antoinette's extravagance (the purchase of a pair of diamond bracelets for 400,000 *livres* in 1776) and a series of scandals. She was portrayed very negatively as the 'Austrian whore'. As the government's debts ballooned, the Queen's fondness for gambling and expensive construction projects suggested that she was widely out of touch with ordinary people. It was believed by many revolutionaries that she influenced the King so that he avoided granting them concessions. Her supporters were labelled the 'Austrian Party' and were suspected of sacrificing the interests of her adopted country for those of her homeland.

The taxation system

Good government benefits greatly from an efficient taxation system that provides it with an adequate income. The taxation system in France was both chaotic and inefficient (see Table 1.1).

Tax collection

Taxes were collected by a system known as **tax farming**. The Farmers-General was a company that collected the indirect taxes for the government. They paid the State an agreed sum and kept for themselves anything collected above this

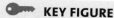

KEY FIGURE

Marie Antoinette (1755–93)

Daughter of the Austrian Empress Maria Theresa, she married Louis in 1770. Suspected of exerting undue influence on her indecisive husband. Nicknamed 'Madame Deficit' because of her extravagant tastes.

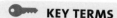

KEY TERMS

Intendants Officials directly appointed by and answerable to the Crown who were mainly responsible for police, justice, finance, public works, and trade and industry.

Généralités The 34 areas into which France was divided for the purpose of collecting taxes and other administrative functions; each area was under the control of an *intendant*.

Livres France's currency during the *ancien régime*. In 1789, 1 *livre* was roughly 8p in today's money.

Tax farming A system where the government agrees a tax assessment figure for an area, which is then collected by a company that bids for the right to collect it.

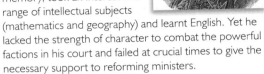

Louis XVI

1754	Born and christened Louis-Auguste
1770	Married Marie Antoinette, daughter of Empress Maria Theresa of Austria
1774	Crowned Louis XVI following the death of his grandfather
1788	Agreed to calls to summon the Estates-General
1789	May, Louis opened the Estates-General at Versailles
	October, Royal family brought forcibly to Paris
1791	20–21 June, 'flight to Varennes'; Louis escaped from Paris
	November, Louis vetoed decrees against the *émigrés* and non-juring priests
1792	10 August, storming of the Tuileries – overthrow of the monarchy
	November, discovery of the *'armoire de fer'* in the Tuileries
	December, trial of Louis
1793	21 January, executed

In the past, historians have portrayed Louis XVI as weak, stupid and indecisive; a man who was ill-suited to the task of governing an absolute state, particularly one with many pressing problems. The view that he was unable to cope with the momentous events unfolding around him has recently been revised. It is acknowledged that Louis had an excellent memory, took an interest in a range of intellectual subjects (mathematics and geography) and learnt English. Yet he lacked the strength of character to combat the powerful factions in his court and failed at crucial times to give the necessary support to reforming ministers.

Louis was clearly aware of the need to resolve his most pressing problems: the lack of revenue and an increasing public debt. When reform plans were submitted to the Assembly of Notables and rejected, he failed to back his ministers and they were dismissed.

Summoning the Estates-General (see page 26) was seen as a sign of desperation, and he again failed to provide leadership. The initiative was seized by the Third Estate while Louis was forced to react to events rather than control them. His attempt to leave France, and the revelation of his true thoughts on the Revolution, further undermined his position. Louis' increasing reliance on the advice of Marie Antoinette confirmed what many suspected, that he lacked leadership skills. The view of one of Louis' biographers, John Hardman, is that Louis was intelligent, hard-working and possessed the sort of skills (financial and naval) which were required by an eighteenth-century French king. In the end he was overwhelmed by the financial crisis and his inability to resolve it.

figure. The French government consequently never received enough money from taxes to cover its expenditure, and so frequently had to borrow. Interest rate payments on the debt became an increasingly large part of government expenditure in the eighteenth century.

SOURCE A

An entry from the private diary of l'Abbé de Veri, 1780.

Louis XVI may be seen passing each morning in his room, observing with his telescope those who arrive at Versailles. He often occupies himself in sweeping and nailing and repairing locks. He has common sense, simple tastes, an honest heart and a sound conscience. That is his good side. On the other hand he has a tendency to indecision, he possesses a rather weak will and he is incapable of ruling effectively. He also lacks an ability to fully appreciate the significance of what is occurring around him.

Read Source A. According to the Abbé de Veri, why might Louis be unsuited to the role of king?

Table 1.1 The main taxes imposed during the *ancien régime*. For a description of the three estates, see pages 6–10

Tax	Description	Indirect (levied on goods)/ direct (levied on incomes)	Who was taxed?
Taille	Land tax – the main direct tax	Direct	In theory, the Third Estate, although in reality, some people had been granted exemption by the Crown, so it was mainly the peasants who were taxed
Vingtième	Five per cent tax on income	Direct	Third Estate
Capitation	Tax on people – frequently called the poll tax	Direct	In theory, Second and Third Estates
Gabelle	Salt tax	Indirect	Everyone
Aidas	Tax on food and drink	Indirect	Everyone
Octrois	Tax on goods entering a town	Indirect	Everyone

 **KEY FIGURE**

Anne-Robert-Jacques Turgot (1727–81)

As Controller General (1774–6), was one of the first of Louis' ministers to attempt to reform French finances. He failed owing to a combination of powerful vested interests and a lack of support from Louis.

Many of the taxes were collected by officials who, under a system known as **venality**, had bought the right to hold their positions. They could not therefore be dismissed. Corruption and wastage were vast, and resulted in the Crown not receiving an adequate income, while the taxpayers knew that much of the tax they paid never reached the treasury.

On his accession in 1774 Louis XVI was aware of many of the problems affecting the finances of the State. He appointed **Turgot** as Controller-General. Turgot was influenced by the ideas of the *philosophes* and embarked on a reform programme. His attempts to abolish the trade **guilds** and the *corvée* and to reform the tax system provoked such a storm of protest from the *parlements* and other interested parties that Louis, for the sake of harmony, withdrew his support and Turgot left office.

The bulk of royal revenue was made up of taxation, yet because of the system of exemptions the Crown was denied an adequate income with which to govern the country. In order to meet the demands of war, the Crown was forced to borrow money. Tax farming meant that not all the revenue paid actually reached the treasury. The issue of taxation weakened the Crown and created resentment among the Third Estate, which bore the burden of tax payment. This was one of the most important long-term causes of the Revolution.

 **KEY TERMS**

Venality The sale and purchase of certain jobs which could be inherited by descendants.

Philosophes A group of writers and thinkers who formed the core of the French Enlightenment.

Guild An organisation that tightly controls entry into a trade.

Corvée Unpaid labour service to maintain roads. In many places money replaced the service.

Parlements The 13 high courts of appeal. All edicts handed down by the Crown had to be registered by the *parlements* before they could be enforced as law.

French society during the *ancien régime*

On the eve of the Revolution it was estimated that the population of France was about 27.5 million. French society in the eighteenth century was divided into three orders known as the Estates of the Realm. The first two estates had many privileges that they frequently used to the disadvantage of the Third Estate. Over the course of the eighteenth century, divisions appeared between and within the estates, and this became a long-term cause of the Revolution.

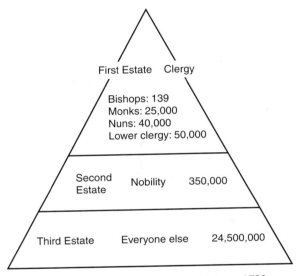

First Estate Clergy

Bishops: 139
Monks: 25,000
Nuns: 40,000
Lower clergy: 50,000

Second Estate   Nobility   350,000

Third Estate   Everyone else   24,500,000

Figure 1.2 The structure of the *ancien régime* c.1780.

The First Estate

The First Estate was the clergy, which consisted of members of religious orders (monks and nuns) and clergy (parish priests). A number of issues contributed to the Church being unpopular with many people. These were:

- plurality and absenteeism
- tithes
- exemption from taxes
- power over the people.

Plurality and absenteeism

Many younger sons of noble families entered the Church and occupied its higher posts, such as bishops and archbishops, which provided large incomes. The Archbishop of Strasbourg received an annual 400,000 *livres*, which contrasted sharply with most parish priests (*curés*) who received only between 700 and 1000 *livres*. Some bishops held more than one bishopric, which meant that they were bishops of more than one **diocese**. This is called **plurality**. Many never visited their diocese: a practice known as absenteeism. This made the Church

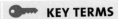

KEY TERMS

Diocese An area served by a bishop. It is made up of a large number of parishes.

Plurality The holding of more than one bishopric or parish by an individual.

very unpopular with many ordinary people who considered that bishops were more interested in wealth than in the religious and spiritual needs of the people.

Tithes

The wealth of the Church came from the land it owned and the tithes paid to it. It was the largest single landowner in France, owning about ten per cent of the land.

The tithe was a charge paid to the Church each year by landowners and was based on a proportion of the crops they produced. This charge varied widely. In Dauphine it amounted to about one-fiftieth of the crops produced, while in Brittany it was a quarter. In most parts of France it was about seven per cent of the crop. The income produced by the tithe provided the Church with 50 million *livres* each year.

Tithes were supposed to provide for parish priests, poor relief and the upkeep of Church buildings, but much of it went instead into the pockets of bishops and abbots. This was greatly resented by both the peasantry and the ordinary clergy and was one of the most common grievances made in their **cahiers** in 1788.

Exemption from taxes

The Church had many privileges apart from collecting the tithe. By far the most important of these was its exemption from taxation. This added to its unpopularity. Its income from property was immense: around 100 million *livres* per year in the closing years of the *ancien régime*. Instead of paying tax the Church agreed to make an annual payment, which it determined, known as the *don gratuit*. It was under five per cent of the Church's income and was much less than it could afford to pay.

Power over the people

France was a very religious country and Catholicism was the official state religion. The influence of the Church was considerable and touched many areas of people's lives. The Church had wide-ranging powers of censorship over books that were critical of it, provided poor relief, hospitals and schools, and kept a list in the parish of all births, marriages and deaths. At a time when communication in general was very poor, the Church acted as a sort of Ministry of Information for the government when parish priests informed their congregations about various policies and initiatives. The vast wealth of the Church and its resistance to new ideas made it unpopular with many people, which contributed to the long-term causes of the Revolution.

The Second Estate

Of the three estates, the nobility was the most powerful. Unlike the British nobility, which were numbered in the hundreds, the French nobility numbered hundreds of thousands, although the exact numbers are disputed. Figures for

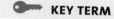 **KEY TERM**

Cahiers Lists of grievances and suggestions for reform drawn up by representatives of each estate and each community and presented to the Estates-General for consideration.

the numbers of nobles by 1789 vary between 110,000 and 350,000. Within the nobility there were great variations in wealth and status:

- The most powerful were the 4000 court nobility, restricted in theory to those whose noble ancestry could be traced back to before 1400; in practice to those who could afford the high cost of living at **Versailles**.
- Second in importance were the *noblesse de robe*: legal and administrative nobles which included the 1200 magistrates of the *parlements*.
- The remainder of the nobility – the overwhelming majority – lived in the country in various states of prosperity. Under the law of primogeniture a landed estate was inherited by the eldest son. Younger sons were forced to fend for themselves and many joined the Church, the army or the administration.

The main source of income for the Second Estate was land, and it owned between a third and a quarter of France. Nearly all the main positions in the State were held by nobles, among them government ministers, *intendants* and upper ranks in the army.

Privileges

In addition to holding most of the top jobs in the State, nobles had many privileges. These included the following:

- They were tried in their own courts.
- They were exempt from military service.
- They were exempt from paying the *gabelle*.
- They were exempt from the *corvée* (forced labour on the roads).
- They received a variety of **feudal** (also known as *seigneurial*) **dues**.
- They had exclusive rights to hunting and fishing.
- In many areas they had the monopoly right (known as banalities) to operate mills, ovens and wine presses.

Perhaps the nobles' greatest privilege was exemption from taxation. Until 1695 they did not pay direct taxes at all. In that year the capitation was introduced and, in 1749, the *vingtième*. Even with these they managed to pay less than they could have done. They were generally exempt from the most onerous tax of all: the *taille*.

Provincial nobles, who were unlikely to be very wealthy, were strongly attached to these privileges, which represented a significant part of their income. They felt that if they were to lose their tax privileges and their seigneurial rights, they would face ruination. Consequently, they were determined to oppose any changes that threatened their position and undermined their privileges. The privileges relating to land ownership and tax exemption were resented by many ordinary people who saw the Second Estate as avoiding their share of the tax burdens borne by others. These issues contributed to the causes of the Revolution.

Joining the nobility

There were various ways of becoming a noble besides the obvious one of inheritance. One of the main ways of acquiring noble status was either by direct appointment from the King or by buying certain offices that carried hereditary titles. These were called venal offices and there were 12,000 of these in the service of the Crown. They carried titles that could be bought, sold or inherited like any other property. Although there were significant benefits to gaining noble status there were also some limitations, the most important of which was that noblemen were not, in theory, allowed to take part in industrial or commercial activities since this would mean they would suffer derogation (loss of their nobility). In reality many did, as the rule was not rigidly enforced.

The Third Estate

In essence, the Third Estate consisted of everyone who did not belong to one or other of the two privileged estates. There were enormous extremes of wealth within this estate.

The bourgeoisie

At the top end were the rich merchants, industrialists and business people. This group of rich commoners, who were not peasants or urban workers, is frequently referred to as the **bourgeoisie**. Among the wealthiest of the bourgeoisie were the merchants and traders who made vast fortunes out of France's overseas trade. Others included financiers, landowners, members of the liberal professions (doctors and writers), lawyers and civil servants. Many were venal office-holders.

As a group, the bourgeoisie was rising not only in wealth but also in numbers. There was a threefold increase in the number of bourgeoisie over the course of the eighteenth century to 2.3 million. Although the bourgeoisie was increasing in importance, there was no real conflict between with the nobility until at least the closing years of the *ancien régime*. The bourgeoisie did, however, feel that its power and wealth should in some way be reflected in the political system as it bore such a substantial part of the tax revenue paid to the Crown. This slowly simmering resentment was one of long-term causes of the Revolution.

The peasantry

At the other extreme of the Third Estate from the bourgeoisie were the peasantry. They were by far the most numerous section of French society, comprising about 85 per cent of the population. This group, however, covered enormous variations in wealth and status.

At the top end was a small group of large farmers who owned their land and employed labourers to produce food to sell to others. More numerous were the labourers who existed at, or near, subsistence levels. For much of the eighteenth century they, and the larger farmers, did well as agricultural conditions were

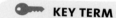 **KEY TERM**

Bourgeoisie Middle-class urban dwellers who made a living through their intellectual skills or business practices.

favourable, particularly in the 1770s. Half of the peasants were sharecroppers who did not own their land but farmed it and gave half of their crops to the landlords instead of rent. About a quarter of the peasants were landless labourers, who owned nothing but their house and garden.

In some parts of France **serfdom** continued to exist. There were a million serfs in the east, mainly in Franche Comté. They were at the bottom of the social structure and their children were unable to inherit even personal property

KEY TERM

Serfdom A system in which people were the property of the landowner.

Look at Source B. Which estate do you think the cartoonist sympathises with?

SOURCE B

A contemporary cartoon showing a peasant crushed by the weight of taxes and dues such as the *taille* and *corvée*, imposed by the privileged First and Second Estates.

without paying considerable dues to their lord. Poor peasants lived in a state of chronic uncertainty. Bad weather or illness could push them into the ranks of the vagrants, who lived by begging, stealing and occasional employment.

Grievances

As the largest group in society, the peasants bore the burden of taxation and this made them extremely resentful. All peasants had to pay a tithe to the Church, feudal dues to their lord and taxes to the State. Nearly all land was subject to feudal dues. These included the *corvée, champart* (a due paid in grain or other crops to the landlord which could vary from five to 33 per cent of the harvest) and *lods et ventes* (a payment to the *seigneur* when property changed hands).

A further grievance was that the peasant could be tried in the seigneurial court, where the lord acted as both judge and jury.

Taxes paid to the State included the *taille*, capitation and *gabelle*. All these increased enormously between 1749 and 1783 to pay for the various wars France was involved in. Taxes took between five and ten per cent of the peasants' income. The heaviest burden on the peasants was the rent they paid to their landlords. This increased markedly during the second half of the eighteenth century as a result of the increase in population, which is estimated to have risen from 22.4 million in 1705 to 27.9 million in 1790. This increased the demand for farms, with the result that landlords could raise rents. The increasing financial burden placed on the peasantry, along with growing resentment of the feudal system, was an important long-term cause of the Revolution.

Urban workers

The remaining part of the Third Estate was made up of urban workers. Small property owners and **artisans** in Paris were known as **sans-culottes**. The majority of workers in the towns lived in crowded insanitary housing blocks known as tenements. They were unskilled and poor.

On the other hand, skilled craftsmen were organised into guilds. In Paris in 1776, 100,000 workers – a third of the male population – belonged to guilds. The standard of living of wage-earners had slowly fallen in the eighteenth century, as prices had risen on average by 65 per cent between 1726 and 1789, but wages by only 22 per cent. In the years immediately preceding the Revolution the worsening economic situation caused considerable resentment among urban dwellers and contributed to the long-term causes of the Revolution. This helps to explain their readiness to become involved in the popular demonstrations that helped to bring about the overthrow of the *ancien régime*.

 **KEY TERMS**

Artisan A skilled worker or craftsman.

Sans-culottes Literally 'those without knee-breeches': those who wore trousers and were classed as workers. It was later used as a label to identify the more extreme urban revolutionaries of 1792–5.

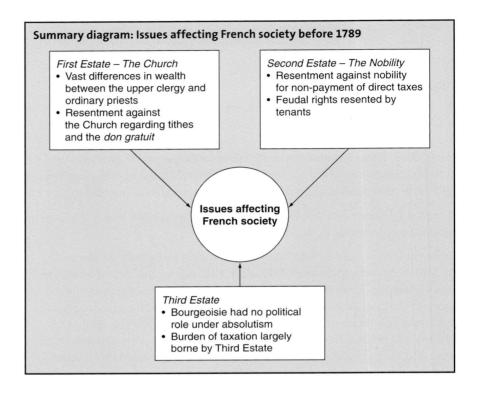

The Enlightenment

During the course of the eighteenth century there emerged in Europe an intellectual movement of writers and thinkers known as the Enlightenment. The movement questioned and challenged a whole range of views and ideas that, at the time, were widely accepted – particularly relating to religion, nature and absolute monarchy. Their analysis of society was based on reason and rational thought, rather than superstition and tradition.

In France these intellectuals were known as the *philosophes* and were writers rather than philosophers. The most famous were Voltaire, Montesqieu and Rousseau. They wrote on the problems of the day and attacked the prejudice and superstition they saw around them. Many of them contributed to the most important work of the French Enlightenment, *The Encyclopaedia* (edited by Diderot, the first volume appeared in 1752, the last of 35 in 1780).

Aims of the *philosophes*

The aim of the *philosophes* was to apply rational analysis to all activities. They were not prepared to accept tradition or revelation, as in the Bible, as a sufficient reason for doing anything. They were much more in favour of liberty – of the press, of speech, of trade, of freedom from arbitrary arrest – than of equality, although they did want equality before the law. The main objects of their attack were the Church and despotic government. The *philosophes* did not accept the literal interpretation of the Bible and rejected anything that could not be explained by reason – miracles, for example – as superstitious. They condemned the Catholic Church because it was wealthy, corrupt and intolerant, and took up Voltaire's cry of '*Écrasez l'infâme*' ('crush the infamous' – meaning the Church).

The *philosophes*, while clearly critical of many aspects of the *ancien régime*, were not essentially opposed to the regime and they were not therefore revolutionary. Yet they did have an impact on the outbreak of the Revolution. Their ideas attacked all the assumptions on which the *ancien régime* was based. They challenged and helped to undermine one of the key pillars of the old order, namely the position of the Church and the role of the King as God's servant. Although not revolutionary themselves, their ideas and approaches did influence many who would become revolutionaries.

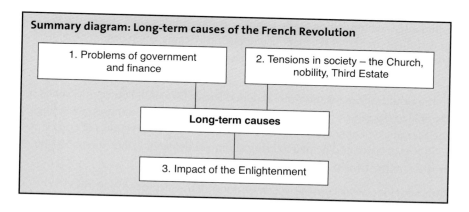

Summary diagram: Long-term causes of the French Revolution

- 1. Problems of government and finance
- 2. Tensions in society – the Church, nobility, Third Estate

Long-term causes

3. Impact of the Enlightenment

2 Short-term causes of the French Revolution

▶ *What short-term factors brought about the crisis that sparked the Revolution?*

In the ten years before the outbreak of the Revolution in 1789, a number of issues, crises and events contributed to the downfall of the *ancien régime* and should be viewed alongside the long-term causes. The main short-term causes were:

- foreign policy
- financial crisis
- political crisis
- economic crisis.

Foreign policy

The Seven Years' War

Since the fifteenth century, France had more often than not had a hostile relationship with both Britain and Austria. Britain was viewed as France's only serious colonial rival and Austria was a rival for the dominance of mainland Europe. By the middle of the eighteenth century, France and Austria had resolved their differences and were allies when the Seven Years' War (1756–63) broke out in 1756. During the course of this war, French forces in India and North America suffered a series of crushing defeats at the hands of the British. Much of France's overseas empire was lost in 1763, although the profitable sugar-producing islands of Martinique and Guadeloupe, and some other lesser territories, were retained.

The American War of Independence

Following the humiliation at the hands of Britain and its ally Prussia, the French government dreamt of revenge. The opportunity came when Britain became involved in a bitter quarrel with its thirteen North American colonies, who rebelled against British rule.

In the resulting American War of Independence (1776–83), France intervened on the side of the rebels, providing both financial and military support, including the Marquis de Lafayette (see profile on page 79). The intervention of France in 1778 was decisive and helped to bring about the defeat of British forces and the creation of the United States of America.

Although France was unable to recover most of the territory lost during the Seven Years' War, the Treaty of Versailles (1783) did satisfy French honour. Few at the time, however, could foresee what the real cost of the war would be: revolution in France. The war cost a great deal of money and in the short term worsened the already weak financial situation of the Crown. French soldiers who had fought in the war had been exposed to ideas such as liberty and democracy and many, on their return home, demanded similar rights for the people of France.

Financial crisis

The main short-term cause of the French Revolution was the financial crisis. By far the most important aspect of this was the huge **deficit** that the government was building up. On 20 August 1786 **Calonne**, the Controller-General, told Louis XVI that the government was on the verge of bankruptcy. Revenue for 1786 would be 475 million *livres*, while expenditure would be 587 million *livres*, making a deficit of 112 million – almost a quarter of the total income. A much more detailed and alarming picture of the situation is provided in the Treasury account of 1788, which has been called the first and last budget of the monarchy (see Table 1.2).

Table 1.2 Royal income and expenditure 1788 (millions of *livres*)

Royal income	Royal expenditure	
	Education and poor relief	12
	Court expenses	36
	Other civil expenditure	98
	Military – army and navy	165
	Debt interest	318
Total 503	**Total**	**629**

The deficit had increased in two years to 126 million *livres* – twenty per cent of total expenditure. It was anticipated that for 1789, receipts would amount to only 325 million *livres* and that the interest payments on the deficit would amount to 62 per cent of the receipts. There are two reasons to explain why there was a deficit and a financial crisis in France:

- *War.* Between 1740 and 1783 France was at war for twenty years, first in the War of Austrian Succession (1740–8), then the Seven Years' War (1756–63) and finally the American War of Independence (1778–83). The cost of helping the American colonists to defeat the British government was approximately 1066 million *livres*. **Jacques Necker**, the finance minister, financed the war by raising loans. While this did not directly lead to revolution, the lack of an elected parliament to guarantee loans, as in Britain, did not give lenders confidence.

- *Tax.* The Crown was not receiving much of the tax revenue (see page 8), and until it recovered control of its finances, no basic reforms could occur. The privileged classes, whose income from property had increased, were an untapped source of revenue that the Crown urgently needed to access. There would, however, be powerful resistance to any change in the taxation structure from those with vested interests in retaining the *status quo*.

 **KEY FIGURE**

Jacques Necker (1732–1804)

A Genevan banker who was in charge of France's finance on a number of occasions. Popular because of his ability to raise loans and thereby avoid creating new taxes.

SOURCE C

From Marquis de Bouillé, quoted in Richard Cobb and Colin James, *The French Revolutions*, Simon & Schuster, 1988, p. 20. Bouillé was a royalist supporter and military commander in 1789.

The most striking of the country's troubles was the chaos in its finances, the result of years of extravagance intensified by the expense of the American War of Independence, which had cost the state over twelve hundred million livres. No one could think of any remedy but a search for fresh funds, as the old ones were exhausted. M. de Calonne the Minister of Finance conceived a bold and wide-reaching plan. Without either threatening the basis of the French monarchy, this plan changed the previous system of financial administration and attacked the vices at their root. The worst of these problems was the arbitrary system of allocation, the oppressive costs of collection, and the abuses of privilege by the richest section of taxpayers. The whole weight of public expenditure was borne by the most numerous but least wealthy part of the nation which was crushed by the burden.

In Source C, what does Bouillé consider to be the main cause of the financial problems affecting France?

Reform

Following Necker's dismissal in 1781, his successor Joly de Fleury discovered the true nature of France's finances. The Treasury was 160 million *livres* short for 1781 and 295 million *livres* short for 1782. To make good the shortfall, Fleury and his successor, Calonne, undid much of Necker's work by resuming the practice of selling offices (many of which Necker had abolished). They both also borrowed much more heavily than Necker.

SOURCE D

From Alexis de Tocqueville, *L'Ancien Régime et la Révolution*, Michel Lévy Frères, 1856. De Tocqueville (1805–59) was one of the first historians to offer an incisive analysis of the origins of the Revolution.

It is not always by going from bad to worse that a society falls into revolution. It happens most often that a people, which has supported without complaint the most oppressive laws, violently throws them off as soon as their weight is lightened. Experience shows that the most dangerous moment for a bad government is generally when it sets about reform.

In 1786, with loans drying up, Calonne was forced to grasp the nettle and embark on a reform of the tax system. His plan consisted of an ambitious three-part programme:

- The main proposal was to replace the capitation and the *vingtième* on landed property by a single land tax. It was to be a tax on the land and not on the person, and would therefore affect all landed proprietors – Church, noble and common alike – regardless of whether the lands were used for luxury purposes or crops. There were to be no exemptions; everyone including the nobles, the clergy and the ***pays d'états*** would pay.
- The second part of the programme was aimed at stimulating the economy to ensure that future tax revenues would increase. To try and achieve this, Calonne proposed abandoning controls on the grain trade and abolishing internal customs barriers, which prevented the free movement of grain from one part of France to another.
- The final part of the programme was to try to restore national confidence so that new loans for the short term could be raised. By doing this Calonne hoped that the *parlements* would be less likely to oppose the registration of his measures. His plan was to achieve some display of national unity and consensus.

The failure of the reform process

The **Estates-General** was the obvious body to summon to approve the reforms, as it was representative of the nation. However, this was rejected as being too

---

In Source D, what does de Toqueville suggest was responsible for the outbreak of the Revolution?

 **KEY TERMS**

Pays d'états Areas that had local representative assemblies of the three estates that contributed to the assessment and collection of royal taxes.

Estates-General Elected representatives of all three estates of the realm. This body was only summoned in times of extreme national crisis, and had last met in 1614.

unpredictable. Calonne and Louis XVI opted instead for a handpicked Assembly of **Notables**. It was anticipated that this would be a pliant body who would willingly agree to rubberstamp the reform package.

The 144 members of the Assembly met in February 1787. They included leading members of the *parlements*, princes, leading nobles and important bishops. On examining the proposals it became clear that they would not collaborate with Calonne and Louis in agreeing the reforms. As representatives of the privileged order they had the most to lose from them.

The Notables were not opposed to all change and agreed that taxation should be extended to all. They claimed that the approval of the nation was needed for Calonne's reforms and urged the summoning of the Estates-General, which had last met in 1614. Realising the strength of opposition to Calonne, Louis dismissed him in April 1787.

Political crisis

Calonne was replaced by one of the Notables, Loménie de Brienne, Archbishop of Toulouse, while another Notable, Lamoignon, president of the *Parlement* of Paris, became head of the judiciary. The Assembly of Notables proved to be no more co-operative with Brienne than it had been with Calonne.

Brienne retained Calonne's land tax and introduced a number of new reforms following on from Necker's earlier plans. These were:

- an end to venal financial officials
- a new central treasury
- laws codified in a printed form accessible to those who needed to consult them
- educational reform
- religious toleration
- reforming the army to make it more efficient and less expensive.

When Brienne presented his reforms to the *Parlement* of Paris for registration, it refused and said that only the Estates-General who represented the whole nation could consent to any new taxes. Louis' reaction was to exile the *Parlement* to Troyes on 15 August.

Louis' action was considered to be high handed and the result was an aristocratic revolt, which proved to be the most violent opposition the government had yet faced. There were riots in some of the provincial capitals where the *parlements* met, such as Rennes in Brittany and Grenoble in Dauphine. In all parts of the country nobles met in unauthorised assemblies to discuss action in support of the *parlements*.

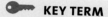

KEY TERM

Notables Rich, powerful individuals; the elite who controlled the political and economic life of France.

SOURCE E

? What is the cartoonist suggesting in Source E?

BUFFET
DE
LA COUR
Calonne 'Audinier'

Contemporary French cartoon depicting the Assembly of Notables as birds. President Monkey (Calonne) addresses the Notables and asks them with which sauce they would like to be eaten. Animals were frequently used to depict people as they were considered to be much less intelligent than humans.

An assembly of the clergy also joined in on the side of the *parlements*, breaking its long tradition of loyalty to the Crown. It condemned the reforms and voted a *don gratuit* of less than a quarter the size requested by the Crown.

Although the opposition was fragmented and dispersed, it continued because of the collapse of the government's finances. At the beginning of August 1788 the royal treasury was empty. Brienne agreed, with Louis' reluctant approval, to summon the Estates-General for 1 May 1789. On 16 August 1788 Brienne suspended all payments from the royal treasury, in effect acknowledging that the Crown was bankrupt. The previous year, the then navy minister, the Marquis de Castries, had perceptively told the King, 'As a Frenchman I want the Estates-General, as a minister I am bound to tell you that they might destroy your authority.'

In September 1788 Louis was forced to back down and allow the Paris *parlement* to return. Following the resignations of Brienne and Lamoignon, the King recalled Necker, in the belief that he was the only one who could restore the government's credit and raise new loans. Necker abandoned his predecessor's reform plans and, while indicating that he would try to raise new loans, stated that he would do nothing until the Estates-General had met.

The crisis had shown the limitations of royal power. Although Louis was in effect an absolute ruler, in reality he was unable to impose his government's reforms on the State. The forces of opposition detected clear signs of weakness in the Crown. The failure to secure reform contributed to a paralysis of the government. In the short term this was very significant, particularly when linked to the economic crisis.

Economic crisis

In the years immediately preceding the outbreak of the Revolution in 1789 the French economy faced a number of crises. The economy was largely based on agriculture and this sector had grown steadily between the 1730s and 1770s. Good harvests had resulted in food surpluses which in turn contributed to an increase in population as people were fed and healthy and more able to withstand diseases.

Bad harvests

During the 1780s the general agricultural prosperity came suddenly to an end. This was brought about by a series of disastrous harvests in 1778–9, 1781–2, 1785–6 and 1787. In 1788 there was a major disaster. There was a very wet spring and freak hailstones in many areas in July resulted in a very poor harvest. This was particularly disastrous for peasants who produced wine as a cash crop. A poor harvest in a pre-industrial society always led to massive unemployment.

The resulting rise in the price of food led to:

- a lower demand for manufactured goods, as more income had to be spent on food
- a significant increase in the price of bread – a key staple food.

Over the period 1726 to 1789 wheat prices increased by about 60 per cent. In normal times it is estimated that about half a labourer's daily wage might be spent on bread. During the severe winter of 1788–9 this proportion was increased to 88 per cent.

The picture in other sectors of the economy was equally gloomy. Production and employment in the textile industries, which accounted for half of industrial production, fell by 50 per cent in 1789. The industry had been badly hit by the Eden Treaty of 1786 which allowed imports of British goods, including textiles, at reduced rates of import duties. This further affected a group who were already suffering economic hardship. The market for wine was also very poor since rising bread prices meant that there was less money to spend on this and other goods. Unemployment was rising at the same time as the cost of living and, as production was either stagnant or falling, workers were unable to increase their wages.

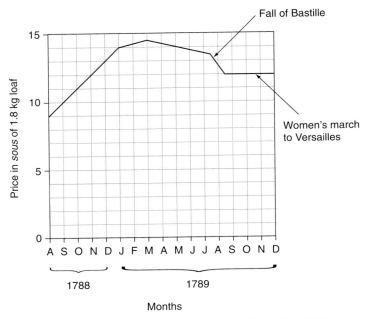

Figure 1.3 Bread prices in Paris, August 1788 to December 1789.

Food shortages

Many ordinary people blamed tithe-owners and landowners for making the situation worse. They were accused of hoarding grain and speculating on prices rising during times of shortage, thereby contributing to the lack of food. In many areas there were food riots and disturbances as people attacked grain stores. These were most frequent in the spring and summer of 1789 when grain prices were at their peak, before the new harvest had been collected.

Many ordinary people in both rural and urban areas believed that the economic crisis was in part the fault of the nobility. Increasing disturbances against the nobility encouraged many ordinary people to take the first tentative steps towards direct political action. The **politicisation** of the majority of the Third Estate began as a result of the economic crisis. Louis' handling of the political crisis further exacerbated the situation in the eyes of ordinary people.

The deep-rooted long-term problems of the *ancien régime*, considered in the first part of this chapter, came to a head in the years immediately preceding 1789. Short-term causes such as poor harvests and rising bread prices helped to bring this about. The attempts at reform were an acknowledgement that changes were needed; the failure of the process showed the depth of the divisions within French society. When the French monarchy declared itself bankrupt and the Assembly of Notables refused to approve the reforms proposed by the King's ministers, the way was paved for the summoning of the Estates-General. Much was expected from this body by all parties.

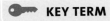

KEY TERM

Politicisation A process in which people who were previously unconcerned with politics take an active interest in political issues which affect their daily lives.

The next chapter will reveal how few could have anticipated the momentous consequences of the decision to summon it.

Summary diagram: Short-term causes of the French Revolution

Foreign policy and the American War of Independence
- Government sought revenge against Britain following 1763
- Supporting American rebels against British 1778–83 resulted in:
  - massive additional debt (1000 million *livres*)
  - awareness of political liberty for USA while no political liberty in France

Financial crisis
- Government on verge of bankruptcy
- Sought new measures to raise taxes

The failure of the reform process
- Assembly of Notables refused to back reform
- Dismissal of Calonne

The political crisis 1787–8
- Louis' political weakness
- Revolt of the Aristocracy

The economic crisis
- Bad harvests – rising bread prices
- Less consumption – unemployment
- Grain and food riots

 # Key debate

▶ *What are the different ways in which the origins of the French Revolution have been interpreted?*

Many historians hold sharply contrasting viewpoints on the origins of the French Revolution. One of the main schools is the Marxist interpretation. **Marxist historians** see the Revolution as part of the class struggle as outlined in the mid-nineteenth century by the German-born philosopher and social economist Karl Marx (1818–83). More recently, **revisionist historians** have rejected this view in favour of different interpretations.

The Marxist interpretation

The dominant interpretation of the French Revolution for much of the past 100 years has been the Marxist interpretation. This was most clearly expressed by Georges Lefebvre and later by his disciple Albert Soboul. Lefebvre regarded the French Revolution as a bourgeois revolution closely tied to social and economic factors. The commercial and industrial bourgeoisie had been growing

 **KEY TERMS**

Marxist historians Those who interpret the Revolution as part of Marx's analysis of history as a series of class-based struggles, resulting ultimately in the triumph of the proletariat.

Revisionist historians Those who reject Marxist analysis and provide a revised interpretation.

in importance in the eighteenth century and had become stronger economically than the nobility. Yet members of the bourgeoisie were kept out of positions of power by the privileged nobility. According to the Marxists, a class struggle developed between the rising bourgeoisie and the declining aristocracy. The bourgeoisie won this struggle because the monarchy became bankrupt owing to the cost of the war in America. The French Revolution was, according to Lefebvre, a struggle for equal rights for the bourgeoisie.

EXTRACT 1

From Albert Soboul, *The French Revolution 1787–1799*, Unwin, 1989, p. 27.

In 1789 French society remained fundamentally aristocratic; it was based on privilege of birth and wealth from land. But this traditional social structure was now being undermined by the evolution of the economy which was giving added importance to personal wealth and was enhancing the power of the middle class. At the same time … the philosophy of the Age of Reason was sapping the ideological foundations of the established order. If France still remained at the end of the eighteenth century a country of peasants and artisans, her traditional economy was being transformed by the growth of overseas trade and the appearance of big industrial concerns. No doubt the progress of capitalism and he demand for economic freedom aroused fierce resistance from those social groups dependent on the traditional economic order; but such resistance did not make them seem any less necessary in the eyes of the bourgeoisie whose spokesmen elaborated a doctrine which conformed to their social and political interests.

The revisionist interpretation

In the aftermath of the Second World War, a group of historians challenged the Marxist interpretation. The first important revisionist critic was Alfred Cobban, who questioned the validity of the **social interpretation** and also whether the Revolution was led by a rising bourgeoisie. For Cobban the Marxist interpretation was too simplistic.

EXTRACT 2

From Alfred Cobban, *The Social Interpretation of the French Revolution*, Cambridge University Press, 1964, p. 162.

In writing the social history of the revolution, I have not intended to suggest that it was other than primarily a political revolution, a struggle for the possession of power and over the conditions in which power was to be exercised. Essentially the revolution was the overthrow of the old political system of the monarchy and the creation of a new one in the shape of the Napoleonic state. However, behind the political regime there is always the social structure, which is in a sense more fundamental and is certainly much

 **KEY TERM**

Social interpretation
An emphasis on changes in society – population trends, social class – as having a significant impact on the Revolution.

more difficult to change. Once we begin to investigate this social background to the revolution we realize how little we really know of the pattern of eighteenth-century French society and the impact on it of the revolution. The supposed social categories of our histories – bourgeois, aristocrats, sans-culottes *– are in fact all political ones.*

The best known of the revisionist historians is François Furet. He went beyond merely questioning the economic and social interpretations of the Revolution as a class-based struggle, favoured by the Marxists, to considering the intellectual and cultural background to 1789. According to Furet, the driving force for change was the advanced democratic ideas of the Enlightenment *philosophes* such as Rousseau.

Towards a post-revisionist consensus

A number of historians have attempted to synthesise the vast amount of historical writing surrounding this issue and reach some sort of balanced judgement. The following extract by Professor J.H. Shennan, which draws on more recent research, is a good example of this.

EXTRACT 3

From J.H. Shennan, *France Before the Revolution*, Methuen, 1983, p. 32.

It seems most likely that the Revolution broke out because long-term problems and resentments were brought to a head by events immediately preceding it. Two of the areas in which deep-seated problems reached a critical point in the 1770s and 1780s were those of finance and government. In the former case the financial stresses induced by the War of American Independence were made worse by the series of bad harvests which caused the price of bread to rise sharply. Behind both of these factors, however, lay the permanent problem posed by conservative social and political attitudes which prevented the rich land of France from yielding its true harvest and the government from acquiring necessary funds.

How far do the historians quoted in Extracts 1, 2 and 3 agree or differ in their interpretations of the origins of the French Revolution?

Chapter summary

The origins of the French Revolution can be examined from the perspective of long- and short-term causes. Different interpretations of these origins are considered in the key debate.

The structure of French society during the *ancien régime*, with its divisions into three estates, created resentments among the least privileged Third Estate. There were tensions within French society before 1789, particularly among the bourgeoisie who were denied any role in government. Ideas of the *philosophes* started to emerge during the middle of the eighteenth century, which helped to undermine the cohesiveness of the absolute State. These can be considered long-term causes of the French Revolution.

The precarious financial position of the Crown deteriorated rapidly following its involvement in the American War of Independence, which hastened the onset of bankruptcy. The Crown's attempt to introduce reforms was mishandled, and resulted in a revolt of the privileged classes that precipitated the summoning of the Estates-General. The escalating crisis resulted in the Crown being forced to make concessions and agree to the creation of a constitutional monarchy. These can be considered short-term causes of the French Revolution.

 Refresher questions

Use these questions to remind yourself of the key material covered in this chapter.

1 What was the nature of royal power?

2 Why was the taxation system an issue?

3 Why was the First Estate unpopular?

4 What were the benefits of belonging to the Second Estate?

5 How could an individual enter the nobility?

6 Why did the Third Estate consider itself to be disadvantaged?

7 What role did the Enlightenment play in bringing about the Revolution?

8 How did foreign policy contribute to the outbreak of the Revolution?

9 How significant was the financial crisis in bringing about the collapse of the monarchy?

10 Why did the reform process fail and with what consequences?

11 What was the significance of the political crisis?

12 How did the economic crisis contribute to the outbreak of the Revolution?

Question practice

ESSAY QUESTIONS

1 'The financial problems of the *ancien régime* were responsible for the outbreak of the Revolution.' Explain why you agree or disagree with this view.

2 How significant a factor was the personality of Louis XVI in the fall of the *ancien régime*?

3 How important were the ideas of the *philosophes* in contributing to the outbreak of the French Revolution in 1789?

4 To what extent was the outbreak of the French Revolution in 1789 primarily due to the poor leadership of Louis XVI?

INTERPRETATION QUESTION

1 Read the interpretation and then answer the question that follows. 'In 1789 French society remained fundamentally aristocratic.' (From Albert Soboul, *The French Revolution 1787–1799*, Methuen, 1989.) Evaluate the strengths and limitations of this interpretation, making reference to other interpretations that you have studied.

SOURCE QUESTIONS

1 Why is Source A (page 4) valuable to the historian studying the role of Louis XVI in the outbreak of the Revolution? Explain your answer using the source, the information given about it and your own knowledge of the historical context.

2 How much weight do you give the evidence of Source D (page 16) in helping to explain why the Revolution broke out? Explain your answer using the source, the information given about it and your own knowledge of the historical context.

3 With reference to Sources A (page 4) and C (page 15), and your understanding of the historical context, which of these two sources is more valuable in explaining why the French Revolution occurred?

4 With reference to Sources A (page 4), C (page 15) and D (page 16), and your understanding of the historical context, assess the value of these sources to a historian studying the origins of the French Revolution.

5 How far could the historian make use of Sources A (page 4) and C (page 15) together to investigate the governmental problems facing France in the years 1774–89? Explain your answer using both sources, the information given about them and your own knowledge of the historical context.

CHAPTER 2

1789: The end of the *ancien régime*

The problems Louis faced compelled him to summon the Estates-General; this met in May 1789. Louis' attempts to control the situation, and the determination of his opponents to resist, resulted in a crisis that ultimately brought about the downfall of the *ancien régime*. The events of this momentous year are considered through the following themes:

★ The Estates-General

★ Revolt in Paris

★ Revolution in the provinces

★ Dismantling of the *ancien régime*

★ Reaction of the monarchy

The key debate on *page 46* of this chapter asks the question: What was the impact of the Declaration of the Rights of Man and the Citizen on France?

Key dates

1789	May 5	The Estates-General met at Versailles	1789	Aug. 4	Decrees dismantling feudalism passed
	June 17	National Assembly proclaimed		Aug. 26	Declaration of the Rights of Man and the Citizen
	June 20	Tennis Court Oath			
	July 10	Formation of the citizens' militia		Oct. 5–6	'October Days'
	July 14	The storming of the Bastille			
	July 20	Start of the Great Fear		Nov. 2	Church property nationalised

 ## The Estates-General

▶ *What was the significance of the debates surrounding the method of voting in the Estates-General?*

By late 1788 the financial and political problems facing the Crown had forced Louis XVI to call the Estates-General. This was the first time it had been summoned since 1614, and presented the government with a number of significant concerns:

- What method would the Estates-General use to vote on any issue presented to it: by head or by estate?
- Who would be elected as deputies to the Estates-General?
- To what extent should the grievances noted in the *cahiers* be addressed?
- What would happen when the Estates-General met?

An important contribution to the debate was made by the Abbé Sieyès in a widely circulated pamphlet which he published at the start of 1789.

SOURCE A

From the Abbé Sieyès, 'What is the Third Estate?', January 1789.

The plan of this work is quite simple. We have three questions to put.

1. What is the Third Estate? – Everything.

2. What has it been hitherto in the political order? – Nothing.

3. What does it demand? – To be something.

We shall see if the answers are right. Until then it would be wrong to condemn as exaggerations truths which are as yet unproven. Then we shall examine the means that have been tried, and those which must be taken, so that the Third Estate may, in fact become something. Thus we shall state:

What ministers have attempted and what the privileged classes themselves propose in its favour;

What should have been done;

Finally, what remains to be done to allow the Third to take the place due to it.

> In Source A, what does Abbé Sieyès consider to be the demands of the Third Estate?

The method of voting

The recently restored Paris *parlement* (see page 18) declared that the Estates-General should meet as in 1614 and that voting should be by estate or order. This would favour the two privileged orders, who wished to protect their privileges and tended to act together. Up to this point the bourgeoisie had taken little part in political agitation. The bourgeoisie had tended to follow the lead given by the privileged classes (the nobles and the clergy) in the *parlements* and the Assembly of Notables.

In 1789 bourgeois leaders of the Third Estate began to suspect that the privileged orders who wanted **voting by order** had opposed the government because they wanted power for themselves and not because they wanted justice for the nation as a whole. The Third Estate now demanded twice the number of deputies (so that they would have as many deputies as the other two orders combined), and **voting by head** instead of voting by order. This form of voting would give them a majority, as many of the First Estate's deputies were poor parish priests who were likely to support the demands of the Third Estate.

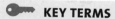 **KEY TERMS**

Voting by order Each estate votes separately on any issue. Any two estates together would outvote the third.

Voting by head Decisions taken by the Estates-General would be agreed by a simple vote with a majority sufficient to agree any policy. This favoured the Third Estate, which had the most deputies.

In December 1788 the King's Council allowed the number of Third Estate deputies to be doubled. Nothing was said about voting by head. When the Estates-General met there was confusion. The Third Estate assumed that there would be voting by head (otherwise doubling served no purpose), while the first two Estates believed that this was not the case.

Electing the deputies

The government made no attempt to influence the elections to the Estates-General and had no candidates of its own. Yet it was to a degree concerned that the deputies who were chosen would in general be sympathetic to the dire economic circumstances it was in, and be supportive to any proposals made by the King.

For the First Estate, the clergy overwhelmingly elected parish priests to represent them: only 51 of the 291 deputies were bishops.

In the Second Estate, the majority of noble deputies were from old noble families in the provinces, many of them poor and **conservative**, but 90 out of the 282 could be classed as **liberals** and these were to play a leading role in the Estates-General.

The 580 deputies elected to represent the Third Estate were educated, articulate and well-off, largely because deputies were expected to pay their own expenses. This was something peasants and artisans could not afford. Not a single peasant

🔑 **KEY TERMS**

Conservatives Those who did not want any reforms. They were deeply suspicious and sceptical of the need for any social or political change.

Liberals Deputies who were far more tolerant of differing political views and who supported a measure of cautious reform.

Abbé Emmanuel Sieyès

1748	Born in Fréjus to a bourgeois family
1773	Ordained as a priest
1787	Elected as a clerical representative at the provincial Assembly of Orleans, where he was particularly interested in issues relating to taxation, agriculture and poor relief
1789	Published a highly influential pamphlet, *What is the Third Estate?*, in which he argued that it was the most important part of the nation. Represented the Third Estate of Paris in the Estates-General. Drew up the Tennis Court Oath and contributed to the Declaration of the Rights of Man
1792	Elected to the Convention and voted for the King's execution but took no active part in the Terror

1793	Following Thermidor he served on the Committee of Public Safety (see page 104)
1794	Elected to the Council of 500
1798	Appointed ambassador to Berlin
1799	Elected Director and plotted the Coup of Brumaire with Bonaparte. Left public office during the Napoleonic Empire and retired from public life
1836	Died

Sieyès was one of the main constitutional planners of the revolutionary period. When asked what he had done during the Terror he declared 'I survived'. He helped to draw up the constitutions linked with the Revolution and was one of its most influential political thinkers.

or urban worker was elected. The largest group of Third Estate deputies were venal office holders (43 per cent), followed by lawyers (35 per cent), although two-thirds of deputies had some legal qualification. Only thirteen per cent were from trade and industry. This meant that the industrial middle class did not play a leading role in events leading to the Revolution or, indeed, in the Revolution itself.

All the adult male members of the two privileged orders had a vote for electing their deputies. The Third Estate, however, was to be chosen by a complicated system of indirect election. Frenchmen over the age of 25 were entitled to vote in a primary assembly, either of their parish or their urban guild, if they paid taxes. At these **primary assemblies** they chose representatives, who in turn elected the deputies.

KEY TERM

Primary assemblies
Meeting places for voters.

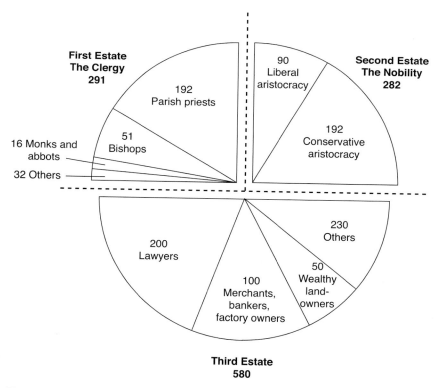

Figure 2.1 The composition of the deputies in the Estates-General 1789.

Cahiers

Before the meeting of the Estates-General, the electors of each of the three orders drew up *cahiers* – lists of grievances and suggestions for reform.

The *cahiers* of the First Estate reflected the interests of the parish clergy. They called for an end to bishops holding more than one diocese, and demanded that those who were not noble be able to become bishops. In return, they were prepared to give up the financial privileges of the Church. They were not, however, prepared to give up the dominant position of the Church: Catholicism should remain the established religion and retain control of education. They did not intend to tolerate Protestantism.

The nobles' *cahiers* were surprisingly liberal: 89 per cent were prepared to give up their financial privileges and nearly 39 per cent supported voting by head, at least on matters of general interest. Instead of trying to preserve their own privileges, they showed a desire for change and were prepared to admit that merit rather than birth should be the key to high office. They attacked the government for its despotism, its inefficiency and its injustice. On many issues they were more liberal than the Third Estate.

The *cahiers* of all three orders had a great deal in common. All were against absolute royal power and all wanted a King whose powers would be limited by an elected assembly, which would have the right to vote taxes and pass laws. Only one major issue separated the Third Estate from the other two orders – voting by head. It was this that was to cause conflict when the Estates-General met.

The meeting of the Estates-General

The year 1789 is not only one of the most important in French history, it is also central to the history of Europe. As events escalated out of Louis' control, resulting in the collapse of the *ancien régime* in France, new structures were created. The emergence of a more democratic system of government as a consequence of popular upheaval set a precedent for other downtrodden people in other countries.

When the Estates-General met on 5 May 1789 the government had the opportunity to take control of the situation. The Third Estate deputies, lacking experience and having no recognised leaders, would have supported the King if he had promised reforms, but the government did not take the initiative and put forward no programme. Necker talked about making taxation fairer but did not mention any other reform. Nothing was said about a new **constitution**, which all the *cahiers* had demanded.

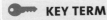 **KEY TERM**

Constitution A written document detailing how a country is to be governed, laws made, powers apportioned and elections conducted.

Although the Estates-General met as three separate groups, the Third Estate insisted that the credentials of those who claimed to have been elected should be verified in a common session comprising the deputies of all three estates. This appeared a trivial matter but was seen by everyone as setting a precedent for deciding whether the Estates-General should meet as one body (and vote by head) when discussing all other matters.

The nobles rejected the Third Estate's demand and declared themselves a separate order by 188 votes to 46, as did the clergy but with a slender majority of nineteen (133 to 114). The Third Estate refused to do anything until the other two orders joined them, so weeks of inaction followed, with the government failing to provide any leadership.

The declaration of the National Assembly

On 10 June the deadlock was broken when the Third Estate passed a motion that it would begin verifying the deputies' credentials, even if the other two orders did not accept their invitation to join in. A trickle of priests joined the Third Estate in the following days. After a debate on 15 June, the deputies of the Third Estate on 17 June voted by 490 to 90 to call themselves the National Assembly. The Third Estate was now claiming that, as it represented most of the nation, it had the right to manage its affairs and decide taxation. Events were rapidly moving out of the control of the government, especially when on 19 June the clergy voted to join the Third Estate.

The Tennis Court Oath

All of this was a direct challenge by the Third Estate to the authority of the King, who was at last forced to act. On 23 June he decided to hold a Royal Session known as a ***séance royale***, attended by all three Estates, at which he would propose a series of reforms. On 20 June 1789 the deputies of the Third Estate found that the hall in which they met had been closed to prepare for the Royal Session. The deputies met instead on a tennis court nearby and took an oath, known as the Tennis Court Oath, not to disperse until they had given France a constitution, thus claiming that the King did not have the right to dissolve them. Only one member voted against the motion; since, only three days before, 90 had voted against a motion to call themselves the National Assembly, it was clear that the deputies were rapidly becoming more radical.

SOURCE B

An engraving of the Tennis Court Oath.

> 🔑 **KEY TERM**
>
> ***Séance royale*** Session of the Estates-General in the presence of the monarch.

> Look closely at Source B. How does the artist seek to portray the great importance and drama of this occasion?

The response of the Crown

To restore a measure of royal authority, Necker advised the King to hold a *séance royale*. It was hoped that the King would ignore the events of 10–17 June and accept voting in common on all important matters. Louis, under pressure from the Queen and his brothers, ignored this advice and came down very firmly on the side of the privileged orders. When the *séance royale* met on 23 June Louis declared the previous decisions taken by the deputies of the Third Estate on 17 June null and void. He would not allow the privileges of the nobility and clergy to be discussed in common.

The King was, however, prepared to accept considerable restrictions on his own power:

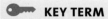

KEY TERM

Lettres de cachet Sealed instructions from the Crown allowing detention without trial of a named individual.

- No taxes would be imposed without the consent of the representatives of the nation.
- *Lettres de cachet* would be abolished.
- Freedom of the press would be introduced.
- Internal customs barriers, the *gabelle* and *corvée*, would be abolished.

If these reforms had been put forward in May, a majority of the Third Estate would probably have been satisfied, but now they did not go far enough. The King ended by ordering the deputies to disperse and meet in their separate assemblies:

- On 24 June 151 clergy joined the Third Estate.
- On 25 June 47 nobles, including one of Louis' leading opponents, the Duc d'Orléans, did the same. There were popular demonstrations in Paris in favour of the Assembly.
- On 27 June the King gave way. He reversed his decision of 23 June and ordered the nobles and clergy to join the Third Estate and vote by head.

Louis was, however, considering another strategy – military force. He had ordered troops to be moved to Paris and Versailles on 22 June. By late June nearly 4000 troops were stationed around Paris. Many of these troops were elite units of the army, the French guards, whose loyalty to the Crown Louis believed to be certain. This caused alarm in the capital despite government claims that they were there simply to preserve order. Further troop movements increased the strength of army units in and around the city from 4000 to over 20,000, in little more than a week. Louis and his advisors appeared to be contemplating using force if necessary to dissolve the National Assembly. In this desperate situation, the Assembly was saved by the revolt of the people of Paris.

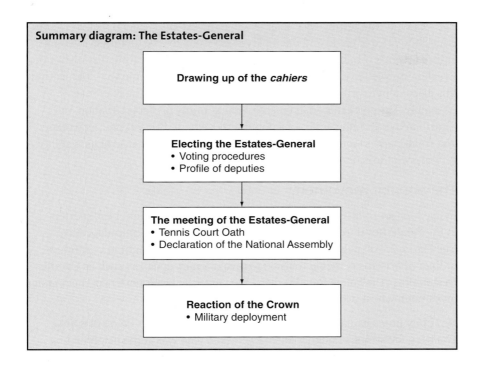

Summary diagram: The Estates-General

Drawing up of the *cahiers*

↓

Electing the Estates-General
- Voting procedures
- Profile of deputies

↓

The meeting of the Estates-General
- Tennis Court Oath
- Declaration of the National Assembly

↓

Reaction of the Crown
- Military deployment

② Revolt in Paris

▶ *What was the importance of the storming of the Bastille?*

The population of Paris was facing difficult times in the spring and summer of 1789. The economic crisis (see page 19) was causing hardship, which led to anti-government feelings and fuelled the rise of the **popular movement**.

The economic crisis in Paris

In normal times, a worker spent up to 50 per cent of his income on bread. In August 1788 the price of a 1.8 kg loaf was 9 *sous* (1 *livre* = 20 *sous* – a *livre* would be equivalent to about eight pence). By March 1789 it had risen to over 14 *sous* per loaf (see Figure 1.3, page 20). By the spring of 1789 a Parisian worker could be spending 88 per cent of his wages on bread. This caused hardship and unrest among the Parisian population. On 28 April, for example, the factory of a prosperous wallpaper manufacturer, Réveillon, was set on fire, following a rumour that he was going to reduce wages. But this riot was more a violent protest against the scarcity and high price of bread than a protest against wages. At least 50 people were killed or wounded by troops.

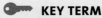 **KEY TERM**

Popular movement
Crowds of politically active Parisians who periodically took to the streets to protest.

The situation was getting very volatile when the Estates-General met. Economic issues (the price of bread and unemployment) were, for the first time, pushing France towards revolution. Falling living standards were creating dissatisfaction, which in turn led to discontent. Political opponents of the King were harnessing this discontent to bring crowds on to the streets to support the National Assembly. The economic crisis created a dangerously unstable situation and contributed to the emergence of a popular movement. Protests among workers and small traders were directed against the government because of its inability to deal with the economic crisis.

The popular movement

In late June journalists and politicians established a permanent headquarters in the Palais-Royal in Paris, home of the Duc d'Orléans. Its central location (see Figure 2.2 on page 35) made it a popular venue. Each night, thousands of ordinary Parisians gathered to listen to revolutionary speakers such as Camille Desmoulins. The Palais-Royal became the unofficial headquarters of the popular movement, whose activities were directed through its speakers.

By 11 July Louis had about 25,000 troops located in the Paris–Versailles area. The King felt strong enough to dismiss Necker, who was at the height of his popularity and was considered as the only minister able to tackle the financial crisis. The deputies of the Estates-General expected Louis to use force to dissolve the Assembly and arrest its leading members. News of Necker's dismissal reached Paris on 12 July, where it inspired large-scale popular demonstrations against the King. Parisians feared that this marked the start of Louis' attempt to restore his power by force. Many flocked to the Palais Royal, where speakers called on them to take up arms. A frantic search began for muskets and ammunition. Gunsmiths' shops were looted and many ordinary people began arming themselves. There were clashes with royal troops guarding the Tuileries.

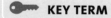 **KEY TERM**

Gardes-françaises An elite royal infantry regiment, many of whom deserted to join opponents of the King in July 1789.

When the ***Gardes-françaises*** were ordered to withdraw from Paris many disobeyed their orders and deserted to the representatives of the people of Paris. Discipline in this elite unit was deteriorating rapidly. Fearing attack by royal forces loyal to the King, barricades were thrown up across many streets to impede their progress.

The capture of the Bastille

The search for weapons by many ordinary Parisian demonstrators drew them to Les Invalides, an old soldiers' retirement home that also served as an arsenal, where over 28,000 muskets and 20 cannon were seized. The demonstrators were still short of gunpowder and cartridges, so they marched on the fortress of the Bastille. This imposing royal prison was a permanent reminder of the power of the *ancien régime*. News of the desertions among the *Gardes-françaises* led the army commanders to advise the King that the reliability of the troops to crush the rising could not be counted on.

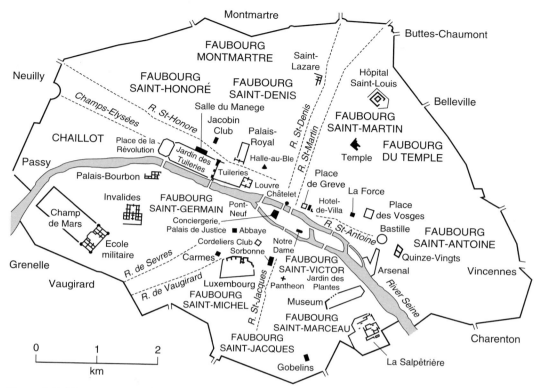

Figure 2.2 The main locations in revolutionary Paris.

Throughout late June, many *Gardes-françaises*, who worked at various trades in Paris in their off-duty hours and mixed with the population, were being influenced by agitators at the Palais-Royal. As early as 24 June two companies had refused to go on duty. By 14 July 1789 five out of six battalions of *Gardes-françaises* had deserted and some joined the Parisians besieging the Bastille. There were 5000 other troops nearby, but the officers told their commander that they could not rely on their men. Troops were removed from the streets of Paris to the Champ de Mars, a wide-open area south of the River Seine, where they did nothing.

The crowd outside the Bastille were denied entry by the governor, de Launay, who also refused to hand over any gunpowder. There was no intention of storming the fortress, although a group managed to enter the inner courtyard. De Launay ordered his troops to open fire on them and 98 were killed. *Gardes-françaises* supporting the crowd, using cannon taken from Les Invalides that morning, overcame the defenders. De Launay was forced to surrender. He was murdered and decapitated by an enraged crowd.

Those who had taken part in the attack on the Bastille were not wealthy middle class but *sans-culottes*. At the height of the rebellion about a quarter of a million Parisians were under arms. This was the first and most famous of the *journées*, which occurred at decisive moments during the course of the Revolution.

The establishment of the Commune of Paris

The popular disturbances in early July 1789 were unplanned and a reaction to the actions of the King and his ministers. Middle-class Parisians, who were worried about their safety and the security of their property, took action to regain control of the situation. On 15 July the Paris electors (representatives of the 60 electoral districts that had chosen the deputies to the Estates-General) set up a new body to govern the city. This was known as the Commune and it would be at the forefront of the clash between Parisians and the King. Sylvain Bailly was elected the mayor of Paris to carry out the Commune's policies.

On 10 July 1789, shortly before the formation of the Commune, the electors of Paris proposed forming a **citizens' militia** to defend the interests of property owners. It was envisaged that the militia would be predominantly bourgeois, and that the *sans-culottes* would be excluded from its ranks. It had the double purpose of protecting property against the attacks of the *menu peuple* and of defending Paris against any possible threat by royal troops. It was these electors and the supporters of the Duc d'Orléans who were to turn what had begun as spontaneous riots into a general rising. On 15 July the citizens' militia became the National Guard and Lafayette was appointed its commander.

SOURCE C

The storming of the Bastille, 14 July 1789.

What does Source C suggest about the storming of the Bastille?

The significance of the storming of the Bastille

The events in Paris on 14 July had far-reaching results:

- The King had lost control of Paris, where the electors set up a Commune to run the city.
- Lafayette (see page 79) was appointed commander of the predominantly bourgeois National Guard.
- The Assembly (which on 9 July had taken the name of the National Constituent Assembly) prepared to draw up a constitution, no longer under threat of being dissolved by the King.
- Real power had passed from the King to the elected representatives of the people. Louis now had to share his power with the National Assembly.
- Louis was no longer in a position to dictate to the Assembly, because he could not rely on the army.
- News of the fall of the Bastille spread through France and intensified activity among the peasantry.
- The revolt of Paris led to the emigration of some nobles, led by the King's brother the Comte d'Artois: 20,000 *émigrés* fled abroad in two months.

KEY TERM

Émigrés People, mainly aristocrats, who fled France during the Revolution. Many *émigrés* joined foreign opponents of the Revolution.

SOURCE D

From a letter written by Horace Walpole to H.S. Conway, 15 July 1789, quoted in *The Letters of Horace Walpole*, Volume VI, Richard Bentley, 1840, p. 328.

I write a few lines only to confirm the truth of much of what you will read in the papers from Paris. Worse news is expected every hour. Some of my friends informed of events in the city. Necker has been dismissed. Paris was in uproar and the courtiers have left. The firing of cannon was heard for four hours. That must have come from the Bastille. It is shocking to imagine what may have happened in such a populous city. Madame de Calonne told my friends that the newly encamped troops deserted in their hundreds. If the Bastille falls, which is possible considering the general spirit of the country, then other fortified places may be seized by the dissidents and whole provinces torn from the authority of the crown. On the other hand if the King prevails what heavy despotism will the Estates by want of their actions have drawn down on their country! They may have obtained many capital points and removed great oppression. No French monarch however will ever summon the Estates again, if this moment has been thrown away.

Read Source D. What does Walpole consider to be the significance of the events taking place in Paris?

On 17 July the King travelled to Paris from Versailles, where the people gave him a hostile reception. Louis recognised the new revolutionary council – the Commune – and the National Guard, and wore in his hat the red, white and blue cockade of the Revolution (red and blue, the colours of Paris, were added to the white of the Bourbons). The significance of the King's humiliation was not lost on foreign diplomats. Gouverneur Morris, later the US ambassador to France, told US President George Washington: 'You may consider the Revolution to be over, since the authority of the King and the nobles has been utterly destroyed.' Far from the Revolution being over, as news of events in Paris spread throughout France, it influenced what occurred elsewhere in the country.

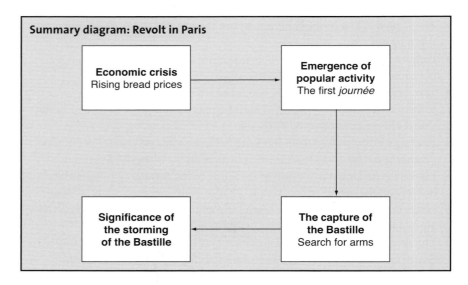

Summary diagram: Revolt in Paris

Economic crisis
Rising bread prices

Emergence of popular activity
The first *journée*

Significance of the storming of the Bastille

The capture of the Bastille
Search for arms

③ Revolution in the provinces

▶ *What were the features of the Revolution when it spread to the provinces?*

News of the capture of the Bastille spread to the provinces, and led to similar challenges to the authority of the Crown. The movement, known as the Municipal Revolution, covered the whole of the month of July 1789. As a consequence of the revolt of Paris, the authority of the King collapsed in most French towns. His orders would now be obeyed only if they had been approved by the newly formed National Constituent Assembly.

Most provincial towns waited to hear what had happened in Paris before they acted. 'The Parisian spirit of commotion', wrote the English traveller and writer Arthur Young, from Strasbourg on 21 July, 'spreads quickly'. Nearly everywhere there was a municipal revolution in which the bourgeoisie played a leading part. This took various forms.

In some towns the existing council merely broadened its membership and carried on as before. In Bordeaux, the electors of the Third Estate seized control, closely following the example of Paris. In most towns, including Lille, Rouen and Lyon, the old municipal corporations which operated during the *ancien régime*, and which excluded ordinary people, were overthrown by force; in others, like Dijon and Pamiers, the former councils were allowed to stay in office, but were integrated into a committee on which they were a minority. Citizens' militias were set up in several towns, such as Marseille, before the National Guard was formed in Paris. In Rouen, revolutionaries seized power at the beginning of July, before the revolt in the capital, following food riots.

In nearly every town a National Guard was formed, as in Paris, it was designed both to control popular violence and to prevent **counter-revolution**. Nearly all *intendants* abandoned their posts. The King had lost control of Paris and of the provincial towns. He was to lose control of the countryside through the peasant revolution.

The rural revolt

The peasants played no part in the events of the Revolution until the spring of 1789. It was the bad harvest of 1788 that gave them a role, because of the great misery and hardship in the countryside. Most peasants had to buy their bread and were, therefore, badly affected by the rise in its price in the spring and summer of 1789. They also suffered from the depression in the textile industry, as many owned handlooms and were small-scale producers of cloth. From January 1789 grain convoys and the premises of suspected **hoarders** were attacked. Since this violence tended to occur when food was scarce it would probably have died out when the new crop was harvested in the summer.

What made these food riots more important than usual were the political events that were taking place. The calling of the Estates-General aroused excitement among the peasants. They believed that the King would not have asked them to state their grievances in the *cahiers* if he did not intend to do something about them.

Events in Paris, particularly the fall of the Bastille, also had a tremendous effect on the countryside. Risings immediately followed in Normandy and Franche-Comté. Demonstrations and riots against taxes, the tithe and feudal dues spread throughout the country; it appeared that law and order had collapsed everywhere.

There were storehouses of grain that had been collected as rents, feudal dues and tithes on the great estates of the Church and other landowners. In the spring and summer of 1789 they were the only places where grain was held in bulk. Landlords were regarded as hoarders. The President of the Grenoble *parlement* wrote on 28 June: 'There is daily talk of attacking the nobility, of setting fire to their châteaux in order to burn all their title-deeds.'

The main features of rural protest were:

- Grain stores were looted.
- Châteaux were attacked and frequently burnt.
- Documents known as 'terriers', which listed peasant obligations, were seized and destroyed.

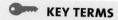

KEY TERMS

Counter-revolutionaries Groups and individuals hostile to the Revolution, who wished to reverse any changes it made at the earliest opportunity.

Hoarders Those who bought up supplies of food, keeping them until prices rose and then selling them at a large profit.

The Great Fear

Although hundreds of châteaux were ransacked and many were set on fire, there was remarkably little bloodshed – landowners or their agents were killed only when they resisted. On 20 July 1789 the attacks on the châteaux started and became part of the Great Fear (*Grande Peur*). These disturbances lasted until 6 August 1789. They began with local rumours that bands of brigands, in the pay of the aristocracy, were going to destroy the harvest. The peasants took up arms to await the brigands and when they did not appear, turned their anger against the landlords. The Great Fear spread the peasant rising throughout most of France. However, some areas that were further away from Paris, such as Brittany, Alsace and the Basque region, were unaffected.

 # Dismantling of the *ancien régime*

▶ *What impact did the reforms have on the lives of ordinary French people?*

The Assembly was in a dilemma. It could not ask the King's troops to crush the peasants, because afterwards they might be turned against the Assembly itself. Yet the Assembly could not allow the anarchy in the countryside to continue. This could be ended, and the support of the peasants gained for the Assembly and for the Revolution, by giving them at least part of what they wanted.

The August Decrees

On 3 August leaders of the **patriot party** drew up a plan for the liberal nobles to propose the dismantling of the feudal system. On the night of 4 August 1789 the Vicomte de Noailles, followed by the Duc d'Auguillon, one of the richest landowners in France, proposed the following:

- Obligations relating to personal service such as serfdom and the *corvée* should be abolished without compensation.
- The abolition of other rights such as *champart* and *lods et ventes* (see page 000). As these were regarded as a form of property they could only be redeemed when a peasant paid compensation to the landowner. As these were the dues that affected the peasant most severely, there was little satisfaction in the countryside with the limited nature of the reforms.

The proposed changes were given legal form in the decrees of 5–11 August, which stated that: 'The National Assembly abolishes the feudal system entirely. It decrees that, as regards feudal rights and dues those relating to personal serfdom are abolished without compensation; all the others are declared to be redeemable.' All seigneurial courts were abolished without any compensation.

Amid great excitement, the example of Noailles and Auguillon was followed by other noble deputies, who lined up to renounce their privileges in a spirit of patriotic fervour. The changes proposed went far beyond those demanded by the *cahiers*. The main ones were:

- Tithes payable to the Church were abolished.
- Venality was abolished.
- All financial and tax privileges relating to land or persons were abolished.
- All citizens were to be taxed equally.
- Special privileges (including tax exemption) for provinces, principalities, pays, **cantons**, towns and villages were abolished.
- All citizens without distinction of birth were eligible for all offices, whether ecclesiastical, civil or military.

When the Assembly adjourned at 2a.m. on 5 August the deputies were weeping for joy. Duquesnoy, one of the deputies, exclaimed 'What a nation! What glory! What honour to be French!'

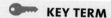

KEY TERM

Canton An administrative subdivision of a department.

SOURCE E

From J.S. Bailly, who was elected president of the National Assembly, and later first mayor of Paris, quoted in J.S. Bailly, *Memoirs*, Volume II, published between 1821 and 1824.

During the evening a proposed proclamation was read out. The proclamation was the cause of an impressive debate and of a scene which was truly magnificent and unforgettable. Vicomte de Noailles proposed a motion that the assembly should decree that seigneurial labour service and personal servitude would be abolished without indemnity, and that feudal rights be redeemed if desired by those who were liable. M. Cotin proposed the abolition of seigneurial courts. The Bishop of Chartres added the abolition of hunting rights. La Rochefoucauld spoke in favour of the abolition of serfdom. Never before have so many bodies and individuals voted such sacrifices at one time, in such generous terms and with such unanimity. This had been a night for destruction and for public happiness. We may view the moment as the dawn of a new revolution, when all the burdens weighing on the people were abolished and France was truly reborn. The feudal regime which had oppressed the people for centuries was demolished at a stroke and in an instant.

Read Source E. What does Bailly consider the significance of the events of the night of 4 August?

Significance of the Decrees

The August Decrees were very important in starting the process of dismantling the *ancien régime*. Although there was still a great deal to be done, they marked the end of noble power and the privilege of birth by establishing a society based on civil equality. All Frenchmen had the same rights and duties, could enter any profession according to their ability and would pay the same taxes. Of course, equality in theory was different from equality in practice. The career open to talent benefited the bourgeoisie rather than the peasant or worker, who lacked the education to take advantage of it. Nevertheless, French society would never be the same again – the *ancien régime* of orders and privilege had gone.

The peasants – the vast mass of the population – were committed to the Revolution as it brought about the end of the hated feudal system. They thought that if they did not support it then those who had lost their power would try to recover it. However, they did not like having to compensate landlords for the loss of their feudal dues. Many stopped paying them until they were finally abolished without compensation in 1793. Some peasants, in areas such as Brittany and the Vendée, were to become active opponents of the Revolution, once it became more extreme (see Chapter 4).

The August Decrees had swept away institutions like the provincial estates and cleared the way for a national, uniform system of administration. As most institutions had been based on privilege, the Assembly now began the laborious task, which would take two years to complete, of replacing institutions and often personnel relating to local government, law, finance, the Church and the armed forces. Yet many thought that those who had lost power would try to recover it. There was a widespread fear of an aristocratic plot and a feeling that, without constant vigilance, the victories of July and August could be quickly reversed.

The Declaration of the Rights of Man and the Citizen

The August Decrees prepared the ground for the creation of a constitution. Before this, the deputies drew up the principles on which this should be based – the Declaration of the Rights of Man and the Citizen. It condemned the practices of the *ancien régime* and outlined the rights of citizens, as demanded in the *cahiers* of all three orders. The following are some of the key points from the Declaration, issued on 26 August:

- All men are born free and equal, in their rights.
- The main rights of man are liberty, property, security and resistance to oppression.
- Power (sovereignty) rests with the people.
- Freedom of worship.
- Freedom of expression – speech and publication.
- Taxation to be borne by all in proportion to their means.
- Freedom to own property.

The Declaration would outlast the constitution to which it was later attached and was to be an important inspiration to liberals throughout Europe in the nineteenth century. For all its well-meaning sentiments, the Declaration mainly represented the interests of the property-owning bourgeoisie. Its significance, according to the historian George Rudé, is that '… it sounded the death-knell of the *ancien régime*, while preparing the public for the constructive legislation that was to follow'.

The nationalisation of Church land

By September the government was facing a serious financial crisis. Tax revenue was not flowing in and the government was unable to raise a loan to meet its costs. Many in the Assembly were contemplating radical action against the Church – one of the largest landowners in the country – in order to raise funds. After prolonged debates during late October and early November 1789, the Assembly agreed on 2 November 1789 that all the property owned by the Church should be placed at the disposal of the nation. The estimated value of all this property was about 2000 million *lives*.

At a stroke, Church land was **nationalised** and the State, for its part, took over responsibility for paying the clergy and carrying out their work of helping the poor. Bonds called ***assignat*** were issued and sold, backed up by the sale of Church land. These were used to settle debts and for purchasing goods and were accepted as currency. Royal land was also sold. It was anticipated that the sale of the first tranche of Church and royal land would raise around 400 million *livres*. This would go a long way towards meeting the financial needs of the government.

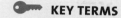

KEY TERMS

Nationalised Taken in to state control.

Assignat Bonds backed up by the sale of Church land that circulated as a form of paper currency.

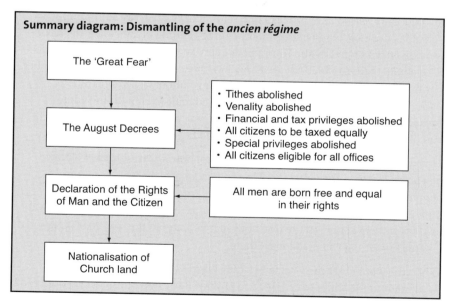

Summary diagram: Dismantling of the *ancien régime*

- The 'Great Fear'
- The August Decrees
  - Tithes abolished
  - Venality abolished
  - Financial and tax privileges abolished
  - All citizens to be taxed equally
  - Special privileges abolished
  - All citizens eligible for all offices
- Declaration of the Rights of Man and the Citizen
  - All men are born free and equal in their rights
- Nationalisation of Church land

5 Reaction of the monarchy

▶ *What effect did the changes have on the power of the monarchy?*

The King did not share the general enthusiasm for the changes that were taking place. On 5 August he wrote to the Archbishop of Arles: 'I will never consent to the spoliation of my clergy and of my nobility. I will not sanction decrees by which they are despoiled.' He could not use force against the Assembly as the loyalty of the army was in doubt, with many officers and men sympathetic to the Revolution. Louis adopted instead a policy of non-cooperation and refused to officially support the August Decrees and the Declaration of Rights. This forced the Assembly to consider the important question of what rights the King should have. Should he be able to veto or delay legislation passed by the Assembly? The deputies decided that the King should have a '**suspensive veto**' – the power to suspend or delay all laws other than financial ones passed by the Assembly for a period up to four years.

No one, at this stage, considered abolishing the monarchy and setting up a **republic**. It was agreed by the deputies that **legislative power** should reside with the National Assembly and that no taxes or loans could be raised without its consent. **Executive power**, it was decided, would be exclusively the preserve of the King.

The October Days

The King's refusal to approve the Assembly's decrees caused considerable tension. That he was forced to do so was the consequence of another revolutionary *journée*. Louis decided to reinforce his guard by summoning to Versailles the loyal Flanders regiment. On the evening of 1 October the troops were given a banquet by the King's bodyguard in the opera house of the palace to celebrate their arrival. Both the King and Queen were present at the banquet, during the course of which there were anti-revolutionary demonstrations. Officers trampled on the tricolour cockade and replaced it with the white cockade of the Bourbons. When news of this reached Paris, feelings ran high and there were demands that the King should be brought back to the capital.

This demand coincided with a food shortage in Paris. On 5 October a crowd of women stormed the Hôtel de Ville, the headquarters of the Commune, demanding bread. They were persuaded to march to Versailles – twenty kilometres away – to put their complaints to the King and the Assembly; 6000 or 7000 of them set off on the five-hour march. Later in the day, 20,000 National Guards, under Lafayette, followed them.

When the women reached Versailles they invaded the Assembly and sent a deputation to the King, who agreed to provide Paris with grain. He also agreed to approve the August Decrees and the Declaration of Rights. On 6 October, at the request of the crowd, the King and Queen appeared on a balcony and were greeted with cries of 'To Paris'. That afternoon the royal family left Versailles. The National Assembly also moved to Paris. These dramatic events are known as the October Days.

SOURCE F

A print showing the women of Paris going to Versailles to bring Louis back to the city.

> What does Source F suggest about the mood of ordinary Parisians in the autumn of 1789? **?**

The significance of the October Days

The October Days were a very significant event in the early phase of the Revolution. The crowd that marched to Versailles aimed to bring the royal family back to Paris, where their freedom of action and political influence would, it was hoped, be significantly reduced. Once in Paris, the King regarded himself as a prisoner of the Paris mob and therefore not bound by anything he was forced to accept.

When Parisians had revolted in July, they had seen the Assembly as their ally. In October, the Assembly had been ignored and humiliated by the decisive action of ordinary Parisians. When the deputies followed the King to Paris, some of them felt as much imprisoned as the King did. Most deputies wanted to work out a compromise with Louis, but this was much more difficult for them in Paris, surrounded by a population which could impose its will on the Assembly by another *journée*.

Following the October Days, the Assembly issued a decree that changed the title and status of the monarch, from 'King of France and Navarre' to 'Louis, by the grace of God and the constitutional law of the State, King of the French'. Louis was now subordinate to the law, and his subjects now became citizens. There had been a shift in the balance of power towards Paris and its increasingly politicised population. Many moderate deputies distrusted the population of Paris almost as much as they did the King, although it was the popular movement and their *journées* that had enabled them to defeat Louis in the first place.

Key debate

> ► *What was the impact of the Declaration of the Rights of Man and the Citizen on France?*

The momentous events which took place in the summer of 1789 paved the way for the reconstruction of France. A keystone in this process was the drawing up of a Declaration of the Rights of Man and the Citizen which paved the way for political reform and ultimately all the other reforms which ended the *ancien régime*. Historians have interpreted the impact of the Declaration on France from a number of different perspectives.

The orthodox Marxist view

George Lefebvre, one of the most eminent historians of the French Revolution in the first half of the twentieth century, summed up the left-wing view of the Declaration in a work first published in 1939 to commemorate the 150th anniversary of the Revolution.

EXTRACT 1

From Georges Lefebvre, *The Coming of the French Revolution*, Vintage Books, 1947, pp. 145, 147, 151.

With despotism destroyed and privilege abolished, nothing prevented the drafting of the Declaration, and the Assembly set to work on August 12. … Men are born free and equal in rights. *This memorable affirmation, standing at the head of Article 1, summarizes the accomplishments of the Revolution from July 14 to August 4, 1789. The rest of the Declaration is so to speak only an exposition and commentary on it. … It is noteworthy that in listing rights, equality does not appear. Equality of Rights was treated at length because special privilege was the foundation of the social hierarchy. The thought in the Declaration looked to the past more than the future.*

One of the central failings of the Declaration, according to Lefebvre, related to the articles dealing with constitutional measures, which contained the seeds of future unrest. While all citizens were to take part in the process of elections, the system that emerged excluded the majority of citizens from all but a very minor role in the process (see Chapter 3, page 52). The common people had fought to destroy the *ancien régime* and had forced the abolition of feudalism. 'It was chimerical to suppose that they would let themselves be excluded forever from the vote, in the name of a declaration which proclaimed men equal in rights.'

An updated interpretation

Among the numerous works published to mark the bicentenary of the Revolution, William Doyle offers a more considered view.

EXTRACT 2

From William Doyle, *The Oxford History of the French Revolution*, Oxford University Press, 1988, pp. 118–19.

Between 9 and 28 July a score of drafts were submitted by various deputies, and on 4 August, the afternoon before the famous all-night session, the assembly agreed to promulgate a declaration as a matter of urgency. On 26 August, after a week of discussion spun out by clerical reluctance to concede total freedom of thought and worship, The Declaration of Rights of Man and Citizen was finally voted. The Assembly reserved the right to add to or alter it when the constitution itself was finally promulgated, but when the moment came two years later nobody dared. The declaration had become the founding document of the Revolution and, as such sacrosanct ... As it was it long outlived the constitution to which it was the preamble; and has been looked to ever since by all who derive inspiration from the French Revolution as the movement's first great manifesto, enshrining the fundamental principles of 1789.

Doyle highlights the longer term impact of the Declaration as an inspirational document, despite its many blemishes.

The declaration reappraised

A more focused examination of the entire text of the Declaration has emphasised the passionate debates surrounding its birth. These debates inevitably resulted in compromise, which meant that the finalised document was ambiguous. Keith Baker suggested that this helped to create a climate of expectation that unresolved issues would be dealt with at some future point. He also argued that as the Revolution became more extreme after 1793, the ambiguities in the Declaration were used to justify a new and more ruthless approach by the republican government (see Chapter 5).

EXTRACT 3

From Keith Michael Baker, 'The idea of a declaration of rights', quoted in Gary Kates, editor, *The French Revolution: Recent Debates and New Controversies*, Routledge, 1998, p. 129.

Though it has often been seen as at once the most striking proof and almost inevitable product of a notorious French nationalism, the text of the Declaration of Rights of Man and Citizen, was far from being a foregone conclusion in 1789. To the contrary, the story of its composition is one of profound uncertainty and conflict over the meaning and essential purpose of any declaration of rights ... It is scarcely surprising, then, that the resulting document bore the marks of its difficult birth. Though it rapidly assumed a virtually sacred status it was left by its authors as a text still provisional and incomplete. Though it appealed to eternal principles it was shaped by acute conflicts over the exigencies of the political moment. Though it held out the

How far do the views of the historians differ on the impact of the Declaration of the Rights of Man and the Citizen in Extracts 1, 2 and 3?

ideal of political transparency, it emerged as a work of textual compromise. Many of the provisions of the Declaration remained profoundly ambiguous. These ambiguities served to inaugurate a radical dynamic that subverted representation in the name of the general will, constitutionalism in the name of political transparency, the rights of individuals in the name of the right of the nation.

Chapter summary

The French Revolution broke out in 1789. The summoning of the Estates-General and the refusal of the Third Estate to accept a junior role in proceedings led to the declaration of the National Assembly. The crisis deepened when suspicions that Louis was going to use force contributed to the storming of the Bastille. Forced to concede a number of reforms, Louis' power was being visibly reduced. All these events were being played out against a rapidly worsening economic crisis. News of events in Paris spread to the provinces, where the authority of the Crown was also being challenged. The August Decrees and the Declaration of the Rights of Man and the Citizen indicated the demands of the revolutionaries and their aim to dismantle the *ancien régime*. The impact of the Declaration is a matter of historical debate. Louis' continued ambivalence towards the Revolution and continuing suspicions that he wished to reverse the process were factors behind the October Days and his forced removal from Versailles to Paris.

Refresher questions

Use these questions to remind yourself of the key material covered in this chapter.

1 Why was the method of voting in the Estates-General important?

2 Who were the deputies elected to the Estates-General?

3 What concerns were reflected in the *cahiers*?

4 How did the demands of the Third Estate lead to the creation of a National Assembly?

5 How did Louis react to the actions of the Estates-General?

6 What impact did the economic crisis have on the population of Paris?

7 How important was the popular movement in the outbreak of the Revolution?

8 What was the significance of the setting up of the Paris Commune?

9 Why was the storming of the Bastille important?

10 What was the significance of the municipal revolution in those areas beyond Paris?

11 Why did events in Paris contribute to revolt in the countryside?

12 How did the actions of the peasantry contribute to the collapse of the *ancien régime*?

13 How important were the August Decrees?

14 What was the Declaration of the Rights of Man and the Citizen and why was it important?

15 Why did the State take over the property of the Church?

Question practice

ESSAY QUESTIONS

1 'The summoning of the Estates-General in 1789 was a momentous event.' Explain why you agree or disagree with this view.

2 How significant a factor in the development of the Revolution was the storming of the Bastille on 14 July 1789?

3 How important were the October Days, 1789, to the course of the French Revolution?

4 To what extent did the National Assembly significantly change France by the end of 1789?

5 Which of the following had the greater impact on the authority of the monarchy in 1789? i) The storming of the Bastille. ii) The October Days. Explain your answer with reference to both i) and ii).

INTERPRETATION QUESTION

1 Read the interpretation of the Declaration of the Rights of Man and then answer the question that follows, 'The thought in the Declaration looked to the past more than the future.' (From Georges Lefebvre, *The Coming of the French Revolution*, 1947.) Evaluate the strengths and limitations of this interpretation, making reference to other interpretations that you have studied.

SOURCE QUESTIONS

1 Why is Source A (page 27) valuable to a historian studying the origin of the French Revolution? Explain your answer using the source, the information given about it and your own knowledge of the historical context.

2 How much weight do you give the evidence of Source D (page 37) about the storming of the Bastille? Explain your answer using the source, the information given about it and your own knowledge of the historical context.

3 With reference to Sources A (page 27) and D (page 37), and your understanding of the historical context, which of these two sources is more valuable in explaining why the events of 1789 developed in the way they did?

4 With reference to Sources A (page 27), D (page 37) and E (page 41), and your understanding of the historical context, assess the value of these sources to a historian studying the significance of 1789.

5 How far could the historian make use of Sources A (page 27) and D (page 37) together to investigate the demands of ordinary people in 1789? Explain your answer using both sources, the information given about them and your own knowledge of the historical context.

CHAPTER 3

Constitutional monarchy: reforming France 1789–92

Following the overthrow of the *ancien régime*, the main aim of the Assembly was to reform France. This would involve changing the country's institutions and restructuring the way in which it was governed. The Declaration of the Rights of Man and the Citizen provided some of the guiding principles which underpinned these reforms. This chapter will consider three important themes:

★ Reform programmes of the National Assembly

★ Rise of the Jacobins and the Cordeliers

★ Emergence of the republican movement

The key debate on *page 72* of this chapter asks the question: What was the impact of the counter-revolution on France?

Key dates

1789	Nov. 2	Nationalisation of Church property
1790	May 21	Creation of the Paris Sections
	July 12	Civil Constitution of the Clergy
	Aug. 16	Reorganisation of the judiciary
1791	March 2	Dissolution of guilds
	June 14	The Le Chapelier Law
	June 20	Flight to Varennes
	July 17	Champ de Mars massacre

1791	Sept. 13	Louis XVI accepted the new constitution
	Nov. 9	Decree against *émigrés* (vetoed by Louis on 12 November)
1792	March	Guillotine to be used for all public executions
	May 27	New decree against refractory priests
1793	July 17	Final abolition of feudalism in France

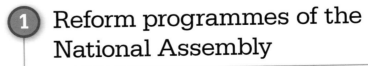

1 Reform programmes of the National Assembly

▶ *In what ways did the reforms of the National Assembly make significant changes to France?*

A significant start had been made to reforming France by the end of 1789. The feudal system had been abolished by the August Decrees (see page 40) and the ground had been prepared for the creation of a constitution. Following this, the deputies drew up the principles on which this should be based – the Declaration of the Rights of Man and the Citizen (see page 42). It condemned the practices of the *ancien régime* and outlined the rights of citizens, as demanded in the *cahiers* of all three orders.

After October 1789 most French people believed that the Revolution was over. For the next year there was broad agreement among the different groups in the Assembly, as they set about reorganising how France was governed and administered. In doing this they tried to apply the principles of the Declaration of Rights to give France a uniform, **decentralised**, representative and humanitarian system which treated people equally and with dignity. Many of the deputies regarded themselves as products of the Enlightenment, and as such sought to end cruelty, superstition and poverty. Most people by the end of 1789 wanted a **constitutional monarchy**, and there were few regrets about the passing of the *ancien régime*. France was fundamentally changed in many ways. New structures, such as the **departments**, were created that have survived until the present day.

The deputies in the National Assembly set about their task of reforming France with considerable dedication. While most people waited in anticipation for reforms which they hoped would improve their lives, many in the privileged classes prepared themselves for the worst. The main areas where changes would be made were as follows:

- local government
- taxation and finance
- economy
- legal system
- the Church
- constitution.

Local government

The reforms to local government involved significantly restructuring it. In restructuring local government the deputies wanted to make sure that power was decentralised, passing from the central government in Paris to the local authorities. This would make it much more difficult for the King to recover the power he had held before the Revolution. It was hoped that the administrative chaos of the *ancien régime* would be replaced by a coherent structure. The Assembly also wanted to ensure that the principle of democracy was introduced to all levels, whereby officials would be elected and would be responsible to those who elected them.

As a result of the decrees of December 1789, February and May 1790:

- France was divided into 83 departments.
- Departments were subdivided into 547 districts and 43,360 **communes** (or municipalities).

KEY TERMS

Decentralised Decision-making devolved from the centre to the regions of a country.

Constitutional monarchy Where the powers of the Crown are limited by a constitution. Also known as a limited monarchy.

Departments On 26 February 1790, 83 new divisions for local administration in France were created to replace the old divisions of the *ancien régime*.

Commune The smallest administrative unit in France.

- Communes were grouped into cantons, where primary assemblies for elections were held and justices of the peace had their courts.
- All these administrative divisions, except the cantons, were run by elected councils.
- In Paris, the local government of the city was reformed into 48 Sections.

The right to vote

The reforms which revealed the real intention of the Assembly related to voting qualifications. It became clear that deputies did not intend that those who had taken part in the popular protests should have a direct role in government. A law in December 1789 introduced the concept of '**active citizens**', of which there were three tiers:

- Men over 25 who paid the equivalent of three days' labour in local taxes. It was estimated in 1790 that almost 4.3 million Frenchmen fell into this category. Citizens who did not pay this amount in taxes had no vote and were known as '**passive citizens**'. In reality the only thing active citizens could do was to choose electors – the second tier.
- Electors – active citizens who paid the equivalent of ten days' labour in local taxes. About 50,000 men met this qualification and they elected members of the canton and department assemblies and could become officials there. They also elected the deputies to the National Assembly – the third tier.
- To be eligible to become a deputy in the National Assembly an 'active citizen' had to pay at least a *marc d'argent* (a silver mark), the equivalent to 54 days' manual labour, in direct taxation. Most Frenchmen were unable to meet this qualification.

The electoral system was, therefore, heavily weighted in favour of the wealthy, although 61 per cent of Frenchmen had the right to take part in some elections (in England only four per cent of adult males had the vote). At a local level, most peasants had the right to vote and were qualified to stand for office. This amounted to an administrative revolution. Before 1789 government officials ran the provincial administration, where there was not one elected council. In 1790 there were no government officials at the local level: elected councils had totally replaced them.

Control of the new councils

In the south, bourgeois landowners controlled the new councils. In the north, the bourgeoisie was largely urban and took office in the towns, which left the rural communes in the hands of *laboureurs*, small merchants and artisans. People belonging to social groups which had never held any public office now had the opportunity of doing so. It is estimated that in the decade 1789–99 about a million people were elected to councils and gained experience in local administration.

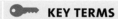

KEY TERMS

Active citizens Citizens who, depending on the amount of taxes paid, could vote and stand as deputies.

Passive citizens Approximately 2.7 million citizens who enjoyed the civic rights provided by the Declaration of the Rights of Man, but paid insufficient taxes to qualify for a vote.

Laboureurs The upper level of the peasantry who owned a plough and hired labour to work their land.

(b) New France: the departmental framework 1790–9.

Look closely at both maps. How do you think that people would have benefited from the reorganisation that took place?

(a) Old France: the provinces of *ancien régime* France.

Figure 3.1 Local government in old France (a) and new France (b).

These councils had an enormous burden of work thrust on them in December 1789 – much more than the *cahiers* had asked for. They had to assess and collect direct taxes, maintain law and order, carry out public works, see to the upkeep of churches and control the National Guard. Later legislation added to their responsibilities: they had to administer the clerical oath of loyalty, register births, marriages and deaths, requisition grain, and keep a watch on people suspected of opposing the Revolution.

In the towns there was usually an adequate supply of literate, talented people who provided a competent administration. It was often impossible, however, in the villages, to fill the councils with men who could read and write. Rural communes, therefore, often carried out their duties badly. In strongly Catholic areas officials disliked persecuting priests who had refused to take the oath of loyalty (see page 60). Consequently, many resigned and areas were left without any effective local government.

Taxation and finance

After the royal administration collapsed in 1789 very few taxes were collected. The Assembly needed money quickly, particularly when it decided that venal office-holders should be compensated for the loss of their offices. Yet a new tax system could not be set up immediately as considerable planning would be required before any new systems could be created.

It was decided that the existing system of direct and indirect taxation should continue until 1791. This was very unpopular. People wanted the demands made in the *cahiers* to be met at once. When there were outbreaks of violence in Picardy, one of the most heavily taxed areas under the *ancien régime*, the government gave way. The *gabelle* was abolished in March 1790 and within a year nearly all the unpopular indirect taxes, except for external customs duties, were also abolished.

The sale of Church land

As a first step to dealing with the financial crisis, Church land was nationalised on 2 November 1789 and *assignats* were introduced. The National Assembly had three main reasons for selling Church land:

- To provide money for the State in the period before the new and fairer taxation system was introduced.
- To guarantee the success of the Revolution, since those who bought Church lands would have a vested interest in maintaining the revolutionary changes, and would be more likely to oppose a restoration of the *ancien régime*, which might lead to the Church recovering its land.
- It was also hoped that the clergy would support the new regime, as they would be dependent on it for their salaries.

The government would issue bonds, known as *assignats,* which the public could buy and use for the purchase of Church lands. In April 1790 the Assembly converted the bonds into paper money, which could be used like bank notes in all financial transactions.

Buying Church land

Sales of land in 1791–2 were brisk. In Haute-Marne, for example, nearly 39,000 hectares of Church land, representing a tenth of the arable land in the department, were sold. The main beneficiaries were the bourgeoisie, as they had the ready cash. This was necessary because the **biens nationaux** were sold off in large plots. Members of the bourgeoisie bought most of the available land near the towns. Peasants fared better away from the towns.

A leading historian of the French Revolution, George Lefebvre, in a special study of the Nord department, found that 25 per cent of the Church land there had been sold by 1799: of this peasants had bought 52 per cent and the bourgeoisie 48 per cent. About a third of the peasants were first-time owners, so land did not only go to the wealthier *laboureurs.* Even where the bourgeoisie bought most of the land, they often resold it in smaller quantities to the peasants. It is estimated that the number of peasant smallholders increased by a million between 1789 and 1810.

Reforming the taxation system

Before the reforms were introduced the Assembly abolished the following:

- indirect taxes: *aidas, traites, octrois, gabelle* (see page 5)
- the **State monopoly** on growing, distributing and selling tobacco
- the old direct taxes: *taille,* capitation, *vingtièmes*
- tax farming.

The new financial system, which came into effect in January 1791, established three new direct taxes:

- the *contribution foncière*: a land tax from which there were no exemptions or special privileges
- the *contribution mobilière*: a tax on movable goods such as grain, payable by active citizens
- the *patente*: a tax on commercial profits.

In line with the principle of equality, citizens would pay according to their ability to do so. It was planned that the new taxes would be collected by the municipal councils.

This system might have worked well if there had been a systematic valuation of the land, but for this a large number of officials were needed. The Assembly would not provide them, as they would cost too much. Consequently, a survey of land values was not begun until 1807 and was not completed until the 1830s.

KEY TERMS

Biens nationaux The nationalised property of the Church as ordered by the decree of 2 November 1789.

State monopoly A system whereby the State exercises total control over an industry and can set whatever price it wishes.

Meanwhile, the new **tax rolls** were based on those of the *ancien régime*, so that great regional variations remained. People in the Seine-et-Marne department, for example, paid five times as much in taxes as those in the Ariège. It was also easier to avoid paying direct taxes than indirect ones, since it was easier to conceal incomes than goods.

The new system did, however, benefit the poor, as with the abolition of indirect taxes, the burden of taxation fell on producers rather than consumers. It was a fairer system, as all property and income were to be taxed on the same basis. There would no longer be any special privileges or exemptions. Citizens would pay according to their means. Much of the new financial structure would last throughout the nineteenth century.

Economy

Economic progress in France during the *ancien régime* was much slower than the rapid developments taking place across the Channel in Britain. The restrictive social structures and internal barriers inhibited economic development. The Revolution presented opportunities for reform. All the deputies in the Constituent Assembly believed in **laissez-faire**. Therefore, they introduced **free trade** in grain in August 1789 and removed price controls. These measures were extended to other products in 1790–1, although this is not what the people as a whole desired. They wanted the price and distribution of all essential goods to be controlled, in order to avoid scarcity, high prices and possible starvation.

In October 1790 internal tariffs were abolished, so a national market was created for the first time. All goods could now move freely from one part of France to another without having to pay internal customs duties. This was helped by the creation of a single system of weights and measures – the metric system – which applied to the whole of France.

Employer–worker relations

The deputies were determined to get rid of any organisations that had special privileges and restrictions regarding employment. The aim was to open up a range of crafts and occupations to more people. Guilds were, therefore, abolished in 1791, as they had restricted the entry of people into certain trades in order to ensure that wage levels and prices charged for goods and services had remained high.

In June 1791 a coalition of 80,000 Parisian workers was threatening a general strike to obtain higher wages, so the Assembly passed the Le Chapelier law, named after the deputy who proposed it, which forbade trade unions and employers' organisations. **Collective bargaining**, **picketing** and strikes were declared illegal. No one in the Assembly objected to the measure. Strikes remained illegal until 1864. The ban on trade unions was not lifted until 1884.

Relief

The Assembly regarded relief for the poor as a duty of the State. In the past the Church had provided help for the poor, but was unable to do so after losing its land and its income. Therefore, there was an urgent need for a national organisation, financed by taxation, to take over this role. The Assembly set up a committee which, in 1791, showed for the first time just how serious the problem was. It concluded that nearly 2 million people could support themselves only by begging. When it came to taking practical measures, there was simply not enough money available to deal with such an appalling problem, so nothing was done.

Legal system

The Constituent Assembly applied the same principle of uniformity to the legal system as it had done to local government. It abolished many features on 16 August 1790 and imposed a new structure. Among those areas removed were the following:

- the different systems of law in the north and south of the country
- the different types of law court, the *parlements*, seigneurial and ecclesiastical courts
- the *lettres de cachet* (see page 32): in place of the old structure a new, uniform system, based on the administrative divisions of the reformed local government, was introduced.

The main features of the new system were as follows:

- In each canton there was to be a justice of the peace, dealing with cases previously handled by seigneurial courts.
- The justice's main task was to persuade the different parties to come to an agreement; he could also judge minor civil cases, such as trespass, without appeal.
- Serious civil cases such as property disputes were dealt with in a district court.
- A criminal court would be located in each department, where trials would be held in public before a jury. The idea of having a jury, like that of having justices of the peace, was taken from English law.
- At the head of the judicial system was a Court of Appeal, whose judges were elected by the department assemblies.
- All judges were elected by active citizens but only those who had been lawyers for five years were eligible. This ensured that all judges were well qualified and accountable.

There were other improvements in the quality of French justice. The **penal code** was made more humane: torture and mutilation were abolished. Anyone arrested had to be brought before a court within 24 hours. The number of capital crimes was significantly reduced. In March 1792 a new and more efficient

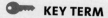 **KEY TERM**

Penal code A list of the laws of France and the punishments for breaking those laws.

KEY TERMS

Guillotine A machine introduced in 1792 for decapitating victims in a relatively painless way. It became synonymous with the Terror.

Legislative Assembly Came into existence in October 1791 and was the second elected Assembly to rule during the Revolution. It differed from the National/Constituent Assembly in that all members were directly elected.

Annates Payments made by the French Church to the Pope.

method of execution – the **guillotine** – was approved by the **Legislative Assembly**. It replaced all other forms used on those condemned to death. This mechanical device with its angular blade would become one of the most feared and lasting images of the Revolution following its first use in April 1792.

The new judicial system was to prove one of the most lasting reforms of the Constituent Assembly. For the first time, justice was made free and equal to all, and was therefore popular. The French system of justice had been one of the most backward, barbarous and corrupt in Europe. In two years it became one of the most enlightened.

The Church

The Constituent Assembly wanted to create a Church that was:

- free from abuses such as absenteeism and plurality
- free from foreign (papal) control – independent of Rome
- democratic
- linked to the new system of local government – primarily the department
- linked more closely to the State in order to strengthen the Revolution.

The deputies were not in the main anti-religious or anti-Catholic, and simply wanted to extend to religion the principles they applied elsewhere. They certainly had no intention of interfering with the doctrines of the Church or with its spiritual functions.

In August 1789 the Assembly abolished the tithe, **annates** and pluralism. It also ended the privileges of the Church, such as its right to decide for itself how much tax it would pay. Most parish clergy supported these measures. They also accepted the sale of Church lands, because they would be paid more than they had been under the *ancien régime*.

In February 1790 a decree distinguished between monastic orders which did not work in the community and those which provided education and charity. The former were suppressed, as they made no direct contribution to the common good. The latter were allowed to remain 'for the present', although the taking of religious vows was forbidden.

These changes took place without creating much of a stir among the clergy as a whole. Less popular was the decree in December 1789 giving civil rights to Protestants. These rights were extended to Jews in September 1791.

The Civil Constitution of the Clergy

There was no serious conflict with the Church until the Civil Constitution of the Clergy was approved on 12 July 1790. This measure reformed the Catholic Church in France, and adapted the organisation of the Church to the administrative framework of local government. **Dioceses** were to coincide with departments. This meant that the number of bishoprics would be reduced from 135 to 83. There would be not only fewer bishops but fewer clergy generally, as all other clerical posts except for parish priests and bishops ceased to exist. The attempt to extend democracy to all aspects of government was also applied to the Church. But there was no intention of ending the Catholic Church's position as the State Church in France.

Some of the key terms of the Civil Constitution of the Clergy were as follows:

- Each department would form a single diocese.
- There would be no recognition of any bishop appointed by the Pope but not approved by the French State.
- All titles and offices, other than those mentioned in the Civil Constitution, were abolished.
- All priests and bishops were to be elected to their posts.
- All elections were to be by ballot and by absolute majority of those who voted.
- Priests were to be paid by the State.
- There was to be no absenteeism by priests or bishops – no bishop could be away from his diocese for more than fifteen days consecutively in any year.

SOURCE A

Study Source A carefully. What do you think is the significance of the large storm cloud gathering behind the priest?

A constitutional priest taking the civic oath.

Most clergy opposed the principle of election, which was unknown in the Church, but even so, the majority (including many bishops) were in favour of finding a way of accepting the Civil Constitution and avoiding a split in the Church. They demanded that the reforms be submitted to a **national synod** of the French Church. This would have made a compromise possible but the Constituent Assembly would not agree to this, as it believed that it would give the Church a privileged position in the State once again, something which had just been abolished.

The oath of loyalty

As a Church assembly was not allowed to discuss the matter, the clergy waited for the Pope to give his verdict. He delayed coming to a decision, as he was involved in delicate negotiations with the French over the status of **Avignon**. The Assembly grew tired of waiting and on 27 November 1790 decreed that clergy must take an oath to the constitution. This split the clergy. In the Assembly only two of the 44 bishops and a third of the other clergy took the oath. In France as a whole seven bishops and 55 per cent of the clergy took the oath. When the Pope finally condemned the Civil Constitution in March and April 1791, many clergy who had taken the oath retracted it.

Two Churches

The Civil Constitution of the Clergy had momentous results. It was one of the defining moments of Revolution. It effectively destroyed the revolutionary consensus that had existed since 1789. Deputies in the Assembly were shocked when it was rejected by so many clergy and by the Pope.

There were now, in effect, two Catholic Churches in France. One was the constitutional Church, which accepted the Revolution but was rejected by Rome. The other was a **non-juring** Church of **refractory priests**, approved by the Pope but regarded by patriots as rejecting the Revolution. Nigel Aston, a modern historian, concludes: 'Faced with what was crudely reduced to a stark choice between religion and revolution, half the adult population (and the great majority of women) rejected revolution.'

A major effect of this split was that the counter-revolution, the movement which sought to overturn the Revolution, received mass support for the first time. Before this, it had been supported only by a few royalists and *émigrés*. In the most strongly Catholic areas – the west, north-east and south of the Massif Central – few clergy took the oath. On 27 May 1792 the Legislative Assembly attempted to take a firmer line with those priests who refused to take the oath by passing a measure which enabled their deportation, if twenty citizens were prepared to denounce them.

Many villagers complained that the Assembly was trying to change their religion, especially when refractory priests were expelled. They felt a sense of betrayal which, combined with their hostility to other measures of the Assembly, such as **conscription**, was to lead to open revolt in 1793 in areas like the Vendée.

Disaffection with the Revolution, which eventually turned into civil war, was, therefore, one result of the Civil Constitution of the Clergy. Another was the King's attempt to flee from France in June 1791, precipitating a series of events which was to bring about the downfall of the monarchy (see pages 67–9).

Constitution

One of the main aims of the Constituent Assembly had been to draw up a constitution that would replace an absolute monarchy with a constitutional one. Under the new proposals power would pass from the Constituent Assembly

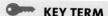 **KEY TERM**

Conscription Compulsory military service.

SOURCE B

What does Source B suggest about the character of the King?

Louis XVI facing both ways. In this contemporary cartoon Louis is shown promising both to support and to destroy the constitution.

(which would be dissolved) to a legislative assembly of 745 members. These members would be elected every two years and would have significant power. Much of the constitution – that the King should have a suspensive veto and that there should be one elected assembly – had been worked out in 1789, but the rest was not finally agreed until 14 September 1791. Under the terms of the constitution, the King had the following constraints:

- He had the right to appoint his ministers (although they could not be members of the Assembly) and military commanders.
- He was given a suspensive veto, although this could not be applied to financial or constitutional matters such as new taxes.
- He was dependent on the Assembly for his foreign policy, as he needed its consent before he could declare war.
- It was agreed that his office, although hereditary, was subordinate to the Assembly, as it passed the laws which the King had to obey. 'In France there is no authority superior to the law … it is only by means of the law that the King reigns.'

In September Louis XVI reluctantly accepted the constitution. Marie Antoinette's attitude was that it was 'so monstrous that it cannot survive for long'. She was determined to overthrow it at the first opportunity.

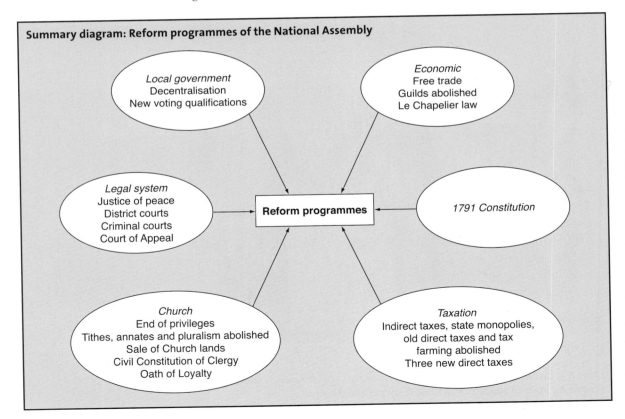

Summary diagram: Reform programmes of the National Assembly

- **Local government** Decentralisation, New voting qualifications
- **Economic** Free trade, Guilds abolished, Le Chapelier law
- **Legal system** Justice of peace, District courts, Criminal courts, Court of Appeal
- **Reform programmes**
- **1791 Constitution**
- **Church** End of privileges, Tithes, annates and pluralism abolished, Sale of Church lands, Civil Constitution of Clergy, Oath of Loyalty
- **Taxation** Indirect taxes, state monopolies, old direct taxes and tax farming abolished, Three new direct taxes

2 Rise of the Jacobins and the Cordeliers

▶ *What impact did the revolutionary clubs have on French citizens?*

In the absence of political parties, clubs were established to support the popular movement. They were set up soon after the Estates-General met in May 1789. For many ordinary people they provided a stage from which speakers could debate the great issues of the day. The majority of Frenchmen who had never been involved in political life discovered that they provided a crash course in political education. This section will examine two of the most important of these clubs and the growth of popular activity which they helped to foment.

The revolutionary clubs

As there were no political parties, the clubs played an important part in the Revolution. They kept the public informed on the major issues of the day, supported election candidates, and acted as pressure groups to influence deputies in the Assembly and to promote actions which the deputies seemed reluctant to undertake. In essence, they provided education in political participation.

The Jacobin Club

The Jacobin Club originated in meetings of radical Breton deputies with others of similar views. When the Assembly moved to Paris after the October Days these deputies and their supporters rented a room from the monks of a Jacobin convent in the Rue Saint-Honoré, hence the name by which they are now universally known. Their official title remained the 'Society of the Friends of the Constitution'. At the club, members debated measures that were to come before the Assembly.

The Jacobin Club set a high entrance fee for its members. There were 1200 members by July 1790 and they came mainly from the wealthiest sections of society. To begin with they associated themselves with the ideas of the **physiocrats**. They raised no serious objections to the introduction of free trade in grain, or the abolition of guilds in 1791. That they started to move towards accepting a more controlled economy can be explained by the problems posed by war and counter-revolution. Even then these measures were forced on them by their more extreme supporters – the *sans-culottes*.

Jacobin ideology was based on a combination of Enlightenment thought and revolutionary practice. They came to reject the notion of monarchy. What distinguished the Jacobins from other contemporary clubs was that they were highly political men of action. As the Jacobins moved further to the left in the summer of 1792 they favoured increased **centralisation** of government in order to defend the republic. The key figure to emerge during this period was

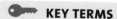

KEY TERMS

Physiocrats A group of French intellectuals who believed that land was the only source of wealth and that landowners should therefore pay the bulk of taxes.

Centralisation Direct central control of the various parts of government, with less power to the regions.

Maximilian Robespierre (1758–94)

The most important member of the Committee of Public Safety. Deeply committed to the ideal of a Republic based on popular sovereignty and prepared to take all measures necessary to preserve it from its enemies.

Jacques Pierre Brissot (1754–93)

Leading figure among the Girondin group of deputies. Believed passionately in the need to spread the ideals of the Revolution. Called for war with France's neighbours to achieve this.

Insurrection An uprising of ordinary people, predominantly *sans-culottes*.

Maximilian Robespierre, leader of a minority group of radical Jacobin deputies (see page 107).

A national network of Jacobin clubs soon grew up, all linked to the central club in Paris with which they regularly corresponded. By the end of 1793 there were over 2000 Jacobin clubs across France. It has been estimated that between 1790 and 1799 the movement involved two per cent of the population (about 500,000 people). The significance of the clubs is that they enabled for the first time large numbers of people to become directly involved in the political life of their country.

The Cordeliers Club

The Cordeliers Club, founded in April 1790, was more radical than the Jacobin Club and had no membership fee. It objected to the distinction between 'active' and 'passive' citizens and supported measures which the *sans-culottes* favoured, namely:

- direct democracy where voters choose deputies
- the recall of deputies to account for their actions, if these went against the wishes of the people
- the right of **insurrection** – rebellion, if a government acted against popular wishes.

It had much support among the working class, although its leaders were bourgeois. Georges Danton (see profile on page 122) and Camille Desmoulins were lawyers. Jacques-René Hébert was an unsuccessful writer who had become a journalist when freedom of the press was allowed. **Brissot** was also a journalist. But the most notorious writer of all was Marat, a failed doctor turned radical journalist. He hated all those who had enjoyed privileges under the old regime and attacked them violently in his newspaper, *L'Ami du Peuple*. He became the chief spokesman of the popular movement.

During the winter of 1790–1 the example of the Cordeliers Club led to the formation of many 'popular' or 'fraternal' societies, which were soon to be found in every district in Paris and in several provincial towns. In 1791 the Cordeliers Club and the popular societies formed a federation and elected a central committee. The members of the popular societies were drawn mainly from the liberal professions such as teachers and officials, and skilled artisans and shopkeepers. Labourers rarely joined, as they did not have the spare time for politics.

SOURCE C

Jean-Paul Marat, 'Illusion of the Blind Multitude on the Supposed Excellence of the Constitution', *L'Ami du Peuple* No. 334, 8 January 1791. Jean-Paul Marat Archive, **www.marxists.org/history/france/revolution/marat/**.

The public's infatuation with the constitution is the folly of the moment.... When it enters the head of a people who have broken their chains, nothing in the world is more apt to flatter self-love than the idea of an indefinite freedom supported by the supreme power. Many among the press have represented the constitution as sublime, the guarantor of the nation's happiness. These pompous views have been circulated throughout the country. New chains are being forged. Credulous Parisians! Remember the inscriptions that decorated the altar of the Fatherland. It said to the people: You are the sovereign. Yet the law is still against you. The blind multitude didn't see that this whole foolish apparatus had no other goal than that of turning the soldiers of the Fatherland into instruments of executive power, maintaining the evil decrees that returned authority to the hands of the King. I repeat to you today: the constitution is a complete failure ... it forms the most dreadful of governments, it is nothing but an administration of royal sympathisers ... a true military and noble despotism.

> According to Source C, what does Marat think of the proposed constitution?

Popular discontent in rural and urban areas

By the start of 1790 many peasants had become disillusioned with the Revolution. The sense of anticipation which followed the 'Night of 4 August' quickly diminished once they realised in the spring of 1790 that their feudal dues were not abolished outright but would have to be bought out (see pages 40–2).

A rural revolution started in 1790 in Brittany, central France and the south-east. This lasted until 1792 and placed pressure on the Jacobins. Peasants fixed the price of grain, called for the sale of Church land in small lots and attacked châteaux. The rising in the Midi (Languedoc, Provence and the Rhône valley) in 1792 was as important as any in 1789 in size and the extent of the destruction. These risings, and the deteriorating military situation, contributed to the most serious crisis of the Revolution. After the overthrow of the monarchy in August 1792, all feudal and seigneurial dues which could not be justified were abolished. Feudalism was finally abolished without compensation by the Jacobins on 17 July 1793.

The *sans-culottes*

The *sans-culottes* were urban workers. They were not a class, as they included artisans and master craftsmen, who owned their own workshops, as well as wage-earners. They had been responsible for the successful attack on the Bastille and for bringing the royal family back to Paris in the October Days, yet they had received few rewards. Many of them were 'passive' citizens (see page 52), who did not have the vote. They suffered greatly from **inflation**. To meet its

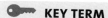
KEY TERM

Inflation A decline in the value of money, which leads to an increase in the price of goods.

expenses, the government printed more and more *assignats* (paper money), whose value therefore declined. There was a wave of strikes by workers against the falling value of their wages early in 1791. Grain prices rose by up to 50 per cent after a poor harvest in 1791. This led to riots, which resulted in shopkeepers being forced to reduce prices.

SOURCE D

From 'What is a sans-culottes?', April 1793, an anonymous document held in the Archives Nationales in Paris and quoted in D.I. Wright, editor, *The French Revolution: Introductory Documents*, University of Queensland Press, 1975, p. 171.

Reply to the impertinent question: What is a sans-culottes? A sans-culottes you rogues? He is someone who always goes about on foot, who has not got the millions you would all like to have, who has no chateaux, no servants to wait on him, and who lives simply with his wife and children if he has any on the fourth or fifth storey. He is useful because he knows how to till a field, to forge iron, to use a saw, to roof a house, to make shoes, and to spill his blood to the last drop for the safety of the Republic. And because he is a worker, you are sure not to meet him in the cafes or gaming houses where others plot and wager … In the evening he goes to the assembly of his Section, not powdered and perfumed or well dressed, in the hope of being noticed by the women citizens, but rather to support good motions with all his strength, and to crush those from the despised faction of politicians. Finally, a sans-culottes always has his sword sharpened, ready to cut off the ears of all opponents of the Revolution; but at the first sound of the drum you see him leave for the Vendée, for the army of the Alps or for the Army of the North.

? According to Source D, what do the *sans-culottes* consider to be their role?

The discontent of the urban workers was harnessed by the popular societies. They skilfully linked economic protests and grievances to the demand for a republic whose representatives were directly elected by the people. This made the Revolution more radical in ways which the bourgeois leaders of 1789 had neither intended nor desired.

Summary diagram: Rise of the Jacobins and the Cordeliers		
	Jacobins	*Cordeliers*
Key members	Maximilian Robespierre	Georges Danton Camille Desmoulins Jacques-René Hébert Jacques Pierre Brissot Jean-Paul Marat
Supporters	Wealthy radical deputies	Bourgeois and working-class radicals
Key ideas	Centralisation	Direct democracy Right of insurrection

3 Emergence of the republican movement

▶ *What factors contributed to the emergence of the republican movement?*

The outstanding politician and orator in the Constituent Assembly was **Comte de Mirabeau**, a nobleman who was elected for the Third Estate in 1789. His willingness to deal directly with the King cost him a great deal of popular support by the time of his death in April 1791. He was fairly typical of a group of moderate politicians who were becoming increasingly influential in the Assembly.

Barnave, Du Port and Lameth (the triumvirate) sought to try and heal the divisions between the aristocracy and bourgeoisie that had emerged during 1789. They feared the extremism of the new clubs and the emergence of the popular movement and wished to bring the Revolution to an end. In order for this to happen there had to be a compromise with the King. This was difficult, as anyone suspected of negotiating with the King was likely to be accused of selling out to the Court. There was also no means of knowing if the King was sincerely prepared to co-operate with the moderates. Louis dashed all their hopes by attempting to flee from Paris.

The flight to Varennes

Louis XVI was a devout man who deeply regretted accepting the Civil Constitution of the Clergy, which offended his conscience. He decided to flee from Paris, where he felt restricted by the Constituent Assembly, to Montmédy in Lorraine, on the border of Luxembourg, and put himself under the protection of the military commander of the area. He hoped that from there, in a position of strength, he would be able to renegotiate with the Constituent Assembly the parts of the constitution he disliked. Military action would, he hoped, be unnecessary, although the King was aware that there was a danger that his flight might open up divisions and bring about civil war.

Louis left Paris with his family on 20 June 1791. When he reached Varennes, during the night of 21–22 June, he was recognised by the local postmaster, Drouet, and stopped. He was brought back to Paris in an atmosphere of deathly silence. Louis' younger brother, the Comte de Provence, was luckier than the King. He also fled from Paris on 20 June with his wife but he arrived safely in Brussels the next day.

How significant was the flight to Varennes?

The flight to Varennes was one of the key moments of the early phase of the French Revolution. Before leaving, Louis had drawn up a proclamation to the

KEY FIGURE

Comte de Mirabeau (1749–91)
A nobleman of liberal beliefs and an outstanding orator who represented the Third Estate in the Estates-General. He worked in secret to support royal interests.

French people which set out in great detail his true feelings regarding the developments that had taken place.

SOURCE E

Study Source E.
According to Louis, who is to blame for the crisis?

From the King's declaration on leaving Paris, 20 June 1791. He writes in the third person, quoted in John Hardman, *The French Revolution Sourcebook*, Arnold, 2002, pp. 135–6.

The king does not think it would be possible to govern so large and important a kingdom as France by the means established by the National Assembly such as they exist at present. His Majesty in giving his assent which he knew well he could not refuse, to all decrees without distinction was motivated by his desire to avoid all discussion which experience had taught him to be pointless. The nearer the Assembly approached the end of its labours the more wise men were seen to lose their influence. The mentality of the clubs dominated everything; thousands of incendiary papers and pamphlets are circulated every day … Did you want anarchy and the despotism of the clubs to replace the monarchical form of government under which the nation has prospered for fourteen hundred years? Did you want to see your king heaped with insults and deprived of his liberty whilst he was exclusively occupied with establishing yours?

The significance of the event was as follows:

- In the declaration it is obvious that Louis had failed to understand the popularity of the changes which had taken place since 1789.
- It became clear that once again (see the Civil Constitution of the Clergy, pages 58–61) the French people would have to make choices that many of them would have preferred to avoid.
- Louis in his declaration had emphatically renounced the Revolution. Could he continue to remain as head of state?
- The credibility of the new constitution was undermined before it had even been implemented.
- Support for a republic started to grow, while the popularity of the King declined.

On 24 June 30,000 people marched to the National Assembly in support of a petition from the Cordeliers Club calling for the King's dismissal from office.

Results of the flight

One immediate result of the flight was that the King lost what remained of his popularity, which had depended on his being seen to support the Revolution. Royal inn signs and street names disappeared all over Paris. His flight persuaded many who had hitherto supported him that he could no longer be trusted. People started to talk openly of replacing the monarchy with a republic.

The deputies in the Assembly acted calmly in this situation. They did not want a republic. They feared that the declaration of a republic would lead to civil war in France and war with European monarchs. Nor did they want to concede victory

SOURCE F

A satirical drawing published in 1791. 'The family of pigs brought back to the sty.'

Study Source F. What is the significance of the way the artist has chosen to portray the royal family in this contemporary cartoon?

to the radicals, who sought more democratic policies. 'Are we going to end the Revolution or are we going to start it again?' one deputy asked the Assembly.

On 16 July the Assembly voted to suspend the King until the constitution was completed. Governing without the head of state would encourage those who favoured republicanism. He would be restored only after he had sworn to observe it. This was going too far for some deputies: 290 abstained from voting as a protest. For others, suspension did not go far enough.

Division among the Jacobins

After the flight to Varennes, radicals were appalled when the King was not dethroned or put on trial. Their anger was directed against the Constituent Assembly, which they claimed no longer represented the people. The Cordeliers took the lead with the popular societies and persuaded the Jacobins to join them in supporting a petition for the King's deposition. This split the Jacobin Club. Those who did not want the King deposed – and this included nearly all the members who were deputies – left the club. They set up a new club, the **Feuillants**, which for the moment had control of the Assembly. Robespierre remained as leader of a small group of radical members. It seemed as though the Jacobins had destroyed themselves. However, only 72 of the provincial Jacobin clubs in France defected from the control of the Parisian club, and most of these drifted back in the next few months.

The Champs de Mars massacre

On 17 July 1791, 50,000 people flocked to the Champ de Mars, a huge field in Paris where the Feast of the Federation, celebrating the fall of the Bastille, had been held three days previously. They were there to sign a republican petition

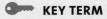 **KEY TERM**

Feuillants Constitutional monarchists, among them Lafayette, who split from the Jacobin Club following the flight to Varennes.

SOURCE G

The shooting of demonstrators at the Champ de Mars.

 **KEY TERMS**

Altar of the fatherland A large memorial to commemorate the Revolution.

Martial law The suspension of civil liberties by the State in an attempt to restore public order when there is severe rioting and mass disobedience.

on the '**altar of the fatherland**'. This was a political demonstration by the poorer sections of the Parisian population. The Commune, under pressure from the Assembly, declared **martial law**. It sent Lafayette with the National Guard to the Champ de Mars, where the Guards fired on the peaceful and unarmed crowd. About 50 people were killed.

This was the first bloody clash between different groups in the Third Estate, and it was greeted with pleasure in the Assembly. Messages of support for the Assembly poured in from the provinces. Martial law remained in force for a month, during which time some popular leaders were arrested. Others, such as Hébert, Marat and Danton, fled or went into hiding. The moderates had won and could now work out a compromise with the King without facing mob violence. It took nearly a year for the popular movement to recover. As far as the extremists were concerned, only the overthrow of the monarchy would satisfy their demands.

The Feuillants were more determined than ever to make an agreement with the King. Although they did not trust him and had lost popular support, for the moment they controlled Paris and the Assembly. Their long-term success, however, depended on the co-operation of Louis, and this was far from certain.

The Legislative Assembly

The acceptance of the constitution by the King on 13 September 1791 marked the end of the Constituent Assembly. Its final meeting was on 30 September. On 1 October the first meeting of the new Legislative Assembly was held. But by now suspicion and hatred among the deputies had replaced the optimism of 1789. The mood among the deputies in the new Legislative Assembly was far from co-operative. This change had come about because:

- the King's reluctance to accept measures he disliked
- suspicions regarding the King's acceptance of the Revolution, as revealed by the flight to Varennes
- the fear of counter-revolutionary plots.

To prevent his political opponents in the Constituent Assembly from dominating the next Assembly, Robespierre proposed a **self-denying ordinance**. This was passed and stated that no member of the Constituent Assembly, including Robespierre, could sit in the new Legislative Assembly.

In the elections for the new Legislative Assembly (29 August to 5 September), under a quarter of the active citizens voted. The Assembly of 745 members which was elected was almost wholly bourgeois. In the semi-circular meeting chamber the seating arrangement in front of the speaker gave rise to new political labels – **left**, **right** and **centre**. There were few nobles, most of whom had retired to their estates and kept themselves to themselves, hoping for better times. Only 23 clergy were elected. There were no peasants or artisans, and few businessmen. At the opening of the Legislative Assembly, it was possible to identify three broad groups of deputies:

- The Left: 136 deputies, most of whom were members of the Jacobin Club. The most prominent were a small group of deputies from the Gironde department, known as the **Girondins**.
- The Right: 264 deputies who were members of the Feuillant Club and considered the Revolution to be over.
- The Centre: 345 deputies making up the largest group who were unattached.

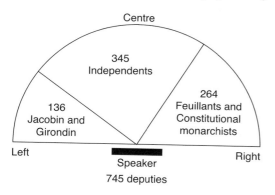

Figure 3.2 below

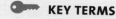

Figure 3.2 Main political groups in the Legislative Assembly, 1 October 1791 to 20 September 1792.

The growth of the counter-revolution

From the very start, the deputies were worried by the non-juring clergy
and by the *émigrés*, whose numbers had increased greatly since the flight to
Varennes. Nearly all the *ancien régime* bishops and many of the great court and
parlementaire families had emigrated to Austria and the small German states
along the River Rhine. What alarmed the Assembly most was the desertion of
army officers. By early 1791, 1200 noble officers had joined the *émigrés*, although
a large majority of pre-Revolution officers remained at their posts. All this
changed after Varennes.

By the end of 1791 about 6000 had emigrated, which was 60 per cent of all
officers. The Assembly passed two laws in November. One declared that all
non-jurors were suspects. The other said that all *émigrés* who did not return to
France by 1 January 1792 would forfeit their property and be regarded as traitors.
When the King vetoed these laws his unpopularity increased. He appeared to be
undermining the Revolution.

4 Key debate

▶ *What was the impact of the counter-revolution on France?*

For a long time historians did not devote much time or effort to examining the
counter-revolution. It was considered to be less fashionable to study than other
aspects of the Revolution. Part of the problem was the lack of agreement about
what exactly the term meant or even when it started. For some it started before
1789 with the revolt of the aristocracy against the Crown's reform proposals of
1787–8. Others saw it emerging rather later with the fusion of opposition against
the religious policies of the National Assembly and dislike of the way Paris was
dictating the pace of change within France.

An additional concern was to what degree the counter-revolution posed a
significant threat to the Revolution. Certainly, in the early years of the Republic
its scale posed a serious problem for the Convention, given the context of a
foreign war which was not progressing well and a deteriorating economy. In
essence, the Revolution was facing simultaneous threats from both internal and
external enemies.

One of the first detailed studies of the counter-revolution was by Jacques
Godechot. In this extract he notes the foreign threat against the Revolution.

EXTRACT 1

**From Jacques Godechot, *The Counter Revolution, Doctrine and Action 1789–
1804*, Routledge & Kegan Paul, 1972, p. 386.**

*Two conclusions emerge at the end of this study: the relatively minor influence
of doctrine on counter-revolutionary action; and an almost complete failure of*

this action in 1804, the year in which this study ends … One of the principal causes of the failure of the counter-revolution in the period under review and particularly in 1799, lies in the lack of synchronization of the attacks launched against France. Each time it had been able to muster upon all its forces to hurl back these assaults. Although the Empire consolidated the work of the Revolution, it also cemented the forces of the counter-revolution and enabled it to triumph in 1814. But the counter-revolution that imposed itself in power at that time bore only a distant resemblance to the counter-revolution of 1804. It had to appropriate many of the ideas and principles of the Revolution.

The Marxist historian George Rudé believed that there was credible threat from the counter-revolution which was held at bay during the Jacobin Republic.

EXTRACT 2

From George Rudé, *Revolutionary Europe 1783–1815*, Fontana, 1964, p. 170.

Royalist and counter-revolutionary agitation had in one form or another been a matter of concern since 1789; but, until war broke out, it had only achieved little success. After the King's execution, royalist activity from both without and within had played a part in fostering rebellion in the Vendée and the 'federalist' departments of the south, west and north. Yet as long as the Jacobins remained in power, these dangers had been held in check and had barely affected the capital. The royalists had however taken fresh heart from the more liberal policies of their successors. By now they were divided into two main groups – the 'ultras' who demanded a return to 1787 and the total restoration of the Old Régime; and the 'constitutionalists', who broadly speaking favoured a restoration of the constitution of 1791. Unfortunately for the 'constitutionalists', the Count of Provence (Louis XVI's brother) was a determined ultra.

J.M. Roberts believed that the term counter-revolution was misleading since it suggested a reply to the Revolution rather than what he considered to be an autonomous existence clearly evident in the revolt of the nobility. He offers the following overview of the counter-revolution.

EXTRACT 3

From J.M. Roberts, *The French Revolution*, Oxford University Press, 1978, pp. 112–13.

Nor did the counter-revolution triumph in 1815. The Bourbon line came back, but on terms, to a constitutional monarchy, with the essential rights of 1789 guaranteed, the revolutionary establishment undisturbed except for a few hard-core regicides, the land settlement untouched, and no return to the old localism and corporatism. Though a more blatantly reactionary programme still seemed feasible to some and lingered as a serious possibility as late as the 1870s, the counter-revolution's practical effect in French history was as negligible as its mythological and intellectual importance was great. Practical conservatism after 1815 increasingly flowed away from it into the channels favoured by the notables who emerged triumphant from the revolution.

To what extent do the historians quoted in Extracts 1, 2 and 3 differ in their interpretations of the success of the counter-revolution?

Chapter summary

The Assembly passed significant reforms which altered many of France's institutions. Many sections of society were politicised as the Revolution took hold in the country. Changes to the way the Catholic Church was organised alienated many who had previously supported the reforms of the National Assembly. The changes were certainly not to everyone's liking, as the growth of the counter-revolution suggests. Whether this had an impact on the Revolution is considered in the key debate.

At the centre of all the events which were unfolding was the King. His distaste for what was happening within France and to his authority became evident during his attempt to flee the country. Whatever assurances he might give to the contrary, he was clearly ill at ease in the role of a constitutional monarch. His opponents for their part were uncomfortable with him, as the growth of republicanism would indicate.

Refresher questions

Use these questions to remind yourself of the key material covered in this chapter.

1 What principles underlay the new political system?

2 How far did the reforms to local government reflect the principles of the Assembly?

3 What was the National Assembly hoping to achieve by selling Church land?

4 What was the underlying aim of the economic reforms?

5 Why were changes made to the French legal system?

6 How significant was the Civil Constitution of the Clergy on the Revolution and counter-revolution?

7 How did the new constitution propose to limit the powers of the Crown?

8 What impact did the political clubs have on the course of the Revolution?

9 In what way did the policies of the Cordeliers Club differ from those of the Jacobin?

10 How did popular societies seek to take advantage of concerns among workers?

11 How did the actions of the King contribute to the emergence of a republican movement?

12 Was the flight to Varennes a turning point in the Revolution?

13 Why were the events on the Champ de Mars important?

14 What effect did the lack of trust between politicians and the King have on the Legislative Assembly?

15 What impact did the flight to Varennes have on the émigrés?

Question practice

ESSAY QUESTIONS

1 'Louis XVI fully supported the establishment of constitutional monarchy in France.' Explain why you agree or disagree with this view.

2 'Louis XVI's flight to Varennes was a pivotal moment in the development of the French Revolution in the years 1789–99.' How far do you agree?

3 Assess the consequences for France of the reforms made to the Catholic Church by the National Assembly.

4 To what extent were the reforms of the National Assembly opposed by more people than supported them?

5 Which had the greater impact on the development of the French Revolution? i) The rise of the Jacobins. ii) The flight to Varennes. Explain your answer with reference to both i) and ii).

INTERPRETATION QUESTION

1 Read the interpretation and then answer the question that follows. 'The counter-revolution's practical effect in French history was as negligible as its mythological and intellectual importance was great.' (From J.M. Roberts, *The French Revolution*, 1978.) Evaluate the strengths and limitations of this interpretation, making reference to other interpretations that you have studied.

SOURCE QUESTIONS

1 Why is Source D (page 66) valuable to the historian studying the *sans-culottes*? Explain your answer using the source, the information given about it and your own knowledge of the historical context.

2 How much weight do you give the evidence of Source E (page 68) to a historian studying the reasons for Louis XVI's overthrow? Explain your answer using the source, the information given about it and your own knowledge of the historical context.

3 With reference to Sources D (page 66) and E (page 68), and your understanding of the historical context, which of these two sources is more valuable in explaining why popular feeling started to move against the Crown?

4 With reference to Sources C (page 64), D (page 66) and E (page 68), and your understanding of the historical context, assess the value of these sources to a historian studying political divisions during the Revolution.

5 How far could a historian make use of Sources C (page 64) and D (page 66) together to investigate the growing power of the popular movement within the French Revolution in the years 1789–99? Explain your answer using both sources, the information given about them and your own knowledge of the historical context.

CHAPTER 4

War, revolt and overthrow of the monarchy 1792–3

The government's reforms led to increased tensions among those opposed to them. Many *émigrés* left France and became active opponents of the government. A number of politicians of widely differing views urged war as a means of dealing with these opponents. The decision to go to war had momentous consequences for both France and Europe. These are examined in three themes:

★ Outbreak of war

★ Overthrow of the monarchy

★ The Republic at war 1792–3

The key debate on *page 96* of this chapter asks the question: How important was the influence of the *sans-culottes* on the French Revolution?

Key dates

1791	Aug. 27	Declaration of Pillnitz	1792	Sept. 22	Proclamation of the Republic
1792	April 20	War declared on Austria		Nov. 6	Battle of Jemappes
	June 13	Prussia declared war on France		Nov. 19	Decree of Fraternity
	Aug. 10	Overthrow of the monarchy	1793	Jan. 21	Execution of Louis XVI
	Aug. 19	Prussian forces entered northern France		Feb. 1	War declared on Great Britain and the Dutch Republic
	Aug. 20	Capture of Longwy		March 11	Revolt in the Vendée
	Sept. 2–6	September Massacres		Oct. 16	Battle of Wattignies

 ## Outbreak of war

▶ *What impact did the decision to go to war have on French politics?*

KEY TERM

The Terror The period roughly covering March 1793 to August 1794 when extreme policies were used by the Jacobin government to ensure the survival of the Republic.

Despite mistrust of the King, it seemed likely that the constitution of 1791 would survive. What prevented this was the outbreak of war with Austria in April 1792. This event had more decisive and far-reaching results than any other in the whole of the Revolution. Almost everything that happened in France after 1792 was caused or affected by this decision. The war finally destroyed the consensus of 1789. It led directly to the fall of the monarchy, to civil war and to **the Terror**.

Foreign reaction to the Revolution

The **Great Powers** had shown no inclination to intervene during the first two years of the French Revolution. Leopold II, ruler of the **Habsburg Empire**, approved of many of the liberal reforms in the Revolution and did not want a return to absolutism in France. He, like other sovereigns, was pleased at the collapse of French power and no longer regarded France as a serious rival. In any case, Russia, Austria and Prussia were preoccupied elsewhere. From 1787 Russia and Austria were at war with the Ottoman Empire. Leopold abandoned the fight in July 1790 to concentrate on the Austrian Netherlands (present-day Belgium), where there was a revolt. He crushed this in the winter of 1790 and then turned his attention to Poland, where Russia and Prussia were seeking to gain territory. All three powers were essentially more interested in trying to secure a partition of Poland to their own advantage, than in what was going on in France.

Declaration of Pillnitz

After the flight to Varennes (see page 67), the Austrians and Prussians felt they had to make some gesture in support of Louis. They made this in the form of a public declaration.

> **SOURCE A**
>
> **From the Declaration of Pillnitz, issued on 27 August 1791, quoted in J.H. Stewart, *A Documentary Survey of the French Revolution*, Macmillan, 1951, pp. 223–4.**
>
> *His Majesty the Emperor and His Majesty the King of Prussia … jointly declare that they regard the present position of his Majesty the King of France as a matter of common concern to all the sovereigns of Europe. They trust that the powers whose aid is supplied will not fail to recognise this fact: and that, accordingly, they will not refuse to co-operate with their said Majesties in employing, in proportion to their forces, the most effective means for enabling the King of France to consolidate with complete freedom the foundations of a monarchical government … In which case their said Majesties, are resolved to act promptly, in mutual accord, with the forces necessary to attain the proposed objective. In the meantime, they will give their troops such orders as are necessary to have them ready for active service.*

The declaration was significant because it appeared to be a threat to interfere in French internal affairs. Enemies of the King considered that the declaration justified their opposition to, and mistrust of, the monarchy. In reality, however, it was no threat at all since the Austrians knew that the other powers, such as Britain, would not join them. This meant that the declaration was unlikely to lead to any action. In France the declaration did not create much of a stir. The Assembly did not debate it and most newspapers ignored it. When the constitution was passed in September, Leopold gave it a warm welcome, so the possibility of Austrian intervention was even more remote.

🔑 KEY TERMS

Great Powers Countries that were more powerful than others on the basis of their military, economic and territorial strength – the major ones were Austria, France, Prussia, Russia and Britain.

Habsburg Empire Territory that roughly corresponds to modern-day Austria, Hungary, the Czech Republic and Slovakia. The empire also considered itself to be the leading German state.

Read Source A. What level of support did the two monarchs offer Louis? **?**

Support for war

In France, people, for very different reasons, came to believe that war was either in their own best interests or in those of France. Marie Antoinette ('the only man in the family', Mirabeau called her) wrote to her brother, the Emperor Leopold II, in September 1791: 'Conciliation is out of the question now. Armed force has destroyed everything and only armed force can put things right.' She hoped for a war in which France would be defeated, enabling Louis to recover his old powers. The King shared her view that France would be defeated. 'The physical condition and morale of France', he wrote, 'is such that it will be unable to sustain even half a campaign.' The deputies were not convinced. There were widespread rumours that the country's foreign policy was being run by an '**Austrian Committee**', headed by Marie Antoinette, and that secret agents were being sent to Koblenz (the headquarters of the *émigrés*) and Vienna to plot counter-revolution. These rumours were well founded.

Army commanders such as Lafayette and Dumouriez also wanted war. Lafayette, the first commander of the National Guard, had brought the King from Versailles to Paris during the October Days and was responsible for the 'massacre' of the Champ de Mars (see page 69). He had become disillusioned by the failure of the Revolution to produce political stability and wanted the authority of the King to be strengthened. This could be done by waging a short, successful war against Austria, which he believed would increase his prestige as a general. It would also enable him to dictate his own terms to both the King and the Assembly.

The desire for war resulted in the co-operation of Lafayette and his followers with the **Brissotins**, who also wanted war. They were followers of Jacques Brissot, one of the first politicians to support demands for a Republic. After the flight to Varennes he argued for the abolition of the monarchy and the trial of Louis XVI. He saw that the King had not really accepted the constitution and that the Court was plotting against the Revolution and seeking the armed intervention of the European powers. Brissot believed that war would force the King to reveal his true sympathies: being either for or against the Revolution. He also argued that it would expose any traitors who were opposed to the Revolution.

There were about 130 Girondins in the 745-member Legislative Assembly, so to obtain a majority they needed the support both of Lafayette and his followers and of the unorganised centre. Brissot obtained this by playing on their hopes and fears by waging a campaign calling for war, which he began in October 1791. The main points in his case for war were:

- A successful conflict would rouse enthusiasm for the Revolution and show the permanence of the new regime.
- A war would allow France to extend its revolutionary ideals abroad.

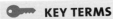

KEY TERMS

Austrian Committee
Influential politicians and close confidants of Marie Antoinette who kept in close secret contact with Vienna, capital of the Habsburg Empire.

Brissotins Supporters of Jacques Brissot who later merged with the Girondins.

- French armies would have the active support of their enemy's own repressed subjects.
- The international situation was favourable as the European powers were unlikely to unite against France – Russia was preoccupied with Poland, and Britain would not join in unless its home security or empire was directly threatened.

Opposition to war

Most deputies were won over by these arguments but some politicians outside the Assembly were not. Robespierre expressed his attitude to the war in these terms: 'You propose to give supreme power to those who most want your ruin. The only way to save the State and to safeguard freedom is to wage war in the right way, on our enemies at home, instead of marching under their orders against their allies across the frontiers.'

Marquis de Lafayette

1757	Born at Chavaniac into an ancient noble family
1774	Married the daughter of the Duc d'Ayen
1777	Used part of his enormous fortune to fit out a ship and set sail for America. Distinguished service in the cause of liberty made him a hero in France and opened up his mind to the need for reform in his homeland
1787	Member of the Assembly of Notables, called for the summoning of the Estates-General, was closely connected with the reform movement
1789	Representative of the nobility to the Estates-General
1790	Occupied a pivotal role in the *Fête de la Fédération* to celebrate the first anniversary of the Revolution. Within weeks the champion of liberty appeared to be supporting repression, when an army mutiny was suppressed
1791	Champ de Mars massacre. This appeared to confirm the popular belief that he was hostile towards ordinary people. His fall from power was rapid
1792	At the outbreak of war he was appointed commander of the Army of the Centre. In June he left his post during the *journées* to try and organise the Legislative Assembly against the Jacobins
1799	Returned to France under Napoleon and retired to farm his estates
1834	Died

Marriage into the great Noailles family gave Lafayette good connections into the circle of courtiers around the young Louis XVI. During the early years of the Revolution he allied himself with the revolutionary bourgeoisie and became one of the most powerful men in France when he was appointed commander of the National Guard in 1789. His soldiers escorted the Royal family back to Paris during the October Days. Despite his apparent sympathy for the Revolution, he steadily became more hostile to it. The popular belief was that he was behind the Champ de Mars massacre in 1791. Overambition proved to be his undoing. After the overthrow of Louis, he tried to turn his army against Paris. He failed and defected to the Prussians.

Robespierre argued that the real threat came from soldiers like Lafayette, who were still popular enough to mislead the public. Robespierre believed that the aim of the European powers was to intimidate France, not to invade. War would be more difficult than Brissot expected, because foreigners would not rise up in support of French invaders. Robespierre (see page 107) memorably observed: 'No one loves armed missionaries.' As a result of his opposition to the war, Robespierre became an isolated and unpopular figure, who was convinced that his opponents were plotting to betray the Revolution. His relations with Brissot were poisoned by bitter personal quarrels and mutual suspicion.

The declaration of war

The Girondins were pressing hard for war but it is doubtful whether they would have gained the support of the majority of deputies without the bungling of Austria and Prussia. On 7 February 1792 Austria and Prussia became allies and thought they could intimidate the French by threatening war. They had great confidence in their own armies: in 1789 a small Prussian army had conquered the **United Provinces** in under a month and in 1790 a small Austrian army occupied Belgium in under two weeks. They expected little resistance from the French army because:

- France was considered to be weak from internal division.
- Mutinies in the army and the loss of so many officers who had fled the country would undermine France's ability to defend itself effectively.
- The bankrupt nature of French finances would limit the purchase of munitions.

It was anticipated that France would have neither the will nor the ability to resist Austrian pressure.

Austrian threats and Girondin attacks on the 'Austrian Committee' at Court forced the King to dismiss his Feuillant ministers in March 1792. He appointed a more radical government, including some Girondins. This was a decisive change. The old ministers had carried out the wishes of the King; the new ones obeyed the Assembly. Both the Assembly and the government now wanted war, especially the new Foreign Minister, General Dumouriez. He hated Austria but had aims similar to those of Lafayette: a short successful war would increase his own personal power and prestige along with that of the Crown.

In Austria, the cautious Leopold had died on 1 March and had been replaced by the young and impetuous Francis II. When rumours reached Austria that Marie Antoinette was to be put on trial, it decided reluctantly on war. But it was the French who actually declared war on 20 April 1792. Only seven deputies voted against it. The French hoped to fight solely against Austria but Prussia declared war on France in June, and took the lead in the campaign under its Commander-in-Chief the Duke of Brunswick.

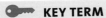

KEY TERM

United Provinces Present-day Netherlands, ruled at the time by the House of Orange.

For very different reasons, influential groups in the Assembly and supporters of Louis XVI decided that war would serve their interests best. They hoped for a short decisive war, but this did not happen. The resulting conflict – known as the **Revolutionary War** – would:

- last ten years until the Treaty of Amiens 1802
- result in the loss of 1.4 million French people
- dramatically alter the whole direction of the Revolution.

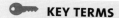

KEY TERMS

Revolutionary War Fought by France against other European powers between 1792 and 1802.

Regular army Full-time professional soldiers. As events unfolded the white uniforms of the *ancien régime* were replaced by ones that reflected the colours of the Revolution: red, white and blue.

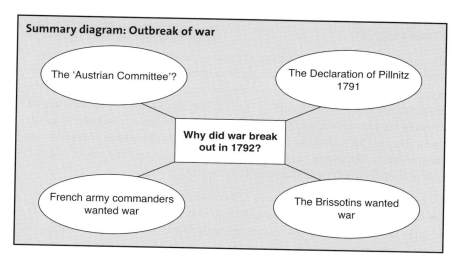

Summary diagram: Outbreak of war

- The 'Austrian Committee'?
- The Declaration of Pillnitz 1791
- **Why did war break out in 1792?**
- French army commanders wanted war
- The Brissotins wanted war

② Overthrow of the monarchy

▶ *What factors contributed to the overthrow of the monarchy?*

Having taken France into war, the early military engagements showed how badly prepared the French army was. Military defeat and the desertion of many commanders to the enemy created tension and fear in Paris that the capital would be captured. The royal family and Louis were suspected of being less than fully committed to gaining a French victory, and some of Louis' actions were seen as hostile to the Revolution. In this climate the King's political opponents became increasingly determined to overthrow the monarchy.

The military crisis

When war was declared, the French army was not well prepared. Over half its 12,000 officers had emigrated. There were 150,000 men under arms in 1791 comprising both regular and newly recruited volunteers. However, a combination of desertion and revolutionary propaganda in the many new newspapers and magazines destroyed the discipline of the **regular army**, while the volunteers were poorly trained and equipped.

When French forces advanced into the Austrian Netherlands (Belgium) on 20 April 1792 they were faced with determined opposition. The army panicked and retreated headlong to Lille, where they murdered their commander. Whole units deserted. By the end of May all three field-commanders were advising that peace should be made immediately. The allies counter-attacked and invaded northern France. Treason and traitors were blamed for French defeats and with some justification: Marie Antoinette had sent details of French military plans to the Austrians.

Royal vetoes

The government also had other problems to cope with. There was opposition from refractory priests and counter-revolutionaries who wanted to restore the authority of the Catholic Church and the monarchy. The Girondins had to satisfy demands for action against 'traitors'. On 27 May the Assembly passed a law for the deportation of refractory priests. Another law disbanded the King's Guard and a third set up a camp for 20,000 National Guards (known as *fédérés*) from the provinces. They were to protect Paris from invasion and the government from a coup by the generals, especially Lafayette.

Louis refused to approve these laws. When Roland, the Girondin Minister of the Interior, protested, Louis dismissed him and other Girondin ministers on 13 June. Dumouriez resigned soon afterwards. On 19 June Louis vetoed the laws on refractory priests and the *fédéré* camp. There was an expectation of a military coup in support of the King.

The rise of the *sans-culottes*

Leaders of the **Paris Sections** responded to these events by holding an armed demonstration on 20 June, the anniversary of the Tennis Court Oath and of the flight to Varennes. Their leaders came from the Cordeliers Club. About 8000 demonstrators, many of them National Guards, poured into the Tuileries. One participant described seeing Louis '… wearing the **bonnet rouge** on his head and drinking from a bottle, to the health of the nation'. Louis behaved with great dignity. He was not intimidated and his calmness may have saved his life. This *journée* did not achieve its desired end: the King did not withdraw his veto or recall the Girondin ministers. However, it did show very clearly the weakness of the King and the Assembly and the growing power of the Sections. The Assembly soon took steps which recognised the growing importance of the *sans-culottes* but which also increased the likelihood of a rising. On 11 July the Assembly declared a state of emergency by issuing a decree '**la patrie en danger**', which called on every Frenchman to fight.

This tilted the balance of power in favour of those who called for greater democracy. How could you ask a man to fight and not give him a vote? The Sections, whose assemblies were allowed to meet in permanent session, and *fédérés* demanded the admission of 'passive citizens' into the sectional assemblies and National Guard. These requests were granted by the end of the

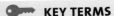

KEY TERMS

Fédérés National guardsmen from the provinces who arrived in Paris to display during the *Fête de la Fédération* commemorating the fall of the Bastille, 14 July 1792.

Paris Sections Paris was divided into 48 Sections to replace the 60 electoral districts of 1789; the Section became the power base of the *sans-culottes*.

Bonnet rouge The red cap popularly known as the cap of liberty, which became an important symbol of the Revolution.

La patrie en danger 'The fatherland is in danger' became a rallying cry to ordinary people to help save the country.

month. The control exerted by the bourgeois since 1789 began to give way to the popular democracy of the *sans-culottes*.

SOURCE B

From the decree 'The country in danger', 11 July 1792.

Large numbers of troops are marching on our frontiers. All those who hate liberty are taking up arms against our constitution. Citizens the country is in danger. May those who have the honour of being the first to march to the defence of that which is dearest to them never forget that they are Frenchmen and free, that their fellow citizens in their homes are upholding the security of the individual and of property, that the magistrates of the people are ever watchful, that with the calm courage of true strength everyone is waiting for the signal from the law to act, and the country will be saved.

> Read Source B. What case did the Assembly make to persuade French citizens to help defend the country? **?**

Tension in Paris

Tension in Paris was increased by the arrival of *fédérés* from the provinces in the summer of 1792, and by the publication of the Brunswick Manifesto.

The *fédérés*

Unlike the Paris National Guard, whose officers were conservative or royalist, many of the *fédérés* were militant revolutionaries and republicans. Their patriotism was expressed in the war song of the Rhine army, composed in Strasbourg by Rouget de l'Isle. It acquired its name **La Marseillaise** as it was sung by the fédérés of Marseille on their march to the capital. Although by July they only numbered 5000 in Paris they were a powerful pressure group in the radical sections, calling for the removal of the King.

As the situation in Paris deteriorated rapidly, extremists became much more active in its political life. With a new insurrection being prepared by radicals and *fédérés* from the middle of July, the Girondins changed their attitude of opposition to the King and tried to prevent a rising. They were alarmed that events were getting out of their control. Girondin leaders warned the King that there was likely to be a more violent uprising than that of 20 June and that it was likely he would be deposed. They offered to do all they could to prevent such an uprising, if he would recall the ministers dismissed on 13 June. Louis rejected their offer.

The Jacobin leader, Robespierre, was co-operating with the central committee of the *fédérés* and on 29 July, in a speech to the Jacobin Club, he put forward his proposals:

- abandonment of the constitution of 1791
- the overthrow of the monarchy
- the establishment of a National Convention, elected by **universal male suffrage**, to replace the Legislative Assembly
- a **purge** of the departmental authorities, many of which were royalist.

> **🔑 KEY TERMS**
>
> **La Marseillaise** The rousing song composed by Rouget de l'Isle in 1792 and adopted as the anthem of the Republic on 14 July 1795.
>
> **Universal male suffrage** A vote for every man over a certain age.
>
> **Purge** Forced removal of political opponents.

Until this date Robespierre had warned the fédérés and the Sections against hasty action, as this might lead to a backlash in the King's favour. Now he felt the moment had come to strike. Petitions were pouring in from the *fédérés*, the clubs and the provinces for the removal of the King.

The Brunswick Manifesto

To add to the worsening tension the Brunswick Manifesto, issued by the commander-in-chief of the Austro-Prussian armies, was published in Paris on 1 August. Its main terms and threats were:

- to ensure the welfare of France, and not to conquer any French territory
- to restore the liberty of Louis XVI and his family
- that the city of Paris set Louis free without delay, and make it responsible for the safety of the royal family
- if the Tuileries Palace was attacked and the royal family harmed then the joint Austrian–Prussian army would inflict 'an exemplary vengeance' on the city and its citizens.

The Manifesto was intended to help the King but it had the opposite effect. Frenchmen were infuriated by what they considered to be foreign intervention in their affairs. Many who had previously supported the monarchy now turned against it.

On 3 August Pétion, the Mayor of Paris, went to the Legislative Assembly and demanded, on behalf of 47 out of the 48 Sections, the abolition of the monarchy. Yet the Assembly refused to depose the King and defeated a motion to put Lafayette on trial. This finally persuaded many that a rising was necessary.

The attack on the Tuileries

On the night of 9 August *sans-culottes* took over the Hôtel de Ville, expelled the city council and set up a revolutionary Commune. Among its leaders was Hébert, who had taken part in the Cordeliers agitation the previous year and had strong links with the Sections and the *fédérés*.

On 10 August 1792 several thousand men from the National Guard, which was now open to 'passive citizens', and 2000 *fédérés*, marched on the Tuileries. The palace was defended by 3000 troops, 2000 of whom were National Guards. The others were Swiss mercenaries who were certain to resist. During the morning, the King sought refuge in the Assembly to protect his family. The National Guardsmen who were defending the Tuileries joined the crowd and entered the courtyards. They believed the attack was over until the Swiss began to fire. The *fédérés* replied with grapeshot and it seemed that a violent battle would start. The King ordered his Swiss guards to cease fire. This left them at the mercy of the attackers: 600 Swiss were massacred. Among the attackers, 90 *fédérés* and 300 Parisians (tradesmen, craftsmen, wage-earners) had been killed or wounded. It was the bloodiest *journée* of the Revolution.

SOURCE C

Storming of the Tuileries Palace 1792.

The rising was as much a rejection of the Assembly as it was of the King. The rebels invaded the Assembly and forced it to recognise the new revolutionary Commune, which had given the orders for the attack on the palace. The deputies had to hand over the King to the Commune, who imprisoned him in the Temple (see the map on page 35). They also agreed to the election, by universal male suffrage, of a National Convention that was to draw up a new, democratic constitution. The Commune was now in control in Paris, although in the rest of France it was the authority of the Assembly alone that was recognised.

The proclamation of the Republic

Following the overthrow of Louis, the **constitutional monarchists** who made up about two-thirds of the deputies did not feel safe, so they stayed away from the Assembly and went into hiding. This left the Girondins in charge, the beneficiaries of a revolution they had tried to avoid. The 300 or so deputies remaining in the Assembly appointed new ministers, including the three who had been dismissed earlier. A surprise appointment was that of Danton (see his profile on page 122) as appointed Minister of Justice to please the *sans-culottes*.

In its final six weeks before the National Convention replaced it, the Assembly did all that the Commune wanted. It passed several radical measures:

- Refractory priests who did not leave France were to be deported to the French colony of Guiana.

> What does Source C suggest about the nature of the attack on the Tuileries?

 **KEY TERM**

Constitutional monarchists Supporters of Louis who welcomed the granting of limited democratic rights to the French people.

- Abolition without compensation of all feudal dues unless the *seigneur* was able to produce title deeds detailing specific rights. This was an attempt to win over the peasantry, many of whom resented the attack on the monarchy. It effectively ended the feudal system, which peasants had unsuccessfully been trying to do since the August Decrees of 1789.
- House-to-house searches were ordered for arms and suspects; many people were arrested.
- Divorce was legalised. Registration of births, deaths and marriages became a State responsibility rather than a Church one.

After the 10 August *journée*, Louis XVI was suspended from exercising his powers. It was left for the National Convention to decide whether or not to dethrone him. The Convention met for the first time on 20 September 1792. By then there was little doubt that Louis would be deposed. Royal documents found in the Tuileries after 10 August confirmed what was widely suspected – that the King had betrayed the nation by maintaining links with France's enemies. On 21–22 September 1792 the monarchy in France was abolished and a Republic was proclaimed. This was in effect a second revolution. Abolishing the monarchy was one thing, how to deal with Louis was an entirely different issue.

Girondins versus Jacobins: the power struggle in the Convention

In the elections to the Convention, which were held at the end of August and the beginning of September 1792, all men over 21 could vote. The results for the new 749-seat Convention were distorted by fear and intimidation. In Paris, all who had shown royalist sympathies were **disenfranchised**. Thus, all 24 members for Paris were Jacobins, republicans and supporters of the Commune. Robespierre came head of the poll in the capital. Among the deputies in the Convention whose allegiance can be identified, there were about 180 Girondins and 300 Jacobins. A total of 250 deputies were uncommitted to either group and were known as **the Plain**. Forty-seven per cent of the deputies were lawyers. The proportion representing business and trade had declined to nine per cent (compared with thirteen per cent in the Constituent Assembly). Only six deputies were artisans.

Until 2 June 1793 the history of the Convention was that of a struggle between the Girondins and Jacobins. The Jacobins were also known as the **Montagnards** ('the Mountain') or simply the Left. Neither group was a party in the modern sense, with an agreed programme and common discipline. People disapproved of parties, which were regarded as pursuing the selfish interests of the members rather than the common good, very much like the corporations and guilds of the *ancien régime* had done. It is, therefore, very difficult to say how many deputies belonged to any one group at any time.

🔑 **KEY TERMS**

Disenfranchised Stripped of the right to vote.

The Plain The majority of deputies in the Convention who sat on the lower seats of the tiered assembly hall.

Montagnards The Mountain – the name given to Jacobin deputies who occupied the upper seats to the left of the speaker in the tiered chamber of the National Assembly.

Table 4.1 The main differences between the Girondins and the Montagnards

	The Girondins	**The Montagnards (the Left)**
Deputies	Bourgeois	Bourgeois
Leaders	Brissot, Roland	Robespierre, Danton, Marat, Couthon, Saint-Just
Policies	Believed in the Revolution and the Republic	Believed in the Revolution and the Republic
	Hated privilege	Hated privilege
	Anti-clerical	Anti-clerical
	Wanted a more enlightened and humane France	Wanted a more enlightened and humane France
	Liberal economic policy market determines wages and prices. **Free market** economics	Tight control over wages and prices by central government. Policies of the 'maximum'
	Favoured federalism – more power given to the provinces	Favoured strong central government control from Paris
	Committed to winning the war	Committed to winning the war but willing to make greater concessions to ordinary people
Areas of support	Most of the Paris press, considerable provincial support from outside Paris. Lost some popular support because they did not fully back the 10 August *journée*	Strong support among the Paris Sections, political clubs in Paris and the Paris deputies. Very popular with the *sans-culottes* and the popular movement
Beliefs and attitudes	Suspected Robespierre of wanting to create a bloody dictatorship. Were accused by the Montagnards of supporting the counter-revolution	Believed that the Girondins were seeking to attract support from the Right – former nobles and royalists – in order to remain in power. Strong government and firm policies needed to ensure survival of the Republic

As neither side had a majority in the Assembly, each needed to gain the support of the Plain, who were also bourgeois, believed in economic liberalism and were deeply afraid of the popular movement. At first they supported the Girondins, who provided most of the ministers and dominated the majority of the Assembly's committees.

The trial of Louis XVI

The Jacobins insisted on the trial of the King, in order to establish the Republic more firmly. While Louis remained alive it might be easier for the royalists to plot a restoration. The *sans-culottes,* on whom the Jacobins came to rely more and more, wanted the King tried and executed, as they held him responsible for the bloodshed at the Tuileries on 10 August 1792. The Girondins tried to prevent a trial and made two attempts to save Louis' life. First, they suggested that the King's fate should be decided by a referendum. When this was rejected and the King was found guilty and sentenced to death, they then proposed a reprieve.

Two factors sealed Louis XVI's fate:

- First, the incriminating royal correspondence between Louis and the Austrian royal family discovered in the *armoire de fer* documents. These were carefully examined by a special commission set up by the Convention.

 **KEY TERMS**

Anti-clericalism
Opposition to the Catholic Church.

Free market A trading system with no artificial price controls. Prices are determined solely by supply and demand.

SOURCE D

Why do you think the artist of Source D has chosen to portray a skeleton in the chest?

The discovery of the *armoire de fer*.

- Second, Marat's proposal that a decision should be reached by ***appel nominal***, 'so that traitors in this Assembly may be known'. In an Assembly of 749 deputies, no one voted that Louis was innocent, while 693 voted that he was guilty.

When it came to the sentence, 387 voted unconditionally for the death penalty and 288 for imprisonment. The Convention then voted against a reprieve by 380 votes to 310. What the voting patterns reveal was the existence of a solid bloc of moderates in the Convention, reluctant to support the execution of the King.

The execution of Louis XVI

Louis XVI was executed on the morning of 21 January 1793. As Saint-Just, a leading Jacobin, said, '… he was executed not for what he had done but for what he was: a menace to the Republic'. An alternative view is that Louis was executed because his actions in the period after 1789 showed that he was not to be trusted; a view confirmed, to all intents and purposes, by the discovery of the *armoire de fer*.

Securing the execution of Louis was the first Jacobin victory in the Convention and it left the factions more hostile to one another than ever. Although over half the Girondin leaders, including Brissot, had voted for the death penalty, they were branded as royalists and counter-revolutionaries by the Montagnards. By securing Louis' execution, the Montagnards gained an ascendancy in the Convention which they rarely lost afterwards. Brissot hardly spoke there after the trial.

SOURCE E

> What do you think would be the purpose behind producing the print in Source E?

The execution of Louis XVI in the *Place de la Revolution*, 21 January 1793.

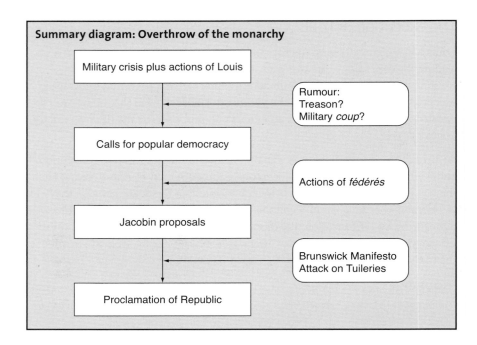

Summary diagram: Overthrow of the monarchy

Military crisis plus actions of Louis

↓

Rumour:
Treason?
Military *coup*?

Calls for popular democracy

↓

Actions of *fédérés*

Jacobin proposals

↓

Brunswick Manifesto
Attack on Tuileries

Proclamation of Republic

3 The Republic at war 1792–3

▶ *What impact did the war have on the course of the Revolution?*

In the summer of 1792 the situation of the French armies on the frontier was desperate. Lafayette had defected to the Austrians on 17 August. With a leading general deserting, who could still be trusted? Panic and fear of treachery swept the country. This was increased when the Prussians crossed the French frontier and captured Longwy. By the beginning of September, Verdun, the last major fortress on the road to Paris, was about to surrender. The French capital was under immediate threat from enemy forces, and the Revolution itself was in danger of being overthrown by foreign powers.

The September Massacres

Against a background of panic and desperation, the authorities appealed to the forces of nationalism and patriotism. The Commune called on all patriots to take up arms. Thousands volunteered to defend the capital and the Revolution. But, once they had left for the front, there was growing concern about the overcrowded prisons, which contained many priests and nobles as counter-revolutionary suspects. A rumour arose that these were plotting to escape, kill the helpless population and hand the city over to the Prussians.

Marat, a powerful figure in the Commune, called for the conspirators to be killed. The massacre of prisoners was the first appearance of the Terror. It began on 2 September and continued for five days. Between 1100 and 1400 of the 2600 prisoners in Paris jails were murdered. Only a quarter were priests and nobles; the rest were common criminals. The killers were the *sans-culottes* of the Sections. The Commune made no attempt to stop them, and neither did Danton, the Minister of Justice. This would have meant **mobilising** the National Guard and risking another Champ de Mars incident.

KEY TERM

Mobilising Calling up part-time soldiers or national guardsmen for military service.

SOURCE F

From a letter written by the leading Girondin supporter Madame Roland, 9 September 1792.

My friend Danton controls everything: Robespierre is his puppet. Marat holds his torch and his dagger: this wild tribune reigns – at the moment we are merely oppressed, but waiting for the time when we become his victims. If you knew the awful details of the killing expeditions! Women brutally raped before being torn to pieces by these tigers, guts cut out and worn as ribbons, human flesh eaten dripping with blood. You know my enthusiasm for the Revolution: well I am ashamed of it! Its reputation is tarnished by these scoundrels, it is becoming hideous. It is degrading to stay here, but it is forbidden to leave Paris. Goodbye, if it is too late for us, save the rest of France from the crimes of these madmen.

Read Source F. What is Madame Roland's main concern in her letter?

SOURCE G

Contemporary print showing the September Massacres 1793.

What does Source G suggest about the actions carried out in early September 1792 in the prisons of Paris?

The massacre cast a shadow over the first meeting of the Convention. Most deputies from the provinces were shocked by the killings and rallied to the Girondins. The hatred of the Girondins for the Jacobins and their *sans-culotte* supporters was intensified. From now on, moderates and foreign opinion regarded Montagnards and *sans-culottes* as bloodthirsty savages: *buveurs de sang* (drinkers of blood).

The Battle of Valmy

Just as the fortunes of war had brought about the September Massacres, they also brought an end to this first phase of the Terror. On 20 September 1792 at Valmy, 52,000 French troops defeated 34,000 Prussians. This was a very significant victory. If the Prussians had won, it was likely that Paris would have fallen and the Revolution would have been brought to an end.

The new forces summoned by the decree of 11 July 1792 (see page 83) were very effective, particularly as they were supplemented by many volunteers and National Guardsmen. In the main, these men were workers and traders who belonged to the *sans-culottes* rather than being the sons of the bourgeoisie. They were passionately committed to the revolutionary cause. Following the Prussian defeat, the German writer Goethe, who witnessed the French victory, wrote: 'This day and this place open a new era in the history of the world.'

Brunswick, the Prussian commander-in-chief, retreated to the frontier. French armies once again took the offensive. Within a month they had occupied much of the left bank of the Rhine. In November Dumouriez defeated the Austrians at Jemappes and occupied most of Belgium. This was the first major battle won by republican forces.

From defence to offence

With the Republic apparently secure from external threat, the government now began to talk about expanding to reach France's **natural frontiers** – the Rhine, the Alps and the Pyrenees – and in January 1793 it passed a decree claiming them for France. This would mean **annexing** territory, which was contrary to the policy laid down by the Constituent Assembly in May 1790: 'the French nation renounces involvement in any war undertaken with the aim of making conquest'.

The change in policy was accompanied by propaganda. On 19 November 1792 the Convention issued the **Decree of Fraternity**, which promised '… to extend fraternal feelings and aid to all peoples who may wish to regain their liberty'. Some politicians were attracted to the prospect of extending the Revolution to other states. Brissot wrote 'We can only be at peace once Europe … is blazing from end to end.' He argued that as long as France was under threat from hostile monarchs there would be little prospect of security. But, if these monarchs could be defeated, the Republic would be secure.

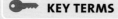 **KEY TERMS**

Natural frontiers Barriers, such as rivers, mountain ranges and the sea, that separate countries.

Annex To incorporate foreign territory into a state, usually forcibly and against the will of the local people.

Decree of Fraternity The Convention offered support to those in any state wishing to overthrow their rulers and establish democratic political systems.

Avignon, which had been papal territory in France since 1273, had been annexed in 1791. Savoy (November 1792) and Nice (January 1793) were the first foreign territories to be added to the Republic. A revolutionary administration was set up in the conquered lands. French armies had to be paid for and fed at the expense of the local population. Church lands and those belonging to enemies of the new regime were confiscated. Tithes and feudal dues were abolished. These measures alienated much of the population, and confirmed Robespierre's prediction that French armies would not be welcomed abroad (see page 80).

The War of the First Coalition

The Republican Convention posed a threat to the European monarchs with its Decree of Fraternity. The Great Powers were alarmed at the annexation of Nice and Savoy. Britain was particularly concerned at the threat France posed to the Austrian Netherlands (modern-day Belgium). These territories possessed good ports from which to launch any potential invasion of Britain. William Pitt, the British prime minister, was determined that both of these should be kept out of French hands. When the French reopened the River Scheldt to navigation it was seen as a direct challenge to British commerce. (Its closure in 1648 had led to the decline of the port of Antwerp as a rival to London.)

The Convention unanimously declared war on Britain and the Netherlands on 1 February 1793. The Spanish royal family, who were related to the French Bourbons, were shocked at the execution of Louis and expelled the French envoy. When it appeared that Spain was preparing to join an anti-French alliance, in March the Convention declared war on its southern neighbour. With the exception of Switzerland, Sweden and Denmark, France was at war with most of Europe.

The French misunderstood the situation in Britain. They mistakenly thought that there would be a revolution there. They also thought that in war Britain would crumble as Prussia and Austria had done at the battles of Valmy and Jemappes. The British, for their part, thought that France was bankrupt and on the verge of civil war. Each side believed that the war would be short and easy and entered into it confidently. **The First Coalition** emerged slowly between March and September 1793. Britain was the driving force binding the other powers together as there was no formal treaty. Its diplomacy persuaded a number of other countries to join the anti-French crusade.

The 1793 campaign

The campaign in 1793 began very badly for the French. A French attack against the Netherlands failed and the French commander, Dumouriez, was defeated by the Austrians at Neerwinden in March. Following his defeat, he plotted with the Austrians to march on Paris to overthrow the Convention and restore the monarchy. His action prompted some politicians to suspect the loyalty of the army commanders. When his army refused to follow him, Dumouriez deserted

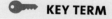

KEY TERM

First Coalition A loose anti-French alliance created by Britain and consisting of the Netherlands, Spain, Piedmont, Naples, Prussia, Russia, Austria and Portugal. Russia refused to commit soldiers to the coalition when Britain did not send money to support Russia's armies.

to the Austrians along with the Duc de Chartres (who later became King Louis Philippe of France 1830–48). Since the Girondins had enthusiastically backed Dumouriez, his defection was very important as it further weakened their position in the Convention and within the Paris clubs.

Meanwhile, the French lost Belgium and the left bank of the Rhine bordering their country. Once again there was fighting on French soil. Leading figures such as Danton were urging conciliation with the coalition. With the military situation deteriorating rapidly, a large rebellion broke out in the Vendée.

The role of Lazare Carnot: organiser of victory

Carnot trained as a military engineer and served as a captain in the Royal army. During the Revolution he was elected first to the Legislative Assembly and following the overthrow of the monarchy, to the National Convention. As the military situation deteriorated, Carnot's military skills were called into use. He was sent to Bayonne, in the south, to organise the defences of the area against a possible attack from Spain.

In the summer of 1793 Carnot joined the **Committee of Public Safety** (CPS), and his military expertise was put to good use. He studied the military problems facing the Republic and presented a number of reports to the CPS. Following one such report, 82 representatives were sent into the departments to speed up the conscription of 300,000 men into the army. The military front causing greatest concern to the Republic was in the north against the Austrians and Prussians. He was sent by the CPS to lend his support to this demoralised and dispirited army. The essence of his contribution was:

- reorganising the army
- re-establishing discipline
- leading by example in military engagements.

Before joining the Army of the North, Austrian forces were besieging Maubeugne. Following the measures suggested by Carnot, the siege was raised and enemy forces were defeated at the Battle of Wattignies on 16 October 1793. During the campaign, Carnot fought alongside the generals and was in the heart of the action. He made a vital contribution to the eventual success of the campaign, and was honoured with the description 'organiser of victory'.

The Vendée Rebellion

By the winter of 1792–3 the counter-revolution in France had virtually collapsed. It is appropriate to describe the Vendée as an 'anti-revolution' rather than a 'counter-revolution' in that it was directed more against the Revolution and its demands rather than for the restoration of the *ancien régime*. The basic causes of the uprising were the expansion of the war and the introduction of conscription. The government ordered a **levy** of 300,000 troops in February 1793. This triggered a massive uprising on 11 March 1793 in four departments

KEY FIGURE

Lazare Carnot (1753–1823)

During the trial of Louis XVI, he voted for execution. Although his political inclination was to the centre, he did lean towards the Jacobins.

KEY TERMS

Committee of Public Safety Effectively, the government of France during 1793–4 and one of the twin pillars of the Terror along with the Committee of General Security.

Levy An assessment to raise an agreed number of conscripts.

south of the Loire, in what became known as the *Vendée militaire* or simply the Vendée.

In reality, discontent in the Vendée had been present long before 1793 and the proposed conscription. Since 1789 peasants in the area had found themselves paying more in the new land tax than they had paid under the taxes of *ancien régime*. They came to dislike the revolutionary government, and with the introduction of the Civil Constitution of the Clergy (see pages 58–60) this dislike turned into hatred and open hostility. The religious changes were strongly resisted in the Vendée, which was deeply attached to the Catholic Church, and there were many non-juring priests in the area.

The sale of Church lands was also unpopular, because most were bought by the bourgeoisie of the towns, who then often raised rents. Those who bought *biens* became supporters of the Revolution, which was a guarantee that they could keep the land (see page 43). Those who were not successful became hostile to the government.

The peasants looked to the nobles as their natural leaders. Many of these were **monarchist**, so the rising became caught up in counter-revolution. New local officials, constitutional priests and National Guards were massacred. By May the situation was considered so grave that 30,000 troops were withdrawn from the front to deal with the rising. Yet the rebels never posed a serious threat to the government in Paris. They were ill-disciplined – better at **guerrilla warfare** than set-piece battles – and unwilling to move far from their local bases.

Economic issues

The economic problems created by the war added to the government's difficulties. To pay for the war more and more *assignats* were printed, which reduced the value of those already in circulation. By February 1793 the purchasing power of the *assignat* had fallen by 50 per cent. This pushed up prices as more *assignats* were needed to buy goods. The harvest in 1792 was good but bread was scarce. Saint-Just pointed out why in a speech in November 1792: 'The farmer does not want to save paper money and for this reason he is most reluctant to sell his grain.' The results of high prices and scarcity were widespread riots against grain stores and demands from the *sans-culottes* for price controls and **requisitioning**.

The Republic saved

Of greater concern to the government in the summer of 1793 was the threat posed by the coalition. The Austrians pushed into France, while the Spaniards invaded Roussillon in the south. An allied army of 160,000 men on the Franco-Dutch border was opposed by a much smaller French force. If the allied commanders had joined forces and moved on Paris, the French would have faced disaster. Fortunately for them, the allies did not co-ordinate their

KEY TERMS

Monarchist Active supporter of the Bourbon monarchy.

Guerrilla warfare Military action by irregular bands avoiding direct confrontation with the larger opposing forces. They did not wear uniforms in order to blend in with civilians.

Requisitioning Compulsory purchase by the government of supplies of food and horses paid for in *assignats* – the new paper currency.

plans. Pitt ordered the Duke of York to capture Dunkirk as a naval base, so he turned west. The Austrians turned east, and the allied army broke in two. This enormous blunder saved France.

Summary diagram: The Republic at war 1792–3

	War	*At home*
1792	Military crisis Battle of Valmy	September Massacres
1793	Decree of Fraternity Annexations Declaration of war on Britain and Holland War went badly for France	Popular discontent: Vendée Rebellion

 # Key debate

▶ *How important was the influence of the* sans-culottes *on the French Revolution?*

The role of the *sans-culottes* on the French Revolution, particularly during the period 1789–94, is certainly one of the issues that rouse passions among historians of the Right and the Left.

The Marxist interpretation

The first major study of the role of the *sans-culottes*, which used previously unexamined local records, was published by a leading Marxist historian, Albert Soboul. He suggested that extreme *sans-culottes* such as Babeuf saw the Revolution in terms of a 'war between the rich and the poor'. Equally important was their initial alliance with the bourgeoisie in helping to overthrow the *ancien régime*. This obvious class-based attitude was one of the features that drew Marxist historians in both France and Russia to study this group.

EXTRACT I

From Albert Soboul, *The Parisian Sans-culottes and the French Revolution 1793–4*, Oxford University Press, 1964, p. 260.

From June 1793 to February 1794 the Parisian sans-culottes *movement played a major role in the political struggle leading to the consolidation of the Revolutionary Government and the organization of the Committee of Public Safety. During the same period, it imposed economic measures upon a reluctant Assembly intended to improve the living standards of the masses … Without the Parisian* sans-culotterie, *the bourgeoisie could not have triumphed in so radical a fashion. From 1789 to the Year II the* sans-culottes *were used as an effective weapon of revolutionary combat and national defence. In 1793, the popular movement made possible the installation of the Revolutionary Government and, consequently the defeat of the counter-revolution in France and the allied coalition in Europe.*

The revisionist view

The first real challenge to the orthodox left-wing view came from the British historian Alfred Cobban. He argued that the significance of the *sans-culottes* had been exaggerated by Marxist historians in order to fit in with their political views.

EXTRACT 2

From Alfred Cobban, *The Social Interpretation of the French Revolution*, Cambridge University Press, 1964, pp. 130–1.

In the light of the Leninist theory it becomes possible to understand why the sans-culottes *movement along with the later* babeuvist *conspiracy, constitute the chief interest in the French Revolution for modern* **Communist** *historians; these movements can be regarded as a dress rehearsal for the Leninist revolution. Hence the enormous concentration of attention on what were after all, only transient episodes which left little permanent mark on the evolution of French society … For the social historian of revolutionary France, the* sans-culottes *have been almost literally a red-herring to divert attention from the basic social problems, both rural and urban of French Revolutionary history.*

KEY TERM

Communist A follower of the political belief that centres on social and economic equality as outlined by Karl Marx.

The moralist view

Gwyn Williams emphasised a different aspect of *sans-culottisme*, namely its moral perspective, although this is still within the context of a developing political movement. Its embodiment was Hébert's *Le Père Duchesne* (see page 121). Reiterating the left-wing view, Williams sees a direct line from Robespierre's despotism of liberty to Marx's dictatorship of the proletariat.

EXTRACT 3

From Gwyn A. Williams, *Artisans and Sans-culottes*, Libris, 1989, p. 25.

Sans-culottisme was a species of morality. This morality had a firm social anchorage. The heart and core of sans-culotterie *was an artisanry of small masters, tradesmen and journeymen; the further one moves from this base the more 'honorary' do* sans-culottes *become … From at least the summer of 1793 onwards, to some extent from the summer of 1792, what we are dealing with is a political movement. In the Year II, indeed, to a* sans-culottes *militant, there was nothing that was not politics. There was a constant reference to first principles, an obsession with sovereignty, equality. After immersion in the records of the sections of Paris, under* sans-culotte *control, one emerges with a vision of a city taken over by workshop Rousseaus.*

The updated view

The decline of communism as a major political force has also been to an extent mirrored in the way the *sans-culottes* are perceived. No longer viewed as a developing political movement, they are more often now seen for what they were – workers who aspired to a share in the gains of the Revolution.

EXTRACT 4

From David Andress, *The Terror: Civil War in the French Revolution*, Abacus, 2006, p. 76.

On the 20 June 1792 a large crowd invaded the Tuileries and confronted the King … The Parisian radicals, who were beginning to refer to themselves and their constituents as sans-culottes, *the 'breechless' who wore the long trousers of the working man, went away feeling satisfied that their message had been put across. Many of the* sans-culottes *were members of the National Guard, and activists in their local Sections – and thus by definition taxpaying 'active citizens' – but they and their spokesmen played on the notion of a common plebeian identity. This was not proletarian, not a modern working class of wage-earners, but more the kind of identity embodied by skilled men possessed of their own resources, but grounded in popular neighbourhood life, demotic sense and the hard-pressed consumer's suspicion of political and economic machinations.*

? How far do the historians quoted in Extracts 1, 2, 3 and 4 agree or differ in their interpretations of the influence of the *sans-culottes* on the French Revolution?

Chapter summary

France's declaration of war in 1792 was supported by most groups within the Assembly, albeit for differing reasons. Yet the early campaigns revealed how unprepared the country was for the war. The conflict exposed the deep differences within France, and suspicions of Louis' motives contributed to his overthrow. The events of August 1792 marked a second French Revolution and the birth of the First Republic. The decision to try and execute Louis not only resulted in a widening of the war but also exposed the deep political divisions within the country as Jacobin and Girondin drew further apart. Against mounting threats from both internal and external enemies, the government became more determined to secure its survival. The role of the *sans-culottes* in the Revolution is considered in the key debate.

Refresher questions

Use these questions to remind yourself of the key material covered in this chapter.

1 Why did France go to war in April 1792?

2 Why did Brissot believe war to be in France's best interest?

3 Why did Robespierre oppose the call for war?

4 Why were the foreign powers confident of victory in any war against France?

5 How well prepared was France for the war in 1792?

6 Why did Louis' actions lead to demands for greater democracy?

7 How did the *fédérés* and the Brunswick Manifesto lead to the removal of the King?

8 What measures did the National Assembly pass in its last six weeks?

9 What were the main divisions in the newly elected Convention?

10 What did the trial and execution of Louis XVI reveal about divisions in the Convention?

11 How serious was the military crisis in August to September 1792?

12 How did the course of the war change during the winter of 1792?

13 What factors led to war between France and the First Coalition?

14 What contribution did Carnot make to military successes in northern France?

15 Why did the Vendée rebel against the republican government?

 # Question practice

ESSAY QUESTIONS

1 'The *sans-culottes* played the key role in bringing about the collapse of the Legislative Assembly'. Explain why you agree or disagree with this view.

2 'The decision to go to war in 1792 was met with universal approval.' How far do you agree?

3 How serious for the survival of the monarchy was Louis XVI's use of the royal veto?

4 To what extent was France's participation in the war entirely responsible for bringing about the overthrow of the monarchy in August 1792?

INTERPRETATION QUESTION

1 Read the interpretation and then answer the question that follows. 'The *sans-culottes* have been almost literally a red-herring to divert attention from the basic social problems, both rural and urban of French Revolutionary history.' (From Alfred Cobban, *The Social Interpretation of the French Revolution*, 1964.) Evaluate the strengths and limitations of this interpretation of the *sans-culottes*, making reference to other interpretations that you have studied.

SOURCE QUESTIONS

1 Why is Source A (page 77) valuable to the historian studying the outbreak of war in 1792? Explain your answer using the source, the information given about it and your own knowledge of the historical context.

2 How much weight do you give the evidence of Source B (page 83) in helping to explain the response of the French government to the crisis facing it in summer 1792? Explain your answer using the source, the information given about it and your own knowledge of the historical context.

3 With reference to Sources B (page 83) and F (page 91), and your understanding of the historical context, which of these two sources is more valuable in explaining why France was facing such a serious crisis in 1792?

4 With reference to Sources A (page 77), B (page 83) and F (page 91), and your understanding of the historical context, assess the value of these sources to a historian studying the revolutionary war in 1792.

5 How far could the historian make use of Sources B (page 83) and F (page 91) together to investigate the impact of the war on the French government in 1792? Explain your answer using both sources, the information given about them and your own knowledge of the historical context.

CHAPTER 5

Government by Terror 1793–4

The Terror was the most dramatic phase of the French Revolution. For opponents of the Revolution it symbolised the chaos and anarchy that France had sunk into. Supporters of the Republic, on the other hand, believed that only the most ruthless policies could ensure its survival. These events are considered in a number of themes:

★ Emergence of government by Terror

★ Dominance of the *sans-culottes*

★ The impact of the Terror

★ The dictatorship of the Committee of Public Safety

★ Overthrow of Robespierre

The key debate on *page 128* of this chapter asks the question: How do historians view the Terror?

Key dates

1793	March 10	Revolutionary Tribunal established	1793	Oct. 5	New revolutionary calendar
	April 6	Committee of Public Safety created		Dec. 4	Law of 14 Frimaire established revolutionary government
	June 2	Girondin deputies purged	1794	March 24	Execution of Hébert and his leading supporters
	June 24	A new constitution approved			
	July 27	Robespierre joined the CPS		April 5	Danton and Desmoulins executed
	Aug. 23	Decree of *levée en masse* issued			
	Sept. 17	Law of Suspects		June 8	Festival of the Supreme Being
	Sept. 22	Year II began		July 27–28	Coup of Thermidor
	Sept. 29	General Maximum introduced		July 28	Execution of Robespierre

Emergence of government by Terror

▶ *Why did government by Terror emerge during the summer of 1793?*

While the Terror is the most dramatic phase of the Revolution, it had less influence on the formation of modern France than the great reforms of the Constituent Assembly. The late twentieth-century French historians François Furet and Denis Richet saw the period from August 1792 to July 1794 as a time when extremist *sans-culottes* knocked the Revolution off course. They forced the country's leaders to adopt policies that were contrary to the liberal reforms of the Constituent Assembly. Their support was necessary to preserve the Revolution but they did not make any permanent gains for themselves or any lasting changes.

Government by Terror came into being because of the need to organise the Republic against internal and external threats to its survival. There were two periods of terror and both were associated with the war abroad:

- The first began with the attack on the Tuileries on 10 August 1792, included the September Massacres, and came to an end with the Battle of Valmy, when the allied invasion was held up and then pushed back (see pages 92–4).
- The second period began with the *journée* of 31 May to 2 June 1793, when some Girondin deputies were arrested, and ended with the execution of Robespierre and his supporters in July 1794. During the start of this second Terror, French armies were doing badly and the country was once again faced with invasion. Its end came shortly after the victory of Fleurus in June 1794, which secured France's frontiers.

The political crisis

In order to fight the war and crush the Republic's internal and external enemies, it was necessary for the government to have the support of the people. To achieve this some popular demands would have to be granted. The Montagnards realised this and drew closer to the *sans-culottes*, just as the Plain was drawing closer to the Montagnards. Its members shared the Girondin hatred of Robespierre and Marat, but they held the Girondins responsible for the failures in the war (Dumouriez had been closely associated with them), the rising in the Vendée and the economic crisis. After all, several ministers were Girondins. The Plain, along with the Montagnards, favoured repressive measures.

Barère, a leader of the Plain, told the Convention that it should recognise three things:

- In a state of emergency, no government could rule by normal methods.
- The bourgeoisie should not isolate itself from the people, whose demands should be satisfied.
- Since it was vital that the bourgeoisie retain control of this alliance with the people, the Convention must take the initiative by introducing the necessary measures.

The machinery of the Terror

Against a background of mounting crisis – military defeat, civil war, severe economic problems and **anti-republican opposition**, which threatened to overturn the Revolution – the Convention passed a range of measures between 10 March and 20 May 1793 designed to deal with these problems and ensure its survival. They had three objectives:

- To identify, place under observation and punish suspects.
- To make government more effective and ensure that its orders were carried out.
- To meet at least some of the economic demands of the *sans-culottes*.

Committee of General Security

The task of rooting out all anti-republican opposition was given to the **Committee of General Security** (CGS). On 10 March 1793 a **Revolutionary Tribunal** was set up in Paris to try counter-revolutionary suspects. It was intended to prevent massacres like those of September 1792 (see pages 90–1). 'Let us embody Terror,' said Danton in the debate on the decree, 'so as to prevent the people from doing so.' This tribunal was to become one of the main instruments of what became known as the Terror.

Owing to the resistance to conscription and the suspicion of generals after Dumouriez's defection, **representatives-on-mission** were sent to the provinces. They had almost unlimited powers over the department administrations and the armies and were intended as the first stage in reasserting central control over the provinces. Plots by royalists were blamed for the rising in the Vendée, so *comités de surveillance* were set up in each commune and all major towns. They provided many victims for the Revolutionary Tribunal.

Severe measures were to be taken against rebels. The **summary execution decree** provided for the trial and execution of armed rebels within 24 hours of capture. These trials were held without a jury and there was no appeal. They condemned many more victims than the Revolutionary Tribunal itself did. Very harsh laws were also passed against *émigrés*: their property was confiscated by government officials and they were to be executed if they returned to France.

 **KEY TERMS**

Anti-republican opposition Forces opposed to the Republic, mainly former members of the nobility, refractory priests and monarchists.

Committee of General Security Had overall responsibility for police security, surveillance and spying.

Revolutionary Tribunal A court specialising in trying those accused of counter-revolutionary activities.

Representatives-on-mission Mainly Jacobin deputies from the Convention sent to various parts of France to reassert government authority.

Comités de surveillance Surveillance or watch committees, sometimes known simply as revolutionary committees.

Summary execution decree From 19 March 1793 any rebels captured with arms were to be executed immediately.

Committee of Public Safety

On 6 April 1793 one of the most important decisions taken by the Convention was to set up the **Committee of Public Safety** (CPS). Its purpose was to supervise and speed up the activities of ministers, whose authority it superseded. The CPS was not a dictatorship; it depended on the support of the Convention, which approved its powers each month.

As to the composition of the new Committee, Danton, supported by the Plain, wanted a committee without extremists. Thus, of the nine members selected in April, seven, including Barère, were from the Plain. There were only two members from the Montagnards, of whom Danton was one, and no Girondins at all. Danton and Robespierre spoke of the need for winning the support of the people for the Republic. This, they felt, could be done by economic concessions. On 4 May a maximum price was fixed for grain (the Girondins were opposed to all price controls, preferring the free market to set the level) and later in the month it became compulsory for the wealthy to loan money to the government.

All these measures – Revolutionary Tribunals, representatives-on-mission, watch committees, the CPS and the summary execution decree – were vital parts of the machinery of the Terror. At first they were applied only partially, if at all, outside the Vendée.

The overthrow of the Girondins

Danton and other Montagnards had asked the Girondins to stop attacking Parisian *sans-culottes* as *buveurs de sang* (see page 108) but to no avail:

- On 26 May Robespierre came down on the side of the *sans-culottes* when he invited 'the people to place themselves in **insurrection** against the corrupt [Girondin] deputies'.
- On 31 May a rising began which spread rapidly when news of the overthrow of the Jacobins in Lyon reached Paris on 1 June.
- On 2 June 80,000 National Guardsmen surrounded the Convention and directed their cannon at it. They demanded the expulsion of the Girondins from the Assembly and a maximum price imposed on all essential goods. When the deputies tried to leave they were forced back. For the first time armed force was being used against an elected assembly.

To avoid a massacre or a seizure of power by a revolutionary commune, the Convention was compelled to agree to the arrest of 29 Girondin deputies and two ministers. Following the purge of the Girondins a young royalist, Charlotte Corday, assassinated Marat in the vain belief that it would end the Revolution.

SOURCE A

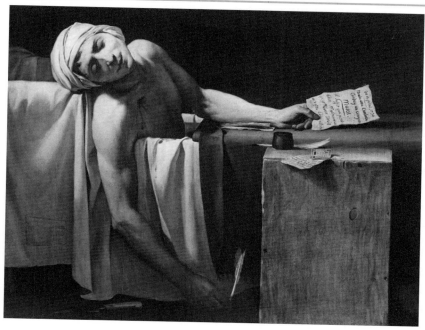

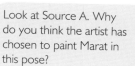

Look at Source A. Why do you think the artist has chosen to paint Marat in this pose?

Marat Assassinated by Jacques-Louis David, 1793. Marat was one of the most extreme of the Jacobin and was very popular with the *sans-culottes*. He suffered from a chronic skin disease and had to bathe regularly in a medicated tub. As a busy man he conducted meetings while bathing: his assassin murdered him in his bath. David presents the body of Marat in a classic pose used by many artists over the centuries to portray Christ after his removal from the cross.

The federal revolt

As the military crisis worsened, the Montagnards turned on the Girondins. During the political crisis of June 1793, Girondin deputies were expelled from the Convention (see pages 104) for supporting revolts backed by royalists, aimed at destroying the unity of the Republic. In fact, both sides believed in the unity of the Republic and the revolts had, initially, nothing to do with royalism or counter-revolution. The Montagnards called these revolts '**federalism**', and were concerned not only that the unity of the Republic was under threat, but that with fighting a war as well, the government's resources would be placed under very severe strain.

In many departments the rebels resented the influence of Paris and its Commune over the Convention and the power of the Jacobins. The first significant city to rebel was Marseille. Its inhabitants turned against the local Jacobin Club. Encouraged by these events, anti-Jacobin supporters took control of many other towns and cities in the south. The most serious revolt occurred in Lyon (30 May) – the Republic's second city. Bordeaux reacted to the purge of the Girondin deputies by declaring the city in revolt until they were restored.

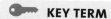

KEY TERM

Federalism A rejection of the central authority of the State in favour of regional authority.

Some form of disturbance occurred in 60 of the 83 departments, although significant resistance to the Convention occurred in only eight. Potentially the most serious revolt was in the great naval base of Toulon. Disillusion with the war and the course of the Revolution led to an uprising which overthrew the town council and closed down the Jacobin Club. The government cut off food supplies to the city. To prevent starvation the town authorities negotiated with the British, who insisted that the monarchy be restored. British troops entered the town on 28 August. As half the French fleet was lying off the coast at Toulon, this was a most serious blow to the Republic.

Once Marseille, Lyon and Toulon had rejected the authority of the Convention, many smaller towns in the Rhône valley and Provence followed suit. Despite the attempts of the Jacobin press to portray them as pro-Church monarchists, many of the federalists were supporters of the Republic. According to rebels in Toulon, all they wanted was 'to enjoy our goods, our property, the fruits of our toil and industry in peace, yet we see them incessantly exposed to threats from those who have nothing themselves'. However, 'Federal' forces were pitifully small. Marseille was able to raise only 3500 men, Bordeaux 400, and none of them wanted to move far from home. This failure to co-operate enabled the government to pick off the rebel areas one by one.

The New Committee of Public Safety

After 2 June most deputies feared and distrusted the Montagnards because of the way they had dealt with the Girondin. However, they did not want to see the Republic overthrown by domestic or foreign enemies and so, for the next fourteen months, they were reluctant accomplices of the Montagnards' Jacobin minority.

A new CPS was formed between July and September 1793; the twelve members were all either Montagnards or deputies of the Plain who had joined them. All were middle class, except for Hérault de Séchelles, who was a former noble. Eight of them were lawyers, two were engineers. Nearly all were young: the

Table 5.1 Leading members of the Committee of Public Safety (CPS)

Name	Role	Fate
Barère	Spokesman for the CPS	Tried, sentenced to deportation, escaped, died 1841
Collot d'Herbois	Responsible for repression in Lyon	Deported to Guiana, died 1796
Billaud-Varenne	Extreme left-winger	Deported to Guiana where he later settled, died 1819
Carnot	Organised movement of supplies	Returned to private life, died 1823
Couthon	Involved in repression of Lyon	Executed after Coup of Thermidor 1794
Lindet	Implemented General Maximum	Retired to private life, died 1825
Saint-Just	Drew up constitution 1793	Executed after Coup of Thermidor 1794
Danton	Urged slowing down	Executed April 1794
Robespierre	Leading figure in CPS of Terror	Executed after Coup of Thermidor 1794
Hérault de Séchelles	Moderate, linked to plots	Executed April 1794

average age was just 30. There was no chairman: all the members were jointly responsible for the Committee's actions. The new Committee was to become the first strong government since the Revolution began.

Maximilian Robespierre

Maximilian Robespierre joined the CPS on 27 July 1793. Owing to his influence in the Jacobin Club and the Commune, he was expected to provide a link between the middle-class Jacobins and the *sans-culottes*. He never had much support in the Convention and many could not stand his narrow self-righteousness. Yet he was known as 'the Incorruptible' because he did not seek power or wealth for himself and was consistent in putting the good of the country above all other considerations. Some have described him as 'a moral fanatic', because his love of '***vertu***' swept aside all human feelings, as when he wrote: 'The spirit of the Republic is virtue, in other words love of one's country, that magnanimous devotion that sinks all private interests in the general interest.'

 **KEY TERM**

Vertu Virtue – meaning moral excellence.

Maximilian Robespierre

1758	Born into a bourgeois family in Arras
1789	Elected deputy for the Third Estate of Artois
1791	Opposed calls for war
1792	Demanded deposing the King
	Elected to the National Convention
1793	Joined the CPS
1794	Overthrown during Coup of Thermidor and executed

In many ways, Robespierre is the most controversial figure of the revolutionary period, linked indelibly with the Terror. His influence was enormous. For Robespierre, nothing should have stood in the way of the sovereignty of the people. Yet, while battling to secure the Republic's survival, countless atrocities and excesses were committed by government officials and zealous republicans.

Robespierre believed that principles were everything, human beings nothing. Anyone who did not put *vertu* first would have to be sacrificed: 'Terror is nothing other than justice, prompt, severe and inflexible; it is therefore an essence of virtue … Break the enemies of liberty with terror, and you will be justified as founders of the Republic.'

It was Robespierre's tactical skill that led him to ally with the *sans-culottes*. He saw the need for the Montagnards to be allied to the people if the Revolution was to survive. During the rising of 31 May to 2 June he wrote in his diary: 'What is needed is one single will … The danger within France comes from the middle classes and to defeat them we must rally the people.'

Although Robespierre shared many ideas with the *sans-culottes* and was popular with the people of Paris, he was never one of them. He dressed with the silk stockings, knee-breeches and powdered wig of the old regime. He never took part in a demonstration and was never carried shoulder-high by the people, as Marat was. Robespierre was a rather remote figure who lived comfortably, although rather modestly, in the petit-bourgeois household of the cabinet-maker Duplay.

One of his most recent biographers, Peter McPhee, in summing up his contribution, states that 'Robespierre and the CPS had led the Republic and Revolution to security. Their achievement was enormous; so were the human costs. By the time the Republic was safe in 1794, Robespierre was ill, exhausted, irrational and in despair.'

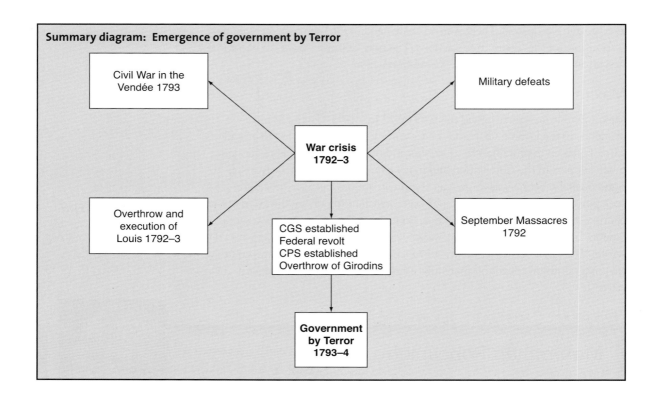

Summary diagram: Emergence of government by Terror

Civil War in the Vendée 1793

Military defeats

War crisis 1792–3

Overthrow and execution of Louis 1792–3

CGS established
Federal revolt
CPS established
Overthrow of Girodins

September Massacres 1792

Government by Terror 1793–4

2 Dominance of the *sans-culottes*

▶ *What did the* sans-culottes *believe in?*

The growth in power of the *sans-culottes* was largely a consequence of the war (see pages 76–83). They had played an important role in the Revolution in 1789 by storming the Bastille, and bringing the King to Paris during the October Days. After that the bourgeois National Guard kept them under control, as at the Champ de Mars. However, when the National Guard was opened up to 'passive citizens' in July 1792 (see page 82) the *sans-culottes* **militants** grew in influence. Their power and domination was important in the overthrow of the monarchy and from the summer of 1792 to the spring of 1794 no one could control Paris without obtaining their support. They were responsible for the *journée* of 31 May to 2 June 1793, which brought the Jacobins to power.

Ideas and organisation

During the period of the Terror, the *sans-culottes* occupied a powerful role in the political life of Paris and many other leading cities. (See page 66 for their own view of themselves in a contemporary document.) The main characteristics of the *sans-culottes* were:

 KEY TERM

Militants Those who differed from ordinary *sans-culottes* in that they adopted an extreme political position such as arguing for a republic, greater democracy and the destruction of privilege.

- hatred of the aristocracy and anyone of great wealth
- **egalitarianism** – they addressed everyone as citizen and *ancien régime* titles were rejected
- the wearing of red caps (*bonnets rouges*), originally associated with freed slaves, symbolising the equality of all citizens, to which they were firmly committed
- passionate anti-clericalism – this was because priests had joined with aristocrats in taking the wealth created by ordinary men and women
- a belief in direct democracy.

For the *sans-culottes*, the sovereignty of the people – their right to exercise power – could not be delegated to representatives. They believed that the people had the right to control and change their elected representative at any time, and if they were betrayed they had the right of insurrection. Political life must take place in the open: the patriot had no reason to hide his opinions. The meetings of the Assembly must therefore be open to the public and deputies must vote aloud.

🔑 KEY TERM

Egalitarianism Derived from 'equality' – the aim to have all citizens equal, with no disparities in wealth, status or opportunity.

SOURCE B

Selected extracts from a petition sent from the *Section des Sans-Culottes* to the Convention, 2 September 1793.

The general assembly of the Section des Sans-Culottes considers it to be the duty of all citizens to propose measures which seem likely to bring about a return of abundance and public tranquillity. It therefore asks the Convention to decree the following:

- *That former nobles will be barred from military careers and every kind of public office.*
- *That the price of basic necessities be fixed at the levels of 1789–90.*
- *That the price of raw materials, level of wages and profits of industry and commerce also be fixed.*
- *That each department be allowed sufficient public money to ensure that the price of basic foodstuffs will be the same for citizens of the Republic.*
- *That there be a fixed maximum on personal wealth.*
- *That no single individual shall possess more than the declared maximum.*
- *That nobody be able to lease more land than is necessary for a fixed number of ploughs.*
- *That no citizen shall possess more than one workshop or retail workshop.*
- *That all who possess goods or land without legal title be recognised as legal proprietors.*

> What does Source B suggest were the main aspirations of the *sans-culottes*? **?**

The Paris Sections

The Commune and the Sections were the administrative units of Parisian local government, with their officials and elected committees. They controlled the National Guard. While there was danger from internal and foreign enemies, they were encouraged by the government to keep a watch on suspects and assist representatives-on-mission in purging local authorities. In 1793 they were often more important than the municipalities, as they issued **certificates of citizenship**.

Each Section was controlled by a small minority of militants, usually the better-off members, who had the time to devote to Section business. Of the 454 members of the Revolutionary Committees in Paris in 1793–4, 65 per cent were shopkeepers, small workshop masters and independent craftsmen while only eight per cent were wage-earners. They exercised power through their own institutions, which were not responsible to the central government.

The Parisian *sans-culottes* had the force with which to seize power but they chose to persuade or intimidate the Convention, never to replace it. They wholeheartedly supported the government on basic issues, such as their hatred of the aristocracy and in their determination to win the war.

Concessions to the *sans-culottes*

As the *sans-culottes* had put the Jacobins in power a series of concessions were made to them by the CPS:

- A new constitution was presented to the people on 24 June 1793, which recognised many of their aspirations, preceded by a new Declaration of Rights, which went much further than that of 1789. It stated the right of people to work, have assistance in time of need and be educated. The right of insurrection was proclaimed. All adult males were to have the vote and there were to be direct elections.
- To fight the war effectively, the Sections demanded conscription. This was part of the *levée en masse*.
- Economic concessions – the maximum legislation to fix prices, making the hoarding of goods a capital offence, anti-hoarding laws (see page 000).

The *levée en masse*

The *levée en masse*, which was decreed on 23 August 1793, marked the appearance of **total war**. It stated that 'Until the enemies of France have been expelled from the territory of the Republic, all Frenchmen are in a state of permanent requisition for the army.'

Nearly half a million conscripts, unmarried men between 18 and 25, were called up to the army. They had to be fed, armed and trained, so all the human and material resources of the nation were put at the government's disposal.

State factories were set up to make arms and ammunition. Church bells were melted down for cannon, and religious vessels, such as chalices, for coinage. The government also took control of foreign trade and shipping. Government control of the economy harnessed the energies of the nation on an unprecedented scale. It was remarkably successful in the short term; without it victory would have been impossible.

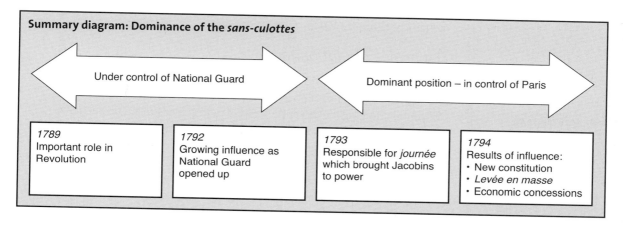

Summary diagram: Dominance of the *sans-culottes*

Under control of National Guard

Dominant position – in control of Paris

1789
Important role in Revolution

1792
Growing influence as National Guard opened up

1793
Responsible for *journée* which brought Jacobins to power

1794
Results of influence:
• New constitution
• *Levée en masse*
• Economic concessions

3 The impact of the Terror

▶ *What measures did the policy of Terror take to restore government authority?*

The firm line imposed by the Jacobin government over most of France did ensure the survival of the Republic in the medium term. Yet many champions of the poor were alarmed that their economic position was getting worse, not better. This section illustrates a much more radical approach to dealing with this issue.

The *Enragés*

The economic situation continued to deteriorate in the summer of 1793. In mid-August the *assignat* was below a third of its face value and drought reduced the grain supplies into Paris by three-quarters.

One group, the **Enragés**, and their spokesman, Jacques Roux, demanded action from the government. As a priest in one of the poorest quarters of Paris, Roux was shocked by what he saw: people starving in crowded attics. These were people for whom the Revolution had brought very little material improvement to their standard of living. His followers were wage-earners, casual labourers, the poor and unemployed. He wanted the Convention to deal immediately with starvation and poverty and when it did nothing, he denounced it. The

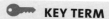 **KEY TERM**

Enragés An extreme revolutionary group led by Jacques Roux which had considerable influence on the Parisian *sans-culottes*.

programme proposed was Economic Terror; he demanded the execution of hoarders who pushed up the price of grain and a purge of ex-nobles from the army. Robespierre wanted to destroy him, because he was threatening the Commune and the Convention with direct action in the streets. Roux was an influential figure in the *journée* of 5 September 1793, which adopted a new, more extreme approach to ensure the movement of food into Paris. During the course of the *journée*, Roux was arrested and after several months in prison, took his own life in February 1794.

The *armée révolutionnaire*

On 4 September a crowd gathered before the Hôtel de Ville to demand bread and higher wages. The following day, urged on by Roux, it marched on the Convention, forcing it to accept a series of radical measures. The Sections imposed on the Convention the proclamation of 'Terror as the order of the day'. The Convention immediately authorised the formation of a Parisian ***armée révolutionnaire*** consisting mainly of *sans-culottes*. The purpose was to confront counter-revolutionary activity and organise the defence of the Republic. In total, 56 other unauthorised armies were set up in the provinces between September and December 1793, and were used in about two-thirds of the departments.

The purpose of these civilian *armée révolutionnaires* was to:

- ensure the food supplies of Paris and the large provincial cities
- round up deserters, hoarders, refractory priests, religious 'fanatics', political suspects and royalist rebels
- mobilise the nation's resources for the war effort by confiscating church silver and bells
- establish revolutionary 'justice' in the areas of the south and west, which had shown little enthusiasm for the Revolution.

The operation of the Parisian army extended over 25 departments. Its main task was to ensure the capital's food supplies by requisitioning grain in the major producing areas of the north. A third of its men took part in the savage repression of the federal revolt at Lyon. Both the Parisian and provincial armies were engaged in **dechristianisation** (see page 117).

The Parisian army was remarkably successful in supplying Paris with bread until the spring of 1794, and so helped to preserve the Revolution. The provincial armies were successful in supplying major towns and the regular army on the eastern frontier. Their success, however, was unlikely to last, because their numbers were small and they met enormous hostility from the rural population. There was great joy in the countryside when they were disbanded. The CPS did not like the revolutionary armies because they were anarchic and outside the control of the authorities. They also disliked them because they created opposition to the Revolution by their heavy-handed methods in dealing with the peasants.

KEY TERMS

Armée révolutionnaire
Sans-culottes sent to the provinces to confront counter-revolutionary forces and ensure the movement of food supplies.

Dechristianisation
Ruthless anti-religious policies conducted by some Jacobin supporters against the Church, aimed at destroying its influence.

Economic Terror

The Convention had bowed to popular pressure from Roux and the *sans-culottes* in July by passing a law that imposed the death penalty for hoarding food and other supplies. On 29 September 1793 the law of the **General Maximum** was passed to control prices. It fixed the price of bread and many essential goods and services at one-third above the prices of June 1790. Wages, which largely determined prices, were also fixed at 50 per cent above the level of 1790. When peasants refused to sell grain at the maximum price that was set, the government was compelled to requisition supplies.

The Maximum set the common people against each other. Peasants hated it because the rate was often below the cost of production, while the *sans-culottes* wanted it so that they could afford to buy bread. When *sans-culottes* went into the countryside with the *armée révolutionnaire* to enforce the Maximum they clashed with the peasants and the conflict between town and country was deepened. The government was in a difficult position, as farmers would simply stop sowing if they could not make a profit. The co-operation of the wealthy peasants, who controlled most of the harvest, was necessary for the government. After all, they were the municipal councillors and tax collectors, who were expected to oversee requisitioning.

Where there was no local revolutionary army in the countryside, the Maximum had to be imposed by the rich. To meet the concerns of farmers and other producers, the government revised prices upwards in February 1794, much to the disgust of the *sans-culottes*. In the short term, the government's measures were successful. The towns and armies were fed and the *assignat*, worth 22 per cent of its face value in August, rose to 48 per cent in December 1793 (see Figure 5.1).

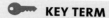

KEY TERM

General Maximum
Tables that fix the prices of a wide range of foods and commodities.

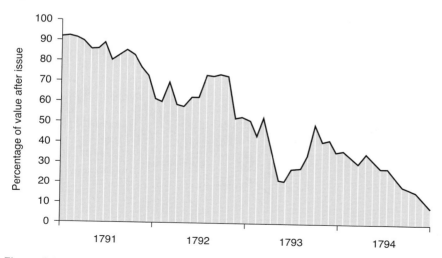

Figure 5.1 The declining value of the *assignat*. How do you think ordinary people would react to the declining value of the *assignat*?

The Political Terror

In October 1793, on the recommendation of the CPS, the recently approved constitution was suspended and it was decreed that 'The government of France will be revolutionary until the peace.' This paved the way for the adoption of extreme policies. The Political Terror took three forms:

- the official Terror, controlled by the CPS and CGS, centred in Paris and whose victims came before the Revolutionary Tribunal
- the Terror in the areas of federal revolt such as the Vendée and Lyon, where the worst atrocities took place
- the Terror in other parts of France, under the control of watch committees, representatives-on-mission and the revolutionary armies.

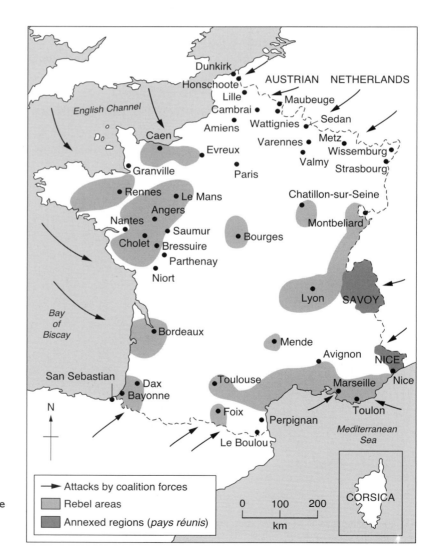

Figure 5.2 The Republic under siege, July to August 1793. Note the extent of the external threat from coalition forces and the rebel areas, which are, in most instances, on the margins of the country where there was the possibility that they could be reinforced by the external enemies of the Republic.

The CGS was largely responsible for bringing cases before the Revolutionary Tribunal in Paris. Up to September 1793 the Tribunal had heard 260 cases and pronounced 66 death sentences (25 per cent of the total). A series of celebrity trials were held which were popular with the masses and removed those regarded as enemies of the Republic. The trial of important figures almost always resulted in their execution. Acquittal would have been regarded as a vote of no confidence in the government. Among those tried and executed by the Revolutionary Tribunal were Marie Antoinette on 16 October, twenty leading Girondin deputies on 31 October, **Philippe Égalité** (formerly known as the Duke of Orleans) on 6 November and Mme Roland, wife of the Girondin ex-minister, three days later.

Provincial repression

By the end of 1793 the federal revolt had been suppressed by the regular army. Marseille, Lyon and Toulon were taken and the Vendéan rebels crushed. Repression followed. From January to May 1794 troops moved through the area, shooting almost every peasant they met, burning their farms and crops and killing their animals. Women were raped and mutilated. When the 'pacification' was over, the Vendée was a depopulated wasteland. Thousands who surrendered crammed the prisons. They could not be released in case they rejoined the rebels, and were shot without trial – 2000 near Angers alone. In the ten departments involved in the Vendée rebellion, revolutionary courts condemned some 8700 people, just over half the 16,600 executions in France during the Terror. Most were ordinary peasants, few were bourgeois.

Representatives-on-mission and the revolutionary armies were often responsible for the worst atrocities. Their actions were fully supported and, indeed, encouraged by the government. At Nantes, the representative Carrier carried out the dreadful *noyades* (drownings) by placing 1800 people, nearly half of them women, into barges, which were taken to the mouth of the Loire and sunk. In Toulon 800 were shot without trial and a further 282 were sent to the guillotine by a Revolutionary Commission.

Lyon, the second city in France, was to pay dearly for its rebellion. On 12 October 1793 the CPS ordered the destruction of Lyon. Collot-d'Herbois, a member of the CPS and a representative-on-mission, restored order in Lyon with great brutality: 1900 victims were either mown down by cannon fire in front of large pits during the *mitraillade* or guillotined. A total of 72 per cent of the executions during the Terror (12,000 victims) took place in these rebel areas of the west and south-east, which covered sixteen departments.

Law of Suspects

In September 1793 the **Law of Suspects** was passed. Under this law the government delegated some of its powers to local revolutionary committees. These committees were packed with fanatical Montagnards and their supporters.

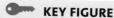

KEY FIGURE

Philippe Égalité (1747–93)

A distant cousin of the Louis XVI and an outspoken critic of the monarchy. He renounced his title and offered his Paris home, the Palais-Royal, as a venue for political meetings.

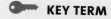

KEY TERM

Law of Suspects Anyone suspected of counter-revolutionary activity and undermining the Republic could be arrested and held without trial indefinitely.

SOURCE C

Print of the drowning of priests in the River Loire at Nantes, November 1793.

? Which side in the civil war do you think published Source C?

SOURCE D

From a letter from Ronsin to the Convention describing events in Lyon, December 1793.

The guillotine and the firing squad did justice to more than four hundred rebels. But the new revolutionary commission has just been established, consisting of true sans-culottes: *my colleague Parein is its president, and in a few days the grape shot, fired by our cannoners, will have delivered to us, in one single moment, more than four thousand conspirators. It is time to cut down the procedure! Delay can awaken, I will not say courage, but the despair of traitors who are still hidden among the debris of that impious town. The republic has need of a great example – the Rhone, reddened with blood, must carry to its banks and to the sea, the corpses of those cowards who murdered our brothers; and whilst the thunderbolt, which must exterminate them in an instant, will carry terror into the departments where the seed of rebellion was sown, it is necessary that the flames from their devastated dens proclaim far and wide the punishment that is destined for those who try to imitate them.*

? What does Source D suggest was the aim behind the methods used by republican forces?

They worked closely with representatives-on-mission and the revolutionary armies to deal with counter-revolutionary activity. Mass arrest of suspects took place (about half a million according to one estimate, of whom 10,000 died in prison). The committees could also send offenders before one of the Revolutionary Tribunals, and purge the local administration, removing moderates and replacing them by *sans-culottes* militants. These committees symbolised the Terror at the local level. By the end of 1793 most rural communes had one. They were the one permanent institution of the Terror in the countryside.

The extent of the Terror

Estimating the human cost of the Terror is difficult because of the absence of reliable figures, which vary from several hundred thousand to tens of thousands. The number of official executions that took place is believed to be 16,600. This figure, however, does not include the large number of deaths resulting from imprisonment, starvation, military action, repression, and so on.

Of the official executions, most took place in the departments involved in the Vendée Rebellion (53 per cent) and the departments in the south-east (twenty per cent). In social terms the official victims were mainly peasants (28 per cent) and urban workers (31 per cent), with the nobility accounting for just eight per cent of the total. What is clear is that the majority of the victims of the Terror perished in the Vendée. The British historian Douglas Johnson suggests a figure of 80,000 deaths for the Vendée, and for the whole of the west a round figure of 200,000 would seem to be realistic.

Table 5.2 Official executions by region during the Terror

Region	No. of deaths	Per cent
Paris	2,639	15.9
Area of the Vendée Rebellion	8,713	52.5
Area of armed federalism round Lyon	1,967	11.9
Area of armed federalism in the Midi	1,296	7.8
Other areas	1,979	11.9
Total	16,594	100.0

Religious Terror: dechristianisation

Dechristianisation was not official government policy. The driving force behind this campaign came from the *sans-culottes* in the Paris Commune, the revolutionary armies and the representatives-on-mission. They hated Catholicism, which they felt had betrayed the Revolution and fomented the cause of the counter-revolution. The Convention was drawn along with it.

Dechristianisation was a deliberate attempt by the First Republic between 1792 and 1794 to use the resources of the State to destroy Christianity as the dominant cultural form of French society. Like the abolition of the monarchy, the destruction of churches was a symbol of the revolutionaries' determination to destroy everything connected with the *ancien régime*.

The attack on the Church took various forms. Churches were closed, church bells and silver were removed, roadside shrines and crosses were destroyed. The Paris Commune stopped paying clerical salaries in May 1793 and in November ordered that all churches in Paris should be closed. Notre Dame, Paris's cathedral, became a Temple of Reason. Other areas of France rapidly followed the lead of Paris so that by the spring of 1794 most of the country's churches had been closed.

Priests were forced to renounce their priesthood and many were compelled to marry. Estimates of the number of priests who gave up their calling vary from about 6000 (ten per cent of all constitutional priests) to 20,000. This brutal attempt to uproot centuries of Christian belief was deeply resented in the villages. For many ordinary people outside the civil war zones, dechristianisation, which left large areas of France without priests, was the aspect of the Terror that most affected them.

Revolutionary calendar

On 5 October 1793 a new revolutionary calendar was introduced. Its aim was twofold: first to emphasise the complete break with the past and its institutions, particularly the Church; second to remove any surviving traces of the *ancien régime*. It was dated from 22 September 1792, when the Republic was proclaimed. Thus, the period from 22 September 1792 to 21 September 1793 became Year I.

The year was divided into twelve months of 30 days, with five supplementary days (soon called *sans-culottides*). Each month was divided into three periods of ten days, every tenth day (*decadi*) being a day of rest. Another decree gave each month a name appropriate to its season: thus Vendémiaire (the month of vintage) ran from 22 September to 21 October, Floréal (the month of flowers) from 20 April to 19 May. The new calendar ignored Sundays and festivals of the Church. In the new calendar, the period of the Terror roughly coincided with Year II, which started on 22 September 1793.

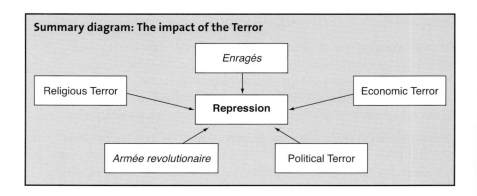

Summary diagram: The impact of the Terror

The dictatorship of the Committee of Public Safety

▶ *What was the extent and nature of the opposition to the policies of the CPS?*

Towards the end of 1793 the government had begun to overcome the problems that had threatened the existence of the Republic:

- The federal revolts had been crushed.
- Food supplies were moving into towns and cities.
- The value of the *assignat* was rising.
- In the west, the defeats of the rebels at Cholet and Le Mans effectively ended the civil war in the Vendée.
- French armies were also doing well in the war. By the end of September they had driven the Spanish armies out of Roussillon and the Piedmontese out of Savoy. The British were defeated at Hondschoote in the same month and the Austrians at Wattignies in October.

It appeared that the CPS's policy for defending France was proving to be successful. With renewed confidence, the Convention's committees could now begin to claw back much of the power which had passed to the *sans-culottes* and their organisations.

Restoring government authority

At some stage it was likely that the government and the *sans-culottes* would come into conflict. There was administrative confusion in many departments in the autumn of 1793 as local revolutionary committees, revolutionary armies and representatives-on-mission, such as Fouché and Carrier, interpreted the law, or ignored it, on a whim. The government could not tolerate anarchy indefinitely as it undermined its authority. Yet it had to act carefully in case it upset its supporters among the *sans-culottes*.

The first steps to tame the popular movement were taken in September 1793. The CPS decided that the general assemblies of the Sections should meet only twice a week. In October the CPS passed a decree that government was to be 'revolutionary until the peace'. This meant the suspension of the constitution of 1793. Although this was planned to be a temporary measure, the constitution was never put into operation.

The Law of Revolutionary Government

A major step to restore central control was taken on 4 December 1793 when the Law of Frimaire established revolutionary government. This law gave the two committees full **executive powers**:

- The CGS was responsible for police and internal security. The Revolutionary Tribunal, as well as the surveillance committees, came under its control.
- The CPS had more extensive powers. In addition to controlling ministers and generals, it was to control foreign policy and purge and direct local government.

KEY TERM

Agents nationaux National agents appointed by, and responsible to, the central government. Their role was to monitor the enforcement of all revolutionary laws.

The chief officials of the communes and departments, who had been elected, were placed under **agents nationaux**. The representatives-on-mission, sent out by the Convention in April, were now put firmly under the control of the CPS. All revolutionary armies, except that in Paris, were to be disbanded. As Robespierre pointed out: 'Revolutionary government … has no room for anarchy and disorder. It is not directed by individual feelings, but by the public interest. It is necessary to navigate between two rocks; weakness and boldness, reaction and extremism.' The new policies resulted in:

- the end of anarchy
- breaking the power of the *sans-culottes*
- providing France with its first strong government since 1787.

However, it rejected many of the principles of 1789. The constitutions of 1791 and 1793 had established decentralisation, elections to all posts, the separation of legislative from executive power and impartial justice. Now all this was reversed. Robespierre justified the policy by arguing that a dictatorship was necessary until the foreign and internal enemies of the Revolution were destroyed. 'We must,' he said, 'organise the despotism of liberty to crush the despotism of kings.' This was contrary to the ideas of democracy and people's rights he had advocated before he took office.

SOURCE E

From a speech delivered by Robespierre outlining the principles of revolutionary government, 25 December 1793.

The function of government is to direct the moral and physical forces of the nation towards its essential aim. The aim of constitutional government is to preserve the Republic: that of revolutionary government is to put the republic on a secure foundation. Revolution is the war of liberty against its enemies: the constitution is the system of victorious and peace-loving liberty. Revolutionary government needs to be extraordinarily active, precisely because it is at war. It is subject to less uniform and less rigorous rules because the circumstances in which it finds itself are tempestuous and changing, and above all because it is continually forced to deploy new resources rapidly, to confront new and pressing dangers. Constitutional government is concerned principally with civil liberty, and revolutionary government with public liberty … Revolutionary government owes good citizens full national protection: to enemies of the people it owes nothing but death.

Study Source E. What does Robespierre consider to be the difference between constitutional and revolutionary government?

Opposition to the government: Hébert

The main challenge to the revolutionary government came from within the ranks of its former supporters. Left-wing opposition came from the publisher Jacques Hébert and his followers. His newspaper *Le Père Duchesne* demanded that more hoarders should be executed and property redistributed. This was very popular with the *sans-culottes*. The Hébertistes had few supporters in the Convention but many in the Cordeliers Club, the Commune, the Paris revolutionary army and the popular societies.

Robespierre disliked their political extremism, particularly their leading part in the dechristianisation campaign, which turned Catholics against the Revolution. When Hébert called for an insurrection at the beginning of March 1794 he was arrested along with eighteen supporters. They were accused of being foreign agents who wanted a military dictatorship that would then prepare the way for a restored monarchy. The populace was taken in by this government propaganda. When Hébert and the Hébertistes were guillotined on 24 March 1794, Paris remained calm.

The CPS took advantage of the situation to strengthen its dictatorship:

- The Parisian revolutionary army was disbanded.
- The Cordeliers Club was closed.
- All popular societies were forced to disband.
- The Commune was purged and filled with supporters of Robespierre.
- Representatives-on-mission, responsible for some of the worst atrocities in the provinces, were recalled to Paris.

Opposition to the government: Danton

Of greater significance, because of the higher profile of its leader, was the opposition of the Right. This centred around Danton (see his profile on page 122), a former colleague of Robespierre, and a leading Montagnard/Jacobin. In order to heal the divisions in the revolutionary movement, the **Indulgents** wanted to halt the Terror and the centralisation imposed in December. To do this, Danton argued that the war would have to come to an end, as it was largely responsible for the Terror.

After leaving office, Danton had become very wealthy. It was not clear where his new-found wealth came from. Nearly 400,000 *livres* were unaccounted for at the Ministry of Justice while he was in charge. He was accused of bribery and corruption. Danton's friend, **Camille Desmoulins**, supported him in his desire to end the Terror. In his newspaper *Le Vieux Cordelier* in December 1793, Desmoulins called for the release of '200,000 citizens who are called suspects'.

Danton, unlike Hébert, had a large following in the Convention, and was regarded as a much more serious threat by the CPS. His call for peace and an end to the Terror would, they felt, leave the door open for a return of the

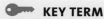

KEY TERM

Indulgents Supporters of Danton and Desmoulins who wished to see a relaxation of the Terror.

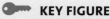

KEY FIGURE

Camille Desmoulins (1760–94)

A skilled journalist and prominent Jacobin who was an ally of Danton. From late 1793 he called for a relaxation of the Terror.

Georges Jacques Danton

1759 — Born into a bourgeois family in Arcis-sur-Aube

1785 — Called to the Bar

1789 — Appointed president of the Cordeliers Club

1791 — Administrator of the Department of Paris

1792 — Appointed Minister of Justice

Elected deputy to the Convention

1793 — Joined the CPS

Retired to the country because of ill health

Urged the slowing down of the Terror

1794 — Labelled by his enemies as an Indulgent, arrested and executed

Georges Jacques Danton was a larger-than-life figure. His presence was great not only in stature (six-foot/182 cm tall) but in the strength and force of his personality. A recent biographer, David Lawday, wrote:

His fate was to take charge of the revolution at a critical moment, when it stumbled and risked collapsing, so that France faced a return to the failed old order from which passionate reformers and an angry populace had torn it free. He was not the instigator of Terror; he resigned himself to it. There is no force on earth he told himself that can stop a revolution from having its dose of blood.

Danton divided opinion. He was loathed and loved in almost equal measure. Many hated him because he was suspected of being corrupt, untrustworthy and in the pay of the royal family. Although there is not much evidence for this, a letter from Mirabeau to Danton in March 1791 does refer to a payment of 30,000 *livres* that he had received. Others loved him for his vast energy, determination and ability to rouse the people to back the causes he championed through the power of his oratory. As minister of justice, he delivered a passionate speech calling for the defence of the nation, after the fall of Verdun to the Prussians (September 1792):

The tocsin [bell] that we are going to sound is no alarm bell, it is the signal for the charge against the enemies of the fatherland. To vanquish them we must show daring, more daring, and again daring; and France will be saved.

As the security of the Republic improved towards the end of 1793, Danton and his leading supporters, the Indulgents (among them the journalist Camille Desmoulins), called for a slowing down of the Terror. Suspected of plotting a coup, they were arrested on 30 March 1794.

monarchy. He was, therefore, brought before the Revolutionary Tribunal on charges based on his political record and on 5 April 1794 was executed with many of his followers, including Desmoulins.

The Terror now seemed to have a momentum of its own. The members of the committees had become brutalised and acted vindictively in ways that would have shamed them only two years earlier. Desmoulins' wife tried to organise a demonstration in his support. She was arrested and in April went to the scaffold, along with the wife of Hébert. They could not in any way be regarded as presenting a threat to the CPS. The effect of the fall of Hébert and Danton was to stifle all criticism of the CPS. Everyone lived in an atmosphere of hatred and suspicion, where an unguarded word could result in death.

The Great Terror

The Great Terror was centred on Paris and lasted from 10 June until 27 July. In order to control all repression, the government in May 1794 abolished the provincial Revolutionary Tribunals. All enemies of the Republic had now to be brought to Paris, to be tried by the city's Revolutionary Tribunal. This did not mean that the Terror would become less severe. Although the 'factions' of Danton and Hébert had been crushed, some of their supporters were still alive, so the Terror would have to continue until they were eliminated. During the Great Terror, approximately 1594 men and women were executed. Robespierre had no desire to protect the innocent, if this meant that dangerous enemies of the Revolution escaped.

Following assassination attempts on Robespierre and Couthon (23 May) they drafted the **Law of Prairial**, which was passed on 10 June 1794. It was directed against 'enemies of the people' but the definitions were so broad and vague that almost anyone could be included. Under it, no witnesses were to be called and judgment was to be decided by 'the conscience of the jurors' rather than by any evidence produced. Defendants were not allowed defence counsel and the only verdicts possible were death or acquittal. This law removed any semblance of a fair trial and was designed to speed up the process of revolutionary justice. In this it succeeded.

More people were sentenced to death in Paris by the Revolutionary Tribunal during June/July 1794 (1594, 59.3 per cent) than in the previous fourteen months of its existence. Many of the victims were nobles and clergymen, while nearly a half were members of the wealthier bourgeoisie. No one dared to make any criticism of the CPS. 'The Revolution is frozen', **Saint-Just** commented.

KEY TERM

Law of Prairial The most severe of the laws passed by the revolutionary government. The purpose of the law was to reform the Revolutionary Tribunal to secure more convictions. The law paved the way for the Great Terror.

KEY FIGURE

Louis Antoine de Saint-Just (1767–94)

A fanatical republican and prominent member of the CPS. He vigorously enforced the Terror against the Republic's enemies, but wished to use it to reorder French society by promoting the redistribution of wealth.

Summary diagram: The dictatorship of the Committee of Public Safety

Measure	Date of introduction	Purpose
CGS	1792 October	Dealt with all matters relating to security
Representatives en mission	1793 March	Sent to Departments to enforce war effort
Revolutionary Tribunal	1793 March	Tried those accused of counter-revolution
Comités de surveillance	1793 March	Monitored movements of strangers
CPS	1793 April	Effectively the government, passed decrees
First Maximum	1793 May	Fixed the prices of grain
Levée en masse	1793 August	Organised France for total war
Death penalty for hoarders	1793 July	Communes and Sections to search for hoarded food
Armée revolutionnaire	1793 September	*Sans-culottes* sent to provinces
Law of Suspects	1793 September	Anyone suspected of counter-revolution arrested
General Maximum	1793 September	Fixed prices on all foods and goods
Law of revolutionary government	1793 December	Extended and centralised power of CPS
Laws of Ventose	1794 February	Distributed property of suspects to the poor
Law of 22 Prairial	1794 June	Reform of Revolutionary Tribunal to speed up executions

Overthrow of Robespierre

▶ *Why was Robespierre overthrown?*

Robespierre loses support

In the spring and early summer of 1794, Robespierre started to lose support in three key areas:

- among Catholics
- among the *sans-culottes*
- on the CPS and CGS.

Catholics

Robespierre believed in God and had a genuine faith in life after death, in which the virtuous would be rewarded. He loathed the dechristianisation campaign of the *sans-culottes*, partly on religious grounds and partly because it upset Catholics and created enemies of the Revolution. He wanted to unite all Frenchmen in a new religion, the **Cult of the Supreme Being**, which he persuaded the Convention to accept in a decree of 7 May 1794. It began: 'The people of France recognise the existence of the Supreme Being and of immortality of the soul.' On 8 June 1794 Robespierre organised a large 'Festival of the Supreme Being' in Paris.

This new religion pleased no one. Catholics were distressed because it ignored Catholic doctrine, ceremonies and the Pope. Anti-clericals, including most members of the CGS, opposed it because they thought it was a first step towards the reintroduction of Catholicism. They felt that Robespierre was setting himself up as the high priest of the new religion.

Sans-culottes

Robespierre's popularity among the *sans-culottes* was falling sharply for a number of reasons:

- the execution of the Hébertistes
- the dissolution of the popular societies
- the end of direct democracy in the Sections
- the raising of the Maximum on prices in March, which led to inflation and a fall in the *assignat* to only 36 per cent of its original value
- the imposing of the Maximum on wages.

While the Commune had been under the control of the Hébertistes it had not applied the Maximum on wages, which had risen considerably above the limit allowed. The government now decided it would have to act, as the profits of manufacturers were disappearing. On 23 July, therefore, the Commune, now staffed by Robespierre's supporters, decided to apply the Maximum to wages.

 KEY TERM

Cult of the Supreme Being Robespierre's alternative civic religion to the Catholic faith.

This led to a fall in wages by as much as a half, and heightened discontent among the majority of *sans-culottes*, who were wage-earners. The Great Terror sickened many ordinary people, workers as well as bourgeoisie. By the spring of 1794 the Republic's armies had driven all foreign troops from French soil, recaptured lost territory in Belgium and moved into the Rhineland. On the domestic front, internal enemies had been defeated and government authority restored over all parts of the country. Many questioned whether it was still necessary to apply the ruthless policies of the Terror now that the threats to the Republic had been dealt with.

CPS and CGS

The dictatorship of the two committees remained unchallengeable, until they fell out between themselves. In April the CPS set up its own police bureau, with Robespierre in charge, to prosecute dishonest officials. The CGS deeply resented this interference with its own control of internal security, so that the two committees became rivals rather than allies. There were also conflicts within the CPS. Some members disliked Saint-Just's **Laws of Ventose** (26 February 1794) and made sure they were never put into practice.

Two members of the CPS, Billaud and Collot, had been closely attached to Hébert and so felt threatened by Robespierre. Robespierre was especially critical of Collot because of the extreme measures he had used to restore order in Lyon (see page 115). Many on the CPS were becoming suspicious of Robespierre, particularly following the introduction of the Cult of the Supreme Being, and he was losing support among former allies.

The Coup of Thermidor

During these divisions, Robespierre took a month away from public life, possibly due to exhaustion. He made no speeches in the Convention between 18 June and 26 July, attended the CPS only two or three times and even gave up his work at the bureau of police. When he did reappear it was to address the Convention, not the CPS. On 26 July (8 **Thermidor**) Robespierre made a speech attacking those colleagues who, he claimed, were plotting against the government. When asked to name them, he declined. This proved to be his undoing. Any denunciation by Robespierre would have resulted in arrest and almost certainly death. Moderates like Carnot and **terrorists** like Fouché and Collot all felt threatened. Fearing that Robespierre was about to denounce them as traitors, a number of his former colleagues conspired to plot against him, before he could order their arrest.

Arrest

When Robespierre attempted to speak at the Convention on 9 Thermidor (27 July) he was shouted down. The Convention then voted for the arrest of Robespierre, his brother Augustin, Couthon, Saint-Just and Hanriot, the

KEY TERMS

Laws of Ventose Property of those recognised as enemies of the Revolution could be seized and distributed among the poor.

Thermidor A month in the new revolutionary calendar, equivalent to 19 July to 17 August.

Terrorist An active supporter of the policies of the Terror.

SOURCE F

How does the cartoon in Source F seek to portray Robespierre?

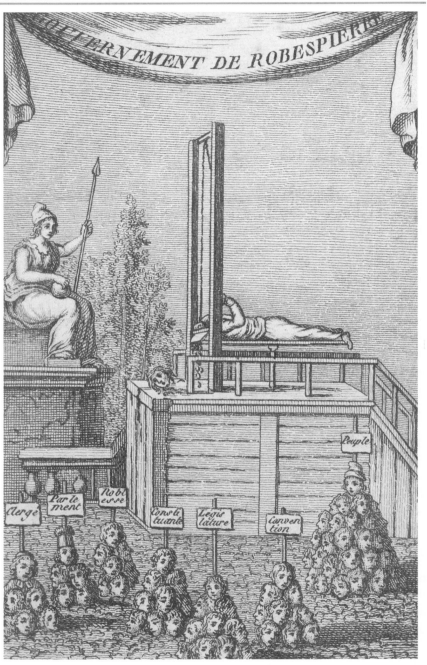

An anti-Robespierre cartoon claiming that most of the victims of the Terror were not from the privileged orders but were ordinary people.

commander of the Paris National Guard. They were taken to prisons controlled by the Commune. Robespierre and his colleagues continued to be popular in the Commune, and its leaders ordered all gaolers in Paris to refuse to accept the prisoners and called for an insurrection in their support. Following their release, they ordered the National Guard of the Sections, still under their control, to mobilise. Hanriot was allowed to escape. However, because of the dictatorship established by the two committees, neither the Jacobin Club nor the Commune could inspire these militants as they had done on 5 September 1792. The CGS now controlled the revolutionary committees of the Sections and the popular societies had been dissolved.

There was great confusion on the evening of 27 July, as the Convention also called on the National Guard to support it against the Commune. Most Sections took no action at first: only seventeen (out of 48) sent troops to support the Commune. They included artillery units and for several hours Hanriot had the Convention at his mercy. Only a failure of nerve on his part and Robespierre's strange reluctance to act saved the Convention.

Robespierre had little faith in a popular rising for which no plans had been made and wanted to keep within the law. Barère proposed that the prisoners be declared outlaws on the basis that they had 'escaped'. This meant that they could be executed without a trial. The decree of outlawry and the enforcement of the law persuaded many Sections that were uncertain about who to support to side with the Convention. When they reached the Hôtel de Ville, where Robespierre and his supporters were based, they found no one defending it.

Amid scenes of great confusion, Robespierre, who had tried to shoot himself, and his leading supporters were arrested for a second time. On 28 July 1794 he and 21 others were executed. In the next few days over 100 members of the Commune followed Robespierre to the scaffold. The events of the **Coup of Thermidor** effectively meant the rejection of government by Terror. The Terror was dead, although the violence would continue.

The end of Terror

The Coup of Thermidor brought to an end the most dramatic period of the Revolution. Through a combination of policies that were attractive to their core supporters and ruthlessness to their enemies, the Jacobin dictatorship ensured the defeat of the Republic's internal and external enemies. Many of the gains made since 1789 were preserved and even extended. In the course of defeating its enemies, the Republic created a highly motivated citizen army, which laid the foundations for future conquests in Europe.

These successful aspects, however, were more than balanced by a number of negative features. There was massive loss of life and devastation in the Vendée and the areas of federalist revolt. The extremist policies of the CPS and CGS alienated many Catholics and the bourgeoisie. Even the *sans-culottes* became

 **KEY TERM**

Coup of Thermidor The overthrow of Robespierre and his closest supporters, which marked the end of the Terror.

disillusioned with the extremist policies of the revolutionary government. The ferocity of the reaction to the Terror, which will be dealt with in the next chapter, indicated the depth of hostility felt by large numbers of men and women towards the system created by Robespierre and his allies.

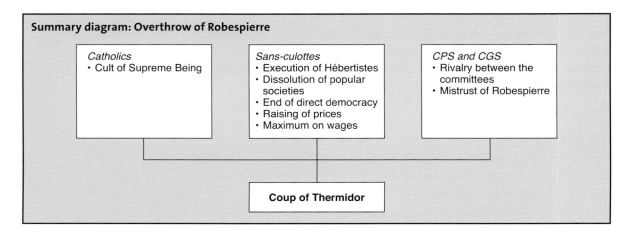

Summary diagram: Overthrow of Robespierre

Catholics	Sans-culottes	CPS and CGS
• Cult of Supreme Being	• Execution of Hébertistes • Dissolution of popular societies • End of direct democracy • Raising of prices • Maximum on wages	• Rivalry between the committees • Mistrust of Robespierre

Coup of Thermidor

 # Key debate

▶ *How do historians view the Terror?*

The Terror is the most dramatic and controversial period of the French Revolution. There has been considerable debate among historians over how to view the Terror. In many ways this debate has divided along the fault lines between Marxist and revisionist historiography. Since the ending of the Cold War there have been attempts to seek a more balanced and non-ideological consensus of what the events of Year II were about.

The modern Marxist interpretation

The Marxist tradition, which views the French Revolution as the first major class struggle, continues to have passionate advocates, despite the collapse of the Soviet Union in the 1990s and the subsequent drift away from historical analysis rooted in communist ideology. Sophie Wahnich argues persuasively in favour of why the Terror was considered necessary by republicans.

EXTRACT I

From Sophie Wahnich, *In Defence of the Terror: Liberty or Death in the French Revolution*, Verso, 2012, p. 97.

The revolutionary Terror, which is attacked for its revolutionary tribunal, its law of suspects and its guillotine, was a process welded to a regime of popular sovereignty in which the object was to conquer tyranny or die for liberty. The

Terror was willed by those who having won sovereign power by dint of insurrection, refused to let this be destroyed by counter-revolutionary enemies. The Terror took place in an uncertain struggle waged by people who tried everything to deflect the fear felt towards the counter-revolutionary enemy into a terror imposed on it. This enemy, for its part, tried everything to bring the revolution to an end. The greatest danger was then that of a weakening of the revolutionary desire. It was this danger that haunted those most committed to the revolutionary process.

Towards a contemporary consensual view

The difficulty posed for republicans in France of how to view the Terror is addressed by David Andress. Without glossing over the brutality of the period he suggests that the unflinching commitment of the terrorists to their cause, namely the preservation of the Republic and all it stood for, was noble and remains relevant.

EXTRACT 2

From David Andress, *The Terror: Civil War in the French Revolution*, Abacus, 2006, p. 372.

For many republicans, the consecration of national glory was thus key to resolving the dilemma of how to treat the Terror – as well as a means of defending their republican heritage against still significant challenges from royalist and Bonapartist traditions. This focus on the 'Frenchness' of the terrorists can, ironically for us, obscure their wider significance, just as the later insistence by twentieth-century Marxist scholars that the Revolution was all about class struggle can make it seem irrelevant in a post-Soviet world. But underpinning the resort to Terror were also ideas that resonate more strongly today: a vivid commitment to a notion of civil society, of personal equality and dignity, and of meaningful individual rights. This after all, was the point of not letting the counter-revolution win.

The revisionist view

The alternative perspective of the revisionists is that the Terror was in essence an anarchic and chaotic descent into a mindless orgy of violence. Simon Schama, while emphasising that '… violence *was* the Revolution itself', does also stress that much of it was directed towards the wealthy. He views this as a brutal example of the politics of envy, made possible as the moral bonds holding society together – the Catholic Church, loyalty to the Crown and deference to the nobility – dissolved and disintegrated before the eyes of the masses.

EXTRACT 3

From Simon Schama, *Citizens: A Chronicle of the French Revolution*, Viking, 1989, pp. 786–7.

The Terror was highly selective in its geography ... For if it operated with crushing effect on areas which were indeed the centres of war and revolt, those same areas happened to be exactly on the economically dynamic periphery of France. Though the Jacobins, as every history relentlessly points out, were great respecters of property, their war was a war on commercial capitalism. They may not have intended it that way at the beginning, but their incessant rhetoric against 'rich egoists' and the incrimination of the commercial and financial elites in federalism meant that, in practice, mercantile and industrial enterprise – unless it had been pulled into the service of the military – was itself attacked. ... The bourgeoisie which Marxist history long believed to be the essential beneficiaries of the Revolution was in fact its principal victim.

? In what way do the historians quoted in Extracts 1, 2 and 3 offer differing interpretations of the Terror?

Chapter summary

The Terror is the most dramatic period of the French Revolution. Confronted with a daunting series of crises and threats, the new Republic was facing almost certain defeat. Against this background the Jacobin government adopted a series of ruthless measures which were enforced with great brutality and efficiency against both its internal and external enemies. The key debate considers how historians have interpreted the Terror. When it had managed to stabilise the situation and was poised to take the initiative against its external enemies, the Jacobin government embarked on an innovative policy of social renewal designed to create a new society. Although it managed to defeat its internal enemies, there were discordant voices from within the ranks of its own supporters. These voices questioned the need for the continuation of the highly centralised governing structure, based around the two great committees. Concerns about Robespierre's motives and methods emboldened his opponents to remove him during the Coup of Thermidor.

Refresher questions

Use these questions to remind yourself of the key material covered in this chapter.

1 What was the reason for introducing government by Terror?

2 Why were the Girondin overthrown?

3 How serious a threat to the government was the federalist revolt?

4 How did Robespierre justify the Terror?

5 Why was Jacques Roux considered to be a threat?

6 What was the purpose behind setting up the *armée révolutionnaire*?

7 What was the impact of the Maximum laws?

8 What measures were used in the provinces to restore the authority of the government?

9 What is significant about the figures relating to deaths during the Terror?

10 What was the impact of the dechristianisation campaign?

11 How did the government deal with those opposed to it?

12 What does the Law of Prairial indicate about revolutionary justice?

13 How did people react to Robespierre's new religion?

14 Why was Robespierre losing support among the *sans-culottes*?

15 How successful was the Terror?

 Question practice

ESSAY QUESTIONS

1 'The civil war in the Vendée was the only significant crisis faced by the republican government during 1793.' Explain why you agree or disagree with this view.

2 'The war crisis was the primary factor behind the emergence of government by Terror in 1793.' How far do you agree?

3 How successful was the Republic in dealing with its enemies during the period 1793–4?

4 To what extent was government by Terror only about defeating the internal and external enemies of the Republic?

INTERPRETATION QUESTION

1 Read the interpretation and then answer the question that follows. 'A regime of popular sovereignty in which the object was to conquer tyranny or die for liberty.' (From Sophie Wahnich, *In Defence of the Terror: Liberty or Death in the French Revolution*, 2012.) Evaluate the strengths and limitations of this interpretation of the Terror, making reference to other interpretations that you have studied.

SOURCE QUESTIONS

1 Why is Source B (page 109) valuable to the historian studying the *sans-culottes*? Explain your answer using the source, the information given about it and your own knowledge of the historical context.

2 How much weight do you give the evidence of Source D (page 116) regarding the activities of the *armées révolutionnaires*? Explain your answer using the source, the information given about it and your own knowledge of the historical context.

3 With reference to Sources B (page 109) and E (page 120), and your understanding of the historical context, which of these two sources is more valuable in explaining why the Revolution became more extreme in late 1793?

4 With reference to Sources B (page 109), D (page 116) and E (page 120), and your understanding of the historical context, assess the value of these sources to a historian studying the emergence of government by Terror in 1793.

5 How far could the historian make use of Sources D (page 116) and E (page 120) together to investigate the justification of government by Terror in 1793–4? Explain your answer using both sources, the information given about them and your own knowledge of the historical context.

CHAPTER 6

Thermidorian reaction and the Directory 1794–9

Following the overthrow of Robespierre and the end of the Terror, a reaction took place among those opposed to revolutionary government. A new system was created – the Directory – which, although the longest lasting of the regimes created during the Revolution, was also in the end replaced. This period is examined as three themes:

★ The Thermidorian reaction

★ The Directory

★ The coup of Brumaire and the overthrow of the Directory

The key debate on *page 160* of this chapter asks the question: Why, ultimately, did the Directory fail?

Key dates

1794	Aug. 1	Law of 22 Prairial repealed, government reorganised
	Sept. 18	State ended financial support of the Church
	Nov. 12	Jacobin Club closed
1795	Feb. 21	Formal separation of Church and State
	April 1–2	Germinal uprising
	May 20–23	Prairial uprising
	Aug. 22	Constitution of Year III

1795	Oct. 5	Vendémiaire uprising; Bonaparte appointed commander of the Army of the Interior
	Nov. 2	Directory established
1796	March 2	Bonaparte appointed to command the army in Italy
1797	Sept. 4	*Coup d'état* of Fructidor
1798	May 11	Law of 22 Floréal
1799	Nov. 9–10	*Coup d'état* of Brumaire; Bonaparte overthrew the Directory
	Dec. 25	Constitution of Year VIII

① The Thermidorian reaction

▶ *What did the Thermidorians do to bring about an end to the Terror?*

There was great delight and relief among many people when Robespierre was executed. The journalist Charles de Lacretelle reported the reactions in Paris: 'People were hugging each other in the streets and at places of entertainment and they were so surprised to find themselves still alive that their joy almost turned to frenzy.'

Those who overthrow Robespierre were known as the **Thermidorians** (after the month of Thermidor when the coup occurred). The Thermidorians were a mixed group – members of the two great committees [the Committee of Public Safety (CPS) and the Committee for General Security (GGC)], ex-terrorists and deputies of the Plain. The Plain now emerged from obscurity to take control. It was made up of the men who had gained from the Revolution by buying *biens nationaux* (land) or by obtaining government contracts. As **regicides** these men were firmly attached to the Republic and did not want to see the return of any form of monarchy. They also disliked the Jacobins, who had given too much power to the *sans-culottes* and had interfered with a free market through the Maximum laws. For them popular democracy, anarchy and the Terror were synonymous. They were also joined by many Montagnards (see pages 86–7).

Ending the Terror

Immediately after Thermidor, the Convention set about dismantling the machinery of the Terror. Between the end of July 1794 and 31 May 1795, the Convention did the following:

- It abolished the Revolutionary Tribunal, following the execution of a further 63 people, including some who had been leading terrorists.
- It released all suspects from prison.
- It repealed the Law of Prairial (see page 123) and closed the Jacobin Club.

The deputies were determined to gain control of the institutions that had made the Terror possible. This meant abandoning the centralisation established by the CPS. The Convention decreed that 25 per cent of the members of the two committees (the CPS and the CGS) had to be changed each month. In August, sixteen committees of the Convention were set up to take over most of the work of the CGS and CPS. The latter was now confined to running the war and diplomacy. In Paris, the Commune was abolished. Power in local government passed to the moderates and property owners, who had been in control before June 1793.

The Thermidorians also decided to deal with religious issues by renouncing the Constitutional Church. In September 1794 the Convention decided that it would no longer pay clerical salaries. This brought about for the first time the **separation of Church and State**. On 21 February 1795 the government restored freedom of worship for all religions, formally ending the persecution waged during the Terror by the dechristianisation campaign. State recognition of the Cult of the Supreme Being was also ended. For the first time in a major European country the State was declaring itself to be entirely neutral in all matters of religious faith, in that it would not favour one belief to the exclusion of others. The consequence of this was that refractory and constitutional priests, Protestants and Jews would be in free competition for popular support.

The uprisings of Germinal and Prairial

The Thermidorians wanted to remove price controls, partly because of their support for a free market and partly because they were considered to be unenforceable. These were abolished in December 1794. Public arms workshops were closed or restored to private ownership. The removal of price controls led to a fall in the value of the *assignat* and massive inflation. The government now had to buy its war materials at market prices. It therefore decided to print more *assignats* to pay for them. In August 1794, before the Maximum was abolished, the *assignat* was 34 per cent of its 1790 value. It dropped to eight per cent in April 1795 and four per cent in May. The situation was made worse by a poor harvest in 1794. Grain shortages led to a huge increase in the price of bread.

The winter of 1794–5 was an unprecedentedly severe one. Rivers froze and factories closed down. A combination of economic collapse and the bitter cold produced an enormous increase in misery, suicides and death from malnutrition, as scarcity turned into famine. The publisher Ruault described the situation: 'The flour intended for Paris is stopped on the way and stolen by citizens even hungrier no doubt than ourselves. Yet there is no lack of corn anywhere! … The farmers absolutely refused to sell it for paper money.'

Germinal

The hungry turned their fury against the Convention. **Germinal** (1 April 1795) was a demonstration rather than a rising. A large crowd of about 10,000 unarmed people marched on the Convention. Many gained access to the main hall and disrupted debates with demands for bread, the constitution of 1793 and the release of former members of the CPS: Barère, Collot and Billaud, who had been imprisoned following the Coup of Thermidor. The demonstrators expected support from the Montagnards in the Assembly but received none. When loyal National Guards appeared, the insurgents withdrew without resisting.

The repression that followed Germinal was light. But to emphasise its authority, the Convention sentenced Barère, Collot and Billaud to be deported to Devil's Island in the French colony of Guiana, off the coast of South America. To safeguard security, other known activists during the Terror were disarmed. During the spring of 1795 disillusionment with the Convention's inability to resolve the famine led to sporadic outbreaks of violence in the provinces, some of which were organised by royalists.

Prairial

Prairial was a much more serious affair. It was an armed rising like those of 10 August 1792 and 2 June 1793 (see pages 84 and 104). On 1 Prairial (20 May 1795) a large crowd of housewives, workers and some National Guard units marched on the Convention to demand bread. In the ensuing chaos a deputy was killed and the mood of the crowd became increasingly hostile. The following day forces loyal to the Convention gathered to confront the crowd and

 KEY TERMS

Germinal Popular demonstration on 1 April 1795 in Paris. Named after a month in the new revolutionary calendar.

Prairial A large popular uprising in Paris on 20–1 May 1795. It was named after a month in the new revolutionary calendar.

a tense situation developed. The Convention's gunners went over to the rebels and aimed their cannon at the Assembly, but no one was prepared to fire. The crisis was resolved when the Convention agreed to accept a petition from the insurgents and to set up a food commission. Loyal National Guards arrived in the evening and cleared the Assembly.

On 3 Prairial (22 May) the Convention took the offensive. The rebel suburbs were surrounded by 20,000 troops of the regular army who forced them to give up their arms and cannon. This time the repression was severe:

- Forty Montagnards were arrested and six were executed.
- A military commission condemned to death a further 36, including the gunners who had joined the rebels.
- About 6000 militants were disarmed and arrested.

Prairial marked the end of the *sans-culottes* as a political and military force. The significance of Prairial was that the defeat of popular movement marked the end of the radical phase of the Revolution. No longer would the *sans-culottes* be able to threaten and intimidate an elected assembly. In Year IV (1795–6) economic conditions were equally as bad as in Year III (1794–5), yet there was no rising. Demoralised, without arms and without leaders, the *sans-culottes* were a spent force.

There were a number of reasons why the uprising of Prairial failed:

- The workers of Paris were divided: the National Guard units in several Sections of the city remained loyal to the Convention.
- There was no institution like the Paris Commune in 1792 to co-ordinate their activities.
- They were politically inexperienced. When they had the advantage and had surrounded the Convention they allowed the opportunity to slip.
- They had lost the support of the radical bourgeoisie, which they had enjoyed between 1789 and 1793.

The key factor, however, was the role of the army. The regular army was used against the citizens of Paris for the first time since the Réveillon riots in the spring of 1789 (see page 33). Its intervention was decisive and made clear just how dependent the new regime was on the military. This would prove to be the first of many instances when the army would interfere in France's internal politics.

The White Terror

The 'White Terror' was an attack on ex-terrorists and all who had done well out of the Revolution by those who had suffered under it. White was the colour of the Bourbons, so 'White Terror' implies that it was a royalist reaction. This was only partly true, as returning *émigrés* and non-juring priests did take advantage of the anti-Jacobin revulsion at the persecution of the Year II. In Nîmes,

'Companies of the Sun' were formed by royalists to attack former terrorists. However, most of those who took part in the White Terror were not royalists and had no intention of restoring the Bourbons and the *seigneurs* of the *ancien régime*. Their main concern was vengeance on all those who had been members of the popular societies and watch committees. The Whites were people who had been victims of the Revolutionary Tribunals. They now turned on those who had done well out of the Revolution, such as purchasers of state land, constitutional priests and government officials.

The White Terror in Paris

The White Terror did not cover the whole of France. It was confined to a score of departments north and west of the Loire and south of Lyon. In Paris it was limited to the activities of the *jeunesse dorée*. These were middle-class youths: bankers' and lawyers' clerks, actors, musicians, army deserters and sons of suspects or of those executed. They dressed extravagantly with square collars, earrings and long hair tied back at the neck, like those about to be guillotined. They formed gangs to beat up and intimidate Jacobins and *sans-culottes*. Yet, although there was certainly some violence, it was not on the same scale as the Terror.

The White Terror in the Vendée

Much more violent was the White Terror in the north-west and south-east of France. Guerrilla warfare was revived in the Vendée in 1794 after the brutal repression of Year II. In the spring, a movement known as **Chouan**, opposed to conscription, began in Brittany under the leadership of Jean Cottereau. Groups of between 50 and 100 men posed a serious threat to law and order as they roamed the countryside, attacking grain convoys and destabilising local government outside the towns by murdering officials.

From the summer of 1794 to the spring of 1796 the Chouans controlled most of Brittany and, under royalist leaders, sought English support. In June 1795, 3000 *émigré* troops based in the Channel Islands were landed at Quiberon Bay and were joined by thousands of Chouans. The total rebel force possibly numbered 22,000.

General Hoche, forewarned, sealed them off with 10,000 troops and compelled them to surrender. Six thousand prisoners were taken, including over 1000 *émigrés*: 640 were shot, along with 108 Chouans, in the biggest disaster suffered by *émigré* forces. The government decided that the Chouan had to be eradicated, and sent Hoche with a huge army of 140,000 to wipe out the Chouan and Vendée rebels. Highly mobile flying columns of soldiers swept across the area north and south of the Loire and by the summer of 1796 they had restored government authority once again to this part of France.

 **KEY TERMS**

Jeunesse dorée 'Gilded youth': young men who dressed extravagantly as a reaction to the restrictions of the Terror. They were also known as Muscadins.

Chouan Guerrilla groups operating in the Vendée between 1794 and 1796.

The White Terror in the south

In the south, the murder gangs of the White Terror were not considered to be a serious threat to the Republic, so little effort was made to crush them. This allowed them to become established and to spread rapidly after the disarming of former terrorists and their supporters. Where the Terror had been at its most savage in Lyon and the Rhône valley, prison massacres reminiscent of the September Massacres in 1792 took place. Gangs of youths, like the *jeunesse dorée* in Paris, killed as many as 2000 in the south-east in 1795. The killing continued throughout 1796 and for much of the following year.

Constitution of Year III, 1795

The Thermidorians wanted a new constitution, which would guarantee the main features of the Revolution of 1789: the abolition of privilege, freedom of the individual, and the control of local and national affairs by an elected assembly and elected officials. They also wanted to ensure that a dictatorship, like that of the CPS, would be impossible in the future and that there would be no return to monarchy or to **popular sovereignty** on the *sans-culotte* model. A new constitution was agreed on 22 August 1795, whose main features were as follows:

- All men over 21 who paid direct taxation were allowed to vote in the primary assemblies to choose electors.
- Real power, however, was exercised by the electors who actually chose the deputies. Electors had to pay taxes equivalent to 150–200 days' labour. This was so high that the number of electors had fallen from 50,000 in 1790–2 to 30,000 in 1795. Electors were, therefore, the very rich, who had suffered from the Revolution in 1793–4.
- In order to prevent a dictatorship arising, the Thermidorians rigidly separated the legislature from the executive.

The legislature

The legislature was divided into two chambers:

- The Council of Five Hundred, all of whom had to be over the age of 30. This Council would initiate legislation and then would pass it on to a Council of Ancients.
- The Council of Ancients: 250 men over the age of 40, who would approve or object to bills but could not introduce or change them.

There was no property qualification for the councillors of either chamber. Elections were to be held every year, when a third of the members retired.

The executive

The executive was to be a Directory of five, chosen by the Ancients from a list drawn up by the Five Hundred. The five directors would hold office for five

KEY TERM

Popular sovereignty
The idea that the people should exercise control over their government, usually by directly electing a representative assembly.

years, although one, chosen by lot, had to retire each year. Directors were not allowed to be members of either council, and their powers were limited. They could not initiate or veto laws or declare war and they had no control over the treasury. Yet they had considerable authority, as they were in charge of diplomacy, military affairs and law enforcement. Government ministers were responsible to the directors, as were government commissioners who saw that government policy was implemented in the provinces.

Weaknesses in the new constitution

In spite of the complex system of **checks and balances** designed to prevent a dictatorship, the new Constitution had many weaknesses:

- The yearly elections promoted instability, as majorities in the councils could be quickly overturned.
- There was no means of resolving conflicts between the legislature and the executive.
- The councils could paralyse the Directory by refusing to pass laws that the government required.
- The directors could neither dissolve the councils nor veto laws passed by them.
- The legislature was not in a strong position either, if it clashed with the executive. It could alter the composition of the Directory only by replacing the one director who retired each year with its own candidate.

The new constitution enforced quite rigidly the **separation of powers**. If a hostile majority dominated the legislature then the constitution allowed it to paralyse the Directory. As the Directory was unable to dissolve the legislature or veto their laws, it came to rely on unconstitutional methods such as cancelling election returns and calling in the army to resolve any disputes.

Having drawn up the new constitution, the Convention, knowing that it was unpopular as an elected chamber, feared that free elections might produce a royalist majority. In order to avoid this it decreed that two-thirds of the deputies to the new councils must be chosen from among the existing deputies of the Convention. The new constitution of Year III was agreed on 22 August 1795. This was then submitted to a **plebiscite** for approval: 1,057,390 were in favour of the constitution, against 49,978 who opposed it. Four million voters did not vote. The two-thirds decree was accepted by only 205,000 to 108,000.

Verona Declaration

As the discussions about the proposed constitution were nearing a close, the royalists sought to promote their cause. Constitutional monarchists, wanting a return to a limited monarchy similar to that in the 1791 constitution, felt they were gaining public support as they appeared to offer a prospect of stability. They had hoped to put Louis XVI's son, a prisoner in the Temple (one of the prisons in Paris) on the throne as 'Louis XVII' but he died in June 1795. From

KEY TERMS

Checks and balances
Ensuring that the power given to the executive was balanced by the power granted to the legislature.

Separation of powers
The division of executive and legislative powers so that the government could not make laws without the support of the legislature.

Plebiscite A popular vote on a single issue.

Verona Declaration
A reactionary statement issued by the new heir to the throne promising to reverse many of the gains made during the Revolution.

northern Italy the Comte de Provence, Louis XVI's brother, immediately proclaimed himself Louis XVIII and on 24 June issued the **Verona Declaration**.

The Declaration, however, turned out to be a reactionary document, which made the task of restoring the monarchy more difficult. Louis promised to restore the 'ancient constitution' of France completely, which meant restoring the three orders and the *parlements*. He also promised to restore 'stolen properties', such as those taken from the Church and the *émigrés*. This antagonised all those who had bought *biens nationaux* and all who had benefited from the abolition of the tithe and seigneurial dues. Although it was not intended as such, the Verona Declaration turned out to be a great boost to those who favoured a Republic.

The Vendémiaire uprising

The Verona Declaration failed to attract mass support for the royalist cause. Although work on the new constitution was proceeding well, news of the two-thirds law came as a shock to many Parisians who had hoped that the Convention would soon be replaced. Its inability to deal with food shortages and inflation turned many ordinary people against the Convention, yet it now appeared that most of its deputies would be returned to the new assembly. Royalists in particular felt that the prospect of any restoration of the monarchy was unlikely given the known hostility of the Convention. Frustration and anger spilled over into rebellion.

On 5 October 1795 (13 Vendémiaire), a large royalist crowd of 25,000 gathered to march on the Convention and seize power. They greatly outnumbered the

SOURCE A

? What does Source A suggest about the methods used by the Directory to maintain order?

The defeat of the royalist uprising of Vendémiaire, 1795. The print shows the force used by the Directory to suppress the uprising. The artillery used by Bonaparte is clearly shown firing into the crowd.

Napoleon Bonaparte

1769 — Born into a minor noble family on the island of Corsica, which had only been part of France since 1768

1785 — Commissioned as an artillery officer

1793 — Commanded artillery at the siege of Toulon

1795 — Put down the Vendémiaire uprising

1799 — Coup of Brumaire, appointed First Consul

1804 — Proclaimed Emperor of the French

1815 — Defeated at Waterloo and exiled to St Helena

1821 — Death and burial at St Helena

Napoleon Bonaparte is one of the most recognisable names in history. His life and career were tied to the French Revolution. He was an individual filled with great energy and a ruthless determination to advance his career, and first came to prominence when he was responsible for raising the siege of Toulon. He was rewarded with promotion to the rank of general. Yet Napoleon was not only a great military strategist but also an astute political operative who knew when to cultivate friendships in high places. When the Directory needed a general to quash popular disturbances, Napoleon was chosen.

As commander of the army in Italy, he defeated Austrian interests in a series of brilliant campaigns and secured a highly beneficial settlement for the French Republic. His attempt to threaten British interests by capturing Egypt ended in failure and the abandonment of his army.

He sailed back to France, and took a role in the coup which toppled the Directory and elevated him to power as First Consul and then Emperor.

A recent British biographer, Andrew Roberts, described Napoleon's career as 'the ultimate triumph of the self-made man'. His reign as Emperor was consumed by war, which ultimately led to his overthrow and exile. At the heart of much of the debate about Napoleon is the question of what his motivation was. Was he driven by preserving and extending the gains of the Revolution to Europe, or simply by self-aggrandisement on an epic scale? Napoleon was a great propagandist and in his years of exile sought to justify his actions. He argued that his universal empire was a means to extend the benefits that France had secured across Europe but that this was thwarted by a coalition of hostile monarchs. Many of his reforms which modernised France survive. His goal of a universal empire, although dismantled with his fall, may yet re-emerge in a very different guise through greater European integration.

The emergence of Napoleon as one of the ablest and most popular generals during the Directory is one of the key features of the Revolution. His use by the Directory to resolve political disputes made him aware of how weak the system was. When invited to join the coup to overthrow the Directory he agreed willingly (see pages 154–5).

7800 government troops but the latter had cannon, under the command of General Bonaparte, whereas the rebels did not. The devastating artillery fire – Bonaparte's famous 'Whiff of grapeshot' – crushed the rebellion. Over 300 were killed or wounded in the fighting, making it one of the bloodiest revolutionary *journées*. It also marked another watershed: the people of Paris would not again attempt to intimidate an elected assembly until 1830.

The divisions among the royalists and the unpopularity of the Verona Declaration all make the rising of Vendémiaire appear rather mysterious. It is usually presented as a royalist rising against the two-thirds decree. Yet, the largest groups of rebels were artisans and apprentices: a third of those arrested were manual workers. The rising was not simply against the two-thirds decree but had economic origins too. Many people, including *rentiers* – small proprietors – and government employees, had been badly hit by inflation. These people, who were among the rebels, had supported the Thermidorians and defended the Convention in the risings of Germinal and Prairial.

The repression that followed was light. Only two people were executed, although steps were taken to prevent further risings. The Sectional Assemblies were abolished and the National Guard was put under the control of the new General of the Army of the Interior, Napoleon Bonaparte. For the second time in six months the army had saved the Thermidorian Republic.

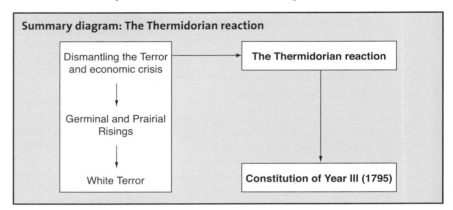

Summary diagram: The Thermidorian reaction

Dismantling the Terror and economic crisis → **The Thermidorian reaction**

Germinal and Prairial Risings

White Terror

Constitution of Year III (1795)

 ## 2 The Directory

▶ *What problems faced the Directory and how did it deal with them?*

KEY TERM

Conventionnels Members of the Convention between 1792 and 1795.

The new third of members elected to the Council of Five Hundred after Vendémiaire and the dissolution of the Convention was mainly royalist, but they were unable to influence the choice of directors. As the Verona Declaration had threatened to punish all regicides, the *conventionnels* elected directors (Carnot was the best known) all of whom were regicides, as this would be a guarantee against a royalist restoration.

The directors wanted to provide a stable and liberal government, which would maintain the gains of the Revolution. Yet the problems they faced were daunting. There was no end in sight for the war, and it had to be paid for. The treasury was empty, taxes were unpaid and the *assignat* had plummeted in value. Many Frenchmen did not expect the Directory to last more than a few months. The Directory did, however, survive and for longer than any of the other revolutionary regimes. There were a number of factors that contributed to this:

● The Directory was committed to restoring the rule of law.
● Many of their key opponents were discredited. Few wanted a return either to the Jacobin Terror of Year II or to the absolute monarchy of the *ancien régime*.
● While many ordinary people were prepared to accept a constitutional monarchy with limited powers, the royalists themselves were deeply divided,

between extremists who supported the Verona Declaration and constitutional monarchists.

- Public apathy also helped the Directory to survive – after six years of revolution and three years of war, revolutionary enthusiasm had all but disappeared.
- Significantly, the army supported the Directory, as a royalist restoration would mean an end to the war. Army officers did not wish to be deprived of any opportunity provided by war for promotion or plunder. It was the army, above all, that enabled the Directory to overcome all challenges to its authority, but this was a double-edged weapon. The army, which kept the Directory in power, would be the most serious threat to its survival if it became dissatisfied.

The Babeuf Plot 1796

The first real challenge to the Directory came from Gracchus Babeuf, a radical pamphleteer and editor of *Tribun du Peuple*. Babeuf disliked the constitution of Year III, because it gave power to the wealthy. He believed that the aim of society should be 'the common happiness', and that the Revolution should secure the equal enjoyment of life's blessings for all. He thought that as private property

SOURCE B

From the 'Doctrine of Babeuf and the Conspiracy of Equals', May 1796, quoted in D.I. Wright, editor, *The French Revolution: Introductory Documents*, University of Queensland Press, 1980, pp. 231–2.

1 *Nature has given to each individual an equal right to the enjoyment of property.*

2 *The purpose of society is to defend such equality ... .*

3 *Nature has imposed upon every individual the obligation to work; anyone who evades his share of work is a criminal.*

4 *Both work and benefits must be common to all.*

5 *There is oppression when one person is exhausted by work and is destitute of everything, while another lives in luxury without doing any work at all.*

...

7 *In a real society there ought to be neither rich nor poor.*

8 *The rich who are not willing to renounce their surplus in favour of the poor are enemies of the people.*

...

10 *The aim of the French Revolution is to destroy inequality.*

11 *The Revolution is not complete, because the rich monopolise all the property and govern exclusively, while the poor toil like slaves and live in misery ... .*

> Study Source B. What does Babeuf suggest is the basis of an ideal society?

produced inequality, the only way to establish real equality was 'to establish the communal management of property and abolish private possession'. These ideas were much more radical than those put forward in Year II and have led many historians to regard Babeuf as the first communist, a forerunner of Karl Marx (1818–83).

KEY TERM

Conspiracy of Equals
Babeuf's theory of how to organise a revolution, using a small group of committed revolutionaries rather than a mass movement.

From March 1796 Babeuf organised a plan to overthrow the Directory by means of a coup. He saw what he called his **Conspiracy of Equals** as a popular rising. Babeuf realised, however, that this would not come about spontaneously but must be prepared by a small group of dedicated revolutionaries. Through propaganda and agitation they would persuade key institutions, like the army and police, who would provide the armed force to seize power. After seizing power, the revolutionary leaders would establish a dictatorship, in order to make fundamental changes in the organisation of society.

Babeuf received no support from the *sans-culottes* and little from former Jacobins. He was arrested in May 1796, after being betrayed to the authorities by a fellow conspirator, and was executed the following year. Marxist historians such as Albert Soboul consider Babeuf's theories to be extremely influential. They argue that his ideas inspired not only nineteenth-century French revolutionaries, like Blanqui, but ultimately Lenin and his followers who set up the first communist state in the Russia in 1917. Babeuf's importance to the French Revolution itself, however, was minimal.

The *coup d'état* of Fructidor 1797

The elections of 1797 revealed a growing popular shift towards the monarchists. People were tired of war abroad and religious conflict at home and found the idea of a constitutional monarchy attractive, believing that it would offer peace and stability. Of the 216 ex-members of the Convention who sought re-election, only eleven were returned. Monarchists won 180 of the 260 seats being contested, bringing their numbers in the councils to 330. The wealthy, populous northern departments returned the largest proportion of monarchists, suggesting that the Directory was losing the support of the richer bourgeoisie.

The elections, where in some departments fewer than ten per cent of electors voted, did not give the monarchists a majority in the councils. However, they did mean that the Directory no longer had majority support and could rely on only about a third of the deputies. All the monarchists needed to do, it appeared, was to wait for the next elections when more *conventionnels* would have to give up their seats and, if voting followed a similar pattern to the elections of 1797, they would obtain a majority. Monarchists would then be in a position to restore the monarchy legally. The opponents of the Directory were also successful in elections to the provincial administrations.

The *coup d'état*

The royalists showed their strength when the councils appointed three of their supporters to important positions. One was elected president of the Five Hundred and another president of the Ancients. Barthélemy, the new director, was regarded as sympathetic to the monarchists, as was Carnot, who was becoming steadily more conservative. Carnot was prepared to give up conquered territory to make a lasting peace and so was disliked by the generals.

Of the remaining directors, two were committed republicans. They were determined to prevent a restoration of the monarchy and sought help from the army. Bonaparte had already sent General Augereau to Paris with some troops to support the republican directors. On the night of 3–4 September 1797 (17–18 Fructidor, Year V) troops were ordered to seize all the strong points in Paris and surround the council chambers. They then arrested two directors, Carnot and Barthélemy, and 53 deputies.

Some of the remaining deputies who attended the councils clearly felt intimidated, and they approved two decrees demanded by the remaining directors. One decree cancelled the elections in 49 departments, removing 177 deputies without providing for their replacement. Normandy, Brittany, the Paris area and the north now had no parliamentary representation at all. A second decree provided for the deportation to the penal settlements in Guiana of Carnot (who had escaped and fled abroad and was sentenced *in absentia*), Barthélemy, the 53 deputies arrested, and some leading royalists. The directors also cancelled the local government elections and made appointments themselves.

It was clear to all that the coup was the end of parliamentary government and of the constitution of Year III, and that the executive had won an important victory over the legislature. The revival of monarchism had been dealt a significant blow. It also meant that the Directory could now govern without facing hostile councils.

Terror

After Fructidor, the new Directory took action against *émigrés* and refractory priests. *Émigrés* who had returned to France were given two weeks to leave, otherwise they would be executed. During the next few months many were hunted down and were sentenced to death. Clergy were now required to take an oath rejecting any support for royalty; those refusing would be deported to Guiana. The 1400 non-juring priests were sentenced to deportation.

The terror that followed Fructidor was limited. It was carried out solely by the government and the army in an attempt to destroy the royalist movement. In the short term it succeeded but, by alienating Catholic opinion, it provided more opponents for the Directory.

Financial reform

Many of the financial problems of the Directory were the legacy of previous regimes, which had printed more and more *assignats* in order to pay for the war. As by February 1796 these were almost worthless, the Directory issued a new paper currency, known as *mandats territoriaux*. They also soon lost value, and by July were worth less than five per cent of their nominal value. In February 1797 they ceased to be legal tender.

The monetary crisis had been catastrophic for government officials, *rentiers* and workers, as they saw a rapid decline in their purchasing power. Metal coins now became the only legal currency and these were in short supply: there were only a billion *livres* in circulation in 1797, compared with 2.5 billion in 1789. This resulted in **deflation**, as producers and retailers lowered prices to try and stimulate demand among consumers who were reluctant to buy goods. The inflation of 1795–7 had made the Directory unpopular with the workers. Now the Directory became unpopular with businessmen since lower prices meant lower profits.

Decreasing the national debt

From the coup of Fructidor to the spring of 1799 the Directory had little trouble with the purged councils, and Dominique-Vincent Ramel, the minister of finance, had an opportunity to introduce some far-reaching reforms. In September 1797 two-thirds of the **national debt** was renounced by a one-off payment to debt holders. Their loans to the government were converted into non-interest-bearing bonds, which could be used to buy national property.

This move was of immediate benefit to the government, as it reduced the annual interest on the national debt from 240 million **francs** (which was about a quarter of government expenditure) to 80 million. It was not of much use to the bondholders who were denied income. Within a year the value of the bonds had fallen by 60 per cent; soon after that they became worthless, when the government refused to accept them for the purchase of *biens*. This was, in effect, a partial declaration of state bankruptcy, as two-thirds of the national debt was liquidated in this way. Although debt holders were unhappy with the measure, the **bankruptcy of the two-thirds**, as it was known, helped to stabilise French finances for a time.

Increasing revenue

In addition to cutting expenditure, Ramel wanted to increase revenue. He put in place a number of policies to achieve this:

- In 1798 four basic forms of direct taxation were established:
  - a tax on trading licences
  - a land tax

- ○ a tax on movable property
- ○ a tax on doors and windows.
- These measures were among the most lasting achievements of the Directory and survived until 1914.
- Ramel changed the method of collecting direct taxes. Whereas, previously, locally elected authorities had been responsible for collection, central control was now introduced. Commissioners appointed by the Directors were to assess and levy taxes.

As there was a continual **deficit** during wartime, the government revived an unpopular practice of the *ancien régime* – indirect taxes. The *octrois* (see page 5) was reintroduced and was again very unpopular, as it raised the price of goods in the towns.

An increasingly lucrative source of income was plunder from those foreign states, especially Italy and Germany, which had been occupied by French armies.

The impact of these policies was positive. Although very unpopular after the bankruptcy of the two-thirds, aided by the reduced military expenditure when peace with Austria was made in October 1797, and new taxes, Ramel was able to **balance the budget** for the first time since the Revolution began.

War 1794–9

The Battle of Fleurus in the Austrian Netherlands in June 1794 was the first of a series of successes, which continued until all the members of the First Coalition, except Britain, had been knocked out of the war. In the summer of 1794 the Austrian Netherlands (Belgium) was occupied and, in the following winter, the United Provinces were invaded. The French conquered the Rhineland and crossed into Spain. Russia had intervened in Poland, which it was clear would be partitioned again. Prussia therefore made peace with France so that it would be free to claim Polish territory for itself. This, in reality, made very little difference as Prussia had played only a minimal part in the war against France since 1793.

At the Treaty of Basel on 6 April 1795, Prussia promised to hand over its territories on the left bank of the Rhine to France. In return it would receive land on the right bank. This treaty freed French troops to attack other enemies.

The Batavian Republic

Meanwhile, the United Provinces had become the Batavian Republic in January 1795, after a revolt against William V, who fled to England. Having lost Prussian support, the Dutch hastily made peace with France, who they were forced to join as an ally. The French hoped that the powerful Dutch navy would help to tip the naval balance against Britain. Spain too made peace in July, giving up to France its part of the island of San Domingo. Of the Great Powers, only Britain and Austria remained in the fight against France.

 **KEY TERM**

Balance the budget To create a situation in which the government's expenditure is equal to its income.

Figure 6.1 France 1789–95. Note how France had extended its territory, particularly in the north-east, in order to establish a natural frontier on the Rhine.

Defeat of Austria

In 1796 the main French objective was to defeat Austria. Carnot drew up the plan of campaign and prepared a pincer movement against Austria. Armies under Jourdan and Moreau would march across Bavaria to Vienna, while the armies of the Alps and Italy would conquer Piedmont and Lombardy and then move across the Alps to Vienna. The main attack was to be by Jourdan and Moreau, who were given 140,000 troops.

Command of the Italian campaign was given to the 27-year-old General Napoleon Bonaparte on 2 March 1796. It was expected that he would play a secondary role as he had no field experience and only 30,000 unpaid and ill-disciplined troops under his command. Yet Napoleon was to turn Italy into the major battleground against Austria. He was able to do this by winning the loyalty of his men, to whom he promised vast wealth.

Within a month of taking command Napoleon had defeated the north Italian state of Piedmont and forced it to make peace. In the same month of May he defeated the Austrians at Lodi and entered Milan. Mantua was the key to the passes over the Alps to Vienna, and Napoleon finally captured it in February 1797. The road to Vienna seemed open but all had not been going well for the French. The Archduke Charles had driven Moreau back to the Rhine, so Napoleon signed an **armistice** with Austria at Leoben in April.

Napoleon decided the terms at Leoben, without consulting the Directory. He was already confident enough to be making his own foreign policy and, in so doing, ignoring specific instructions from the directors. They had wanted to use Lombardy as a bargaining counter when negotiating with Austria to exchange for recognition of French control of the left bank of the Rhine. Instead, Napoleon joined Lombardy to Modena and the Papal Legations to form the Cisalpine Republic. Austria recognised the Austrian Netherlands (Belgium), which the French had annexed in October 1795, as French territory.

As compensation for giving up Lombardy and the Austrian Netherlands, Napoleon gave Austria Venice and part of the Venetian Republic, which provided access to the Adriatic. The fate of the left bank of the Rhine was unclear: it was to be decided by a congress of the Holy Roman Empire. The Directory and the generals on the Rhine were furious that they had no choice but to accept what Napoleon had done. As the royalists had won the elections in France, the Directory knew it might need him. The Peace of Campo Formio, 18 October 1797, confirmed what had been agreed at Leoben.

Britain isolated

With its major allies out of the war, Britain was now isolated. The French wanted to invade Britain, but for this to happen control of the seas was necessary in order to ensure a safe passage for an invasion army. In particular, the French wanted to support **Irish Nationalists** in their attempt to overthrow British rule in Ireland. Control of the sea was also vital if the French hoped to send a military expedition to Ireland. The French hoped that with the aid of the Dutch and Spanish fleets (Spain had become an ally of France in October 1796) they would be able to achieve this. These plans were dashed by two British victories in 1797. In February the Spanish fleet was defeated off Cape St Vincent and the Dutch fleet was almost completely destroyed at Camperdown in October. The war with Britain therefore continued.

KEY TERMS

Armistice An agreement between two countries to end hostilities. This would precede a peace settlement that would formally mark the end of a war.

Irish Nationalists Irish who were staunchly anti-British and wished to be free from what they considered foreign rule. During the Revolution they approached the republicans for support.

Figure 6.2 The expansion of revolutionary France. Note how the French Republic established 'sister republics' along some of her borders. Why do you think the republicans did this?

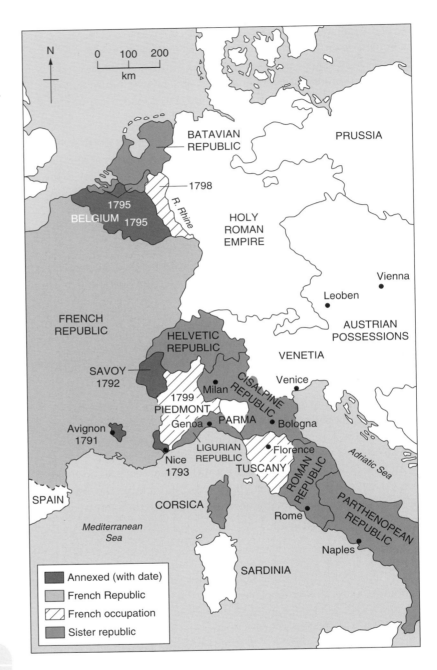

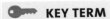

KEY TERM

Satellite republics States that had the appearance of being independent but were in reality under French control. Also known as 'sister republics'.

Creating states

On the European continent the prospects for a permanent peace receded. French foreign policy became increasingly aggressive as the directors sought to keep French conquests and even extend them. France reorganised a number of foreign territories, effectively redrawing the map of Europe in some areas. These new territories were in effect **satellite republics** under French influence or control:

- The Helvetic Republic was set up in Switzerland in January 1798 with the help of Swiss patriots sympathetic to French ideals. This was important to France, as it controlled the main Alpine passes to Italy. Geneva was annexed to France.
- In Italy three small republics were created: the Roman Republic after the French invasion and the flight of the Pope to Tuscany (1798), the Cisalpine Republic based on Milan and the Ligurian Republic, which replaced the Genoese Republic in June 1797.
- The Batavian Republic was established in the United Provinces in January 1795, after a revolt supported by the French against William V, who fled to England.
- The French were busy redrawing the map of Germany in negotiations with the congress of the Holy Roman Empire at Rastatt. In March 1798 the congress handed over the left bank of the Rhine to France and agreed that princes who had lost land there should be compensated by receiving Church land elsewhere in Germany.

The spring of 1798 marked the high point of the Republic's power. In western, central and southern Europe, France had attained a degree of hegemony (domination) unparalleled in modern European history (see the map on page 150). Yet from this position of great external strength, the decline in the Directory's fortunes was equally dramatic. Within eighteen months it would be overthrown.

The Second Coalition

Following his successes in Italy, Napoleon departed for Egypt in May 1798 with the aim of attacking British overland trade routes with India and the east. His fleet, however, was destroyed by Horatio Nelson at the Battle of Aboukir Bay (August 1798). This defeat encouraged other countries to once again take up arms against France. A **Second Coalition** was formed, and Russia, which had not taken part in previous fighting against France, declared war in December. Tsar Paul was incensed at the French seizure of Malta, of which he had declared himself protector in 1797.

France declared war on Austria in March 1799 on the grounds that Austria had allowed Russian troops to move through its territory. Immediately war resumed, France occupied the rest of Italy; Piedmont was annexed to France, and Naples was turned into another 'sister' republic – the Parthenopean.

These early successes were followed by a series of defeats. The French were pushed back to the Rhine by the Austrians, and the Russians advanced through northern Italy. French forces withdrew from the whole of Italy, except Genoa, as the Russians moved into Switzerland. It appeared that France would be invaded

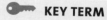 **KEY TERM**

Second Coalition Formed in 1799 and consisting of Britain, Russia, Austria, Turkey, Portugal and Naples.

for the first time in six years, but, as had happened before, France was saved by quarrels among the allies. Austria, instead of supporting Russia in Switzerland, sent its best troops north to the Rhine. This allowed the French to move on to the offensive in Switzerland, where the Russians withdrew in the autumn of 1799. The immediate danger to France was over.

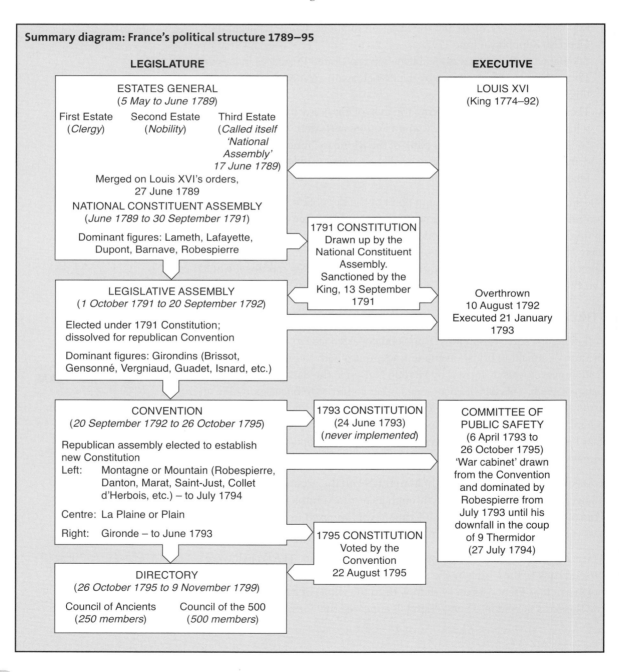

Summary diagram: France's political structure 1789–95

LEGISLATURE — EXECUTIVE

ESTATES GENERAL
(*5 May to June 1789*)

First Estate (*Clergy*) — Second Estate (*Nobility*) — Third Estate (*Called itself 'National Assembly' 17 June 1789*)

Merged on Louis XVI's orders, 27 June 1789

NATIONAL CONSTITUENT ASSEMBLY
(*June 1789 to 30 September 1791*)

Dominant figures: Lameth, Lafayette, Dupont, Barnave, Robespierre

LOUIS XVI
(King 1774–92)

1791 CONSTITUTION
Drawn up by the National Constituent Assembly. Sanctioned by the King, 13 September 1791

LEGISLATIVE ASSEMBLY
(*1 October 1791 to 20 September 1792*)

Elected under 1791 Constitution; dissolved for republican Convention

Dominant figures: Girondins (Brissot, Gensonné, Vergniaud, Guadet, Isnard, etc.)

Overthrown 10 August 1792
Executed 21 January 1793

CONVENTION
(*20 September 1792 to 26 October 1795*)

Republican assembly elected to establish new Constitution

Left: Montagne or Mountain (Robespierre, Danton, Marat, Saint-Just, Collet d'Herbois, etc.) – to July 1794

Centre: La Plaine or Plain

Right: Gironde – to June 1793

1793 CONSTITUTION
(24 June 1793)
(*never implemented*)

COMMITTEE OF PUBLIC SAFETY
(6 April 1793 to 26 October 1795)
'War cabinet' drawn from the Convention and dominated by Robespierre from July 1793 until his downfall in the coup of 9 Thermidor
(27 July 1794)

1795 CONSTITUTION
Voted by the Convention 22 August 1795

DIRECTORY
(*26 October 1795 to 9 November 1799*)

Council of Ancients (*250 members*) — Council of the 500 (*500 members*)

3 The coup of Brumaire and the overthrow of the Directory

▶ *Why was the Directory overthrown?*

The persecution of royalists after Fructidor had been severe, so they tended to keep away from the electoral assemblies in the 1798 election. Although the Jacobins did well in the elections, they captured less than a third of the seats. The Directory could be sure of majority support among deputies in the new legislature, yet the directors persuaded the councils by the Law of 22 Floréal (11 May 1798) to annul the election of 127 deputies, 86 of whom were suspected Jacobins. In another contravention of the 1795 constitution, the directors chose most of the deputies who replaced the expelled members. There was little justification for the *coup d'état* of Floréal as no one could pretend that the Republic was in danger. Once again the Directory had shown its contempt for the wishes of the electors.

Jourdan's law

By 1798 there were concerns about the size of the French army, which was only 270,000 strong. Desertion, low morale and a reluctance to join the military were all taking their toll. Jourdan's law proposed that conscription be reintroduced for the first time since 1793. The councils approved this in September 1798. However, it provoked widespread resistance. Much of the Austrian Netherlands (Belgium), where conscription was also introduced, revolted in November and it took two months to put down the rising. The prospect of conscription was viewed with great reluctance among large numbers of young men who went to great lengths to avoid military service. Of the first draft of 230,000, only 74,000 reached the armies.

The 1799 elections once again showed the unpopularity of the Directory. Only 66 of 187 government candidates were elected. Among the rest there were about 50 Jacobins, including some who had been purged during Floréal. They were still a minority but many moderate deputies were now prepared to follow their lead. The moderates had become disillusioned with the government, as news of military defeats reached Paris. The military situation was regarded as so desperate that the councils were persuaded to pass emergency laws that were proposed by Jacobins. In June 1799 Jourdan called for a new *levée en masse*: all men between the ages of 20 and 25 were to be called up immediately.

Crisis

With its armies being forced back into France, the Republic could no longer pay for the war by seizing foreign assets. A **forced loan** on the rich was decreed. This was intended to raise 100 million *livres*, a sum that meant that the wealthy

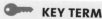

KEY TERM

Forced loan A measure compelling the wealthy to loan money to the government.

might have to give up as much as three-quarters of their income. The **Law of Hostages** of 12 July was even worse for the notables. Any areas resisting the new laws could be declared 'disturbed'. Local authorities could then arrest relatives of *émigrés*, nobles or rebels. They could be imprisoned, fined and their property confiscated to pay for the damage done by those causing disturbances.

SOURCE C

From the Law of Hostages, 18 June 1799.

The kinsmen of émigrés, *their relatives by marriage, and former nobles, the grandfathers, grandmothers, fathers and mothers of persons who, without being nobles or* émigrés *are nevertheless notoriously known as taking part in gatherings or bands of assassins, are personally responsible for the assassinations and acts of brigandage, out of hatred of the Republic, in the departments declared in a state of disturbance. Immediately after publication of the Law, the central administration shall take hostages from the classes noted above. The hostages shall be established at their own expense and in one and the same locality under the supervision of the central and the municipal administrations. The property of deported hostages shall be placed under sequestration.*

Read Source C. Who are the authorities concerned about?

KEY TERMS

Law of Hostages Relatives of any French citizens opposing the Republic would be imprisoned at their own expense and their property seized to pay for damage done by anti-government rebels.

Brigandage Outbreaks of lawlessness and violence by groups of bandits.

These measures appeared to be a return to the arbitrary arrests and harassment of the Terror of the Year II. Yet by November only 10 million *livres* of the forced loan had been collected. Conscription was planned to raise 402,000 troops but, as in 1798, there was widespread resistance and only 248,000 actually joined the army. Many became brigands or royalist rebels to avoid being called up. The Law of Hostages was hardly ever applied, because of opposition from local officials.

In 1799 there was a virtual collapse of government administration in the provinces. There were many reasons for this:

- The Directory could not persuade local notables to accept office and had few troops to enforce its decrees.
- Local authorities were often taken over by royalists, who refused to levy forced loans, persecute non-juring priests or catch deserters.
- The National Guard was not large enough to keep order in the absence of regular troops, so substantial areas of the countryside were not policed at all.
- Government commissioners were killed as quickly as they were replaced.

The result of this administrative collapse was **brigandage**. By November 1799 there was civil war in the Ardèche region in southern France.

The *coup d'état* of Brumaire

The military situation improved in the late summer of 1799. The Russians were driven out of Switzerland in September. Sieyès (page 28), who had become a director, saw this as an opportunity to stage a coup. He wanted to strengthen the executive but knew that the Five Hundred would not agree to this and that it could not be done constitutionally. Therefore a coup was required for which the support of the army would be necessary. But which general could be relied on?

Moreau was approached but recommended Bonaparte, who had returned from Egypt on 10 October. 'There is your man', he told Sieyès. 'He will make your *coup d'état* far better than I can.' On his way to Paris Bonaparte was greeted enthusiastically by the population, as the most successful of the republican generals and the one who had brought peace in 1797. He had made up his mind to play a leading role in French politics. He agreed to join Sieyès' coup but only on condition that a provisional government of three consuls, who would draft a new constitution, should be set up.

The removal to Saint-Cloud

Sieyès wanted to move the councils to **Saint-Cloud**, as the Jacobins in the Five Hundred in Paris were numerous enough to provide opposition to his plans. The Ancients, using as an excuse the fear of a plot, persuaded the councils to move to the safer location at Saint-Cloud. Once there it became clear on 19 Brumaire (10 November) that the only plot was one organised by Sieyès. The Council of Five Hundred was furious, so Bonaparte reluctantly agreed to address both councils.

The appearance of Napoleon in the Five Hundred with armed grenadiers was greeted with cries of 'Outlaw' and 'Down with the tyrant'. He was physically attacked by Jacobin deputies and had to be rescued by fellow officers. It was not at all clear that the soldiers would take action against the elected representatives of the nation. Napoleon's brother Lucien, president of the Five Hundred, came to his rescue when he told the troops that some deputies were trying to assassinate their general. At this the troops cleared the hall where the Five Hundred were meeting.

Some hours later a small group of councillors sympathetic to the plotters met and approved a decree abolishing the Directory.

It was replaced with a provisional executive committee of three members: Sieyès, Roger Ducos and Napoleon. The great beneficiary of Brumaire was Napoleon but it was his brother who was the true hero of the hour.

Constitution of Year VIII

Paris remained calm, but this may have been as a sign of apathy and reluctance to become involved in any more protest, rather than of approval. When news of the coup spread to the provinces there was little rejoicing at the events. Such reaction as there was varied between surprise and mild opposition. A poster that appeared in Paris expressed the disillusionment many felt towards the Directory: 'France wants something great and long-lasting. Instability has been her downfall. She has no desire for a monarchy, wants a free and independent legislature and to enjoy the benefits from ten years of sacrifices.'

 **KEY TERM**

Saint-Cloud A former royal palace in the suburbs of Paris away from the influence of Paris, where the plotters believed that Jacobinism was still a powerful force.

SOURCE D

What does Source D suggest about attitudes within the Council of Five Hundred towards Napoleon?

Napoleon and the Council of Five Hundred at Saint-Cloud by Bouchot. The artist seeks to portray Napoleon in a heroic pose as an isolated figure surrounded by hostile opponents but determined to do what is right for France.

When Napoleon presented the new constitution of Year VIII to the French people on 15 December 1799, he said that it was 'founded on the true principles of representative government, on the sacred rights of property, equality and liberty [see page 42]. Citizens, the Revolution is established on the principles which began it. It is finished.' Many did not realise the significance of the *coup d'état* of Brumaire. The republican phase of the Revolution was drawing to a close, while another, destined to culminate in the Napoleonic Empire, was beginning (see Chapter 8).

SOURCE E

From Napoleon's proclamation to the French nation on 10 November 1799 to explain why he had taken part in the coup.

On my return to Paris I found all authority in chaos and agreement only on the one truth that the constitution was half destroyed and incapable of preserving liberty. Men of every party came to see me, confided their plans, disclosed their secrets and asked for my support. I refused to be a man of party. The Council of the Ancients appealed to me. I answered their appeal. The Ancients resolved, therefore, upon the removal of the legislative bodies to St Cloud. They placed at my disposal the force necessary to secure their independence. I was bound, in duty to my fellow-citizens, to the soldiers perishing in our armies, and the national glory, acquired at the cost of so much blood, to accept of this command … I presented myself before the Council of the Five Hundred, alone, unarmed, my head uncovered, just as the Ancients had received and applauded me. My object was to restore to the majority the expression of its will, and to secure to it its power … Frenchmen, you doubtless recognize in this conduct the zeal of a soldier of liberty, of a citizen devoted to the Republic.

> Read Source E. Why, according to Napoleon, did he agree to take part in the coup?

SOURCE F

> According to Source F, what is Napoleon's role in the history of the Revolution?

A contemporary print that depicts France as a woman being dragged into an abyss by a figure representing revolutionary fanaticism. Napoleon is attempting to draw her back towards justice, unity, peace and plenty.

The failure of the Directory

The directors had wanted to produce a stable government, which maintained the gains of the Revolution of 1789 while avoiding the extremes of Jacobin dictatorship or royalism. In the final analysis they were unsuccessful, and this was due to a combination of factors:

- Their failure to create stability was partly due to the constitution of Year III, with its annual elections and no provision for settling disputes between the executive and the legislature or changing the constitution in a reasonable way.
- In order to try and maintain a non-Jacobin/Royalist majority in the councils, the directors interfered with the election results. During the coups, Fructidor 1797 and Floréal 1798, they purged the councils. The effect of such action on the constitution, as Napoleon told the Ancients, was that: 'Nobody has any respect for it now.'
- Increasing reliance on the army to settle political disputes. This started with the Thermidorians during the risings of Prairial and Vendémiaire and continued under the Directory with the *coup d'état* of Fructidor. This reliance made an army takeover a distinct possibility. Although a politician planned the coup of Brumaire, and assumed the army would merely occupy a supporting role, its most important figure was General Napoleon Bonaparte, who had no intention of leaving the political stage.
- Most of the people who would normally have supported the Directory – owners of *biens*, the wealthy notables – were alienated by its policies, especially its forced loans. They showed this by refusing, in increasingly large numbers, to vote in the annual elections or to take up posts in local government. When the challenge to the Directory came, few were prepared to defend it.
- Any enthusiasm for the war had long since gone and most people wanted peace. Yet war had become a necessity for the Directory – to ensure money for the French treasury to produce the victories and the prestige that would enable the regime to survive, and to provide an opportunity to keep ambitious generals and unruly soldiers out of France. As Napoleon observed '… to exist, it [the Directory] needed a state of war as other governments need a state of peace'. One of the reasons for Napoleon's popularity was that he had brought peace at Campo Formio in 1797.
- The renewal of the war after 1797 also produced a flurry of Jacobin activity. The Jacobins pressed for and secured a forced loan and the Law of Hostages. While Jacobins by the late 1790s were never more than an urban minority, the policies they advocated revived fears of a Terror like that of Year II, and helped to convince many that the Directory could not, and should not, survive.

These events discredited the Directory and produced politicians who were not as attached to the Republic as the *conventionnels* had been:

- Only twelve per cent of those elected to the Councils in 1799 had been members of the Convention.

- Only five per cent were regicides.
- Over half the deputies chosen in 1799 were elected for the first time that year.

These deputies were prepared to accept the view of Sieyès that the constitution should be changed and that this involved getting rid of the Directory.

Deputies who opposed the Directory not only were prepared to welcome the new regime but took part in running it. Of 498 important officials of the **Consulate**, 77 per cent had been deputies under the Directory. These conservatives and moderates wanted stability and were prepared to accept an authoritarian regime to get it. To some extent the regime collapsed because of contradictions within it. The Directory claimed to favour democracy yet used the military to suppress opposition; it needed war for economic purposes, yet the war lost it considerable domestic support.

Achievements of the Directory

Despite the fact that the Directory was the longest lasting of the revolutionary regimes there has been a tendency to dismiss it as a period of little achievement. The trend in recent years has been to consider the period in a more balanced and objective way. Many of the achievements of the Consulate began under the Directory. The financial reforms and reorganisation of the tax system started during the Directory contributed to economic recovery (see pages 146–7). These helped to stimulate industrial and agricultural expansion that would develop much more fully in the Napoleonic era. Changes in administration within the departments preceded the roles later taken by **prefects**. Although its collapse was sudden, the Directory's achievements should not be dismissed as insignificant.

KEY TERMS

Consulate The system of government that replaced the Directory. It took its name from the three consuls, of whom Napoleon was the most important as first consul. They formed the executive in the new constitution of 1799.

Prefect A centrally appointed government official whose task was to administer a department and ensure that government policy was carried out.

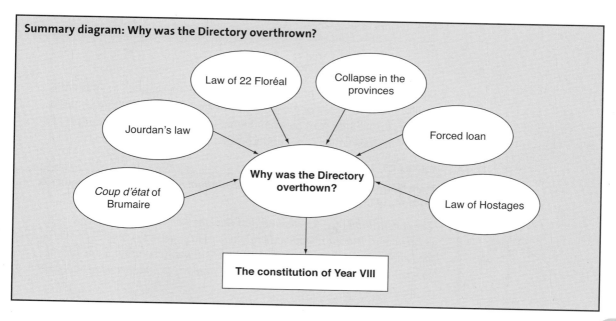

Summary diagram: Why was the Directory overthrown?

Key debate

► *Why, ultimately, did the Directory fail?*

It is possible to dismiss the period of Thermidor and the Directory as being of little importance in the history of the French Revolution, sandwiched as it is between the momentous events of the Revolution and Terror and *la gloire* of the Napoleonic era. It is considered to have lacked the idealism and spirit that drove the great reforms that reshaped the nation. A central issue that engages some historians is why, ultimately, the Directory failed.

The orthodox Marxist view

For many of the Marxist historians of the French Revolution, the Thermidorians and the Directory are the point at which the Revolution came to a juddering halt. The *sans-culottes* had been defeated and the idealism of Year II had been blown away by the chill wind of reaction. Georges Lefebvre sums this up succinctly.

EXTRACT I

From Georges Lefebvre, *The Directory*, Routledge & Kegan Paul, 1965, p. 1.

Thermidorians and Directorials were all one: the same men, the same ends, the same means. They had outlawed the Jacobins and announced their return to liberty; but in destroying the organisation of Year II, they had also ruined the assignat, abandoned the common people to the miseries of inflation, reduced the armies to impotence, and revived the hopes of the counter-revolution. They had forced the electors to choose two-thirds of the new deputies from the Convention, broken the insurrection of Vendémiaire, and revived the exceptional laws against the émigrés and the clergy. The whole history of the Directory lives up to these portents.

A balanced assessment

Many historians of the French Revolution have either tended to ignore the Directory in their books or glossed over the period with rather generalised coverage. British historian Norman Hampson provides a good example of a succinct analysis which is not underpinned by any political ideology.

EXTRACT 2

From Norman Hampson, *The French Revolution: A Concise History*, Thames & Hudson, 1975, p. 161.

The constitution of 1795 ensured that the Directory would be a weak government. It tried to apply liberal policies in a situation where war, inflation, food shortages and the whole violent legacy of the Revolution made liberal government impossible. It has found few supporters and historians have been reluctant to recognize either the achievements of these able men or the extraordinary problems that defeated them. They achieved outstanding military success, but the country was ungovernable by normal constitutional means.

The revisionist view

In adopting a different line from the Marxists, some revisionists emphasise the enormous economic problems that confronted the Thermidorians and the Directory. Alongside this was their need to maintain a balance between the far left and the far right. William Doyle is a prominent British historian of the French Revolution who has sought to provide an analysis which counters that of the Marxists.

EXTRACT 3

From William Doyle, *The Oxford History of the French Revolution*, Oxford University Press, 1988, p. 376.

The Constitution of Year III was never in fact given the chance to work properly. Its first elections were meaningless thanks to the Two Thirds Law, and all subsequent ones were sooner or later discounted. No wonder decreasing numbers of citizens bothered to vote, knowing that after this empty ritual the Directory would exclude those of whom it disapproved anyway. After 1792, for all their talk of national or popular sovereignty, the men who ruled France never accepted the verdict of their electorate. Nor did they accept what all representative regimes sooner or later must; the inevitability of party politics. Neither neo-Jacobin clubs nor monarchist philanthropic institutes were given time to develop into the party organizations they might have become. No serious attempt either was made by the Directors to create an organized centre or moderate party to concentrate their own support. They seem to have considered the virtues of the Thermidorian republic self-evident to all right-thinking men; who would support them without further organization. Bonaparte was right when he declared that the constitution no longer had anyone's respect. Even its self-appointed guardians had never trusted it to function freely.

An analysis of the key figures

The historian M.J. Sydenham applied detailed analysis to the key figures who participated in the Directory. His approach was very much rooted in a close examination of the motives and actions of these politicians. He implied that there was rather more continuity between the Directory and the Terror than might at first appear to be the case.

? How do the authors of Extracts 1, 2, 3 and 4 differ in what they consider to be reasons behind the failure of the Directory?

EXTRACT 4

From M.J. Sydenham, *The First French Republic 1792–1804*, Batsford, 1974, p. 155.

The regime seems to have been in many ways as revolutionary at home as it was in relation to Europe. Far from healing the wounds of France, it prolonged the nation's anguish by renewing the record of political persecution and reviving the attempt to replace Christianity by unrealistic rationalism. Its rule was indeed nothing less than a new manifestation of the Terror similar to that of 1794 in its frank recognition that revolutionaries maintain themselves by force. Nor can the government be called republican even in the more limited sense that it really represented any progressive popular movement. Although the Directorial Terror was aimed at the royalists, at the right, and in all probability at much of the Centre, it was not affected from below but by the power of the police and the army.

Chapter summary

The Directory was the longest lasting of the revolutionary regimes. It was created by the Thermidorians, the right-wing revolutionary reaction to the Jacobin Republic of Year II, following the overthrow of Robespierre. The new constitution of 1795 re-established the power of the revolutionary bourgeoisie. From the outset, the Directory was beset by many economic problems and military setbacks. Opposition to it emerged from both left and right with the revival of Jacobinism and royalism.

The government's response to this was to suspend the democratic process and suppress opposition by force. The army was called in to put down opposition on both sides of the political spectrum. Despite the fact that the Directory stabilised the economic situation and saw its armies go on the offensive, these actions cost it a great deal of popular support. Relying on the army to maintain its position ultimately proved its undoing as the most able, popular and ambitious of the Republic's generals – Napoleon Bonaparte – saw an opportunity to overthrow what had become an unpopular and discredited regime.

Refresher questions

Use these questions to remind yourself of the key material covered in this chapter.

1 Who were the Thermidorians?

2 What measures were taken to end the Terror?

3 What was the significance of the Prairial uprising?

4 What was the motivation behind the White Terror?

5 What did the Thermidorians hope to achieve in a new constitution?

6 Why did the Verona Declaration fail to appeal to the French people?

7 What was unusual about the Vendémiaire uprising?

8 What threat did the revival of monarchism pose to the Directory?

9 What was the importance of the coup of Fructidor?

10 What impact did Napoleon make on the war in Italy?

11 Why was France unable to take advantage of Britain's isolation?

12 How did the creation of new states benefit the Republic?

13 What impact did the defeat of the French at Aboukir Bay have on the war?

14 How effective were the measures introduced in 1799 to deal with the worsening economic and military crisis?

15 What significance did Napoleon attach to the new Constitution?

 Question practice

ESSAY QUESTIONS

1 'The Directory was a period of stability.' Explain why you agree or disagree with this view.

2 To what extent did the Directory consolidate the gains made during the Revolution?

3 How significant a factor was the re-emergence of royalism towards the problems facing the Directory in the years 1795–9?

4 How successful was the Directory in dealing with political threats from the left and the right?

INTERPRETATION QUESTION

1 Read the interpretation and then answer the question that follows. 'Some historians have claimed that the constitution of Year III was never in fact given the chance to work properly.' (From William Doyle, *The Oxford History of the French Revolution*, 1988.) Evaluate the strengths and limitations of this interpretation, making reference to other interpretations that you have studied.

SOURCE QUESTIONS

1 Why is Source B (page 143) valuable to the historian studying opposition to the Directory? Explain your answer using the source, the information given about it and your own knowledge of the historical context.

2 How much weight do you give the evidence of Source E (page 157) of why Napoleon took part in the coup of Brumaire? Explain your answer using the source, the information given about it and your own knowledge of the historical context.

3 With reference to Sources B (page 143) and E (page 157), and your understanding of the historical context, which of these two sources is more valuable in explaining why the Directory ultimately failed?

4 With reference to Sources B (page 143), C (page 154) and E (page 157), and your understanding of the historical context, assess the value of these sources to a historian studying the failure of the Directory.

5 How far could the historian make use of Sources B (page 143) and E (page 157) together to investigate why the Directory failed to survive? Explain your answer using both sources, the information given about them and your own knowledge of the historical context.

CHAPTER 7

The impact of the Revolution

The events in France after 1789 had an impact not only on the lives of French people and society but also on the lives of those living beyond its boundaries. Much of Europe became drawn into the conflict to resist the spread of revolutionary ideas that were first seen in France. This chapter provides an overview of the impact that the French Revolution had on a number of key areas. These are:

★ Dismantling of the *ancien régime*

★ The economy

★ French army and warfare

★ Territorial impact of the Revolution

★ Ideological impact of the Revolution

Key dates

1790	June 19	Abolition of the nobility	1792	Aug. 10	Overthrow of the monarchy
	July 12	Civil Constitution of the Clergy	1793	Feb. 21	Convention accepted the *amalgame*
	Nov. 1	Publication of *Reflections on the Revolution in France*	1796	March–May	Conspiracy of Equals
1791	June 14	Le Chapelier Law	1802	April 18	The Concordat
	Aug. 14	Slave revolt in Saint-Domingue	1814	April 6	Restoration of the Bourbon monarchy

① Dismantling of the *ancien régime*

▶ *How did the Revolution dismantle the* ancien régime?

Most of the *cahiers* in 1789 were moderate and none suggested the abolition of the monarchy. Yet within a short time, beginning with the August Decrees and the Declaration of Rights, fundamental changes had taken place that swept away most of the institutions of the *ancien régime* and ultimately the monarchy itself. This prompted the American historian G.V. Taylor to comment that it was not the revolutionaries who made the Revolution but the Revolution that made the revolutionaries, as they became more confident and ambitious in their plans with each measure that was passed.

The most famous of the institutions destroyed by the Revolution was the Bourbon monarchy, which was overthrown on 10 August 1792. However, this did not prove to be permanent, as the Bourbons were restored on 6 April 1814. Yet the restored monarchy was in many ways different from that of 1789 in that its powers were limited by an elected assembly that had the right to pass laws. Assemblies during the Revolution were hardly democratic as, after the primary assemblies, voting was confined to a small minority of property-holders. An elected legislature, however, was to be one of the permanent changes brought about by the Revolution.

The reforms introduced by the Constituent Assembly (see pages 50–62) were to prove the most radical and the most lasting of the Revolution. The France of the *ancien régime* was dismembered and then reconstructed according to new principles. Most of the institutions of the old regime were abolished, never to return:

- The legal distinction between Estates disappeared.
- The privileges of nobles, Church and *pays d'états* were ended.
- The nobility was abolished (19 June 1790), although it returned under Napoleon.
- Généralités, *intendants*, the old courts of law and the thirteen *parlements* were swept away.
- The entire financial structure of the *ancien régime* was abandoned: direct taxes (the *taille*, capitation and *vingtième*); the Farmers-General; indirect taxes such as the *gabelle* and *aidas*; internal customs; venal offices; the guilds and corporations all came to an end, along with other restrictive practices.
- The Church was drastically transformed by the Civil Constitution of the Clergy – losing the tithe and its lands.
- The sale of the *biens nationaux* was the greatest change in land ownership in France for centuries: a tenth of the land came on to the market at one time.

What replaced all that had been destroyed?

- The administrative structure of modern France with its departments, districts and communes.
- New regular courts of law for both criminal and civil cases.
- A centralised treasury with the power to tax everybody.
- The standardisation of weights and measures through metrication.
- Careers became open to talent in the bureaucracy, the army and the Church.

The three Estates of the *ancien régime* were also significantly affected by the Revolution, although the extent to which they suffered or benefited is a matter for debate among historians. All this – both the destructive and constructive work – was largely achieved in two years and was to be lasting. It was a remarkable achievement.

SOURCE A

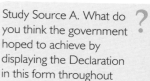

Study Source A. What do you think the government hoped to achieve by displaying the Declaration in this form throughout France?

Poster showing the Declaration of the Rights of Man and the Citizen, August 1789.

The Church

The Church suffered enormously during the Revolution. At an early stage it lost most of its wealth: its income from the tithe, its lands and its financial privileges, none of which were ever recovered. Later, its monopoly of education was removed, as was its control of poor relief and hospitals. The clergy, in effect, became civil servants, as they were paid by the State. Many were better off, as they received higher salaries from the government than they had received from the Church. Yet the Civil Constitution of the Clergy, which was passed on 12 July 1790, produced a deep division within the Church (see pages 58–60). Those who did not accept it (about half the clergy) were persecuted as counter-revolutionaries. Over 200 were killed in the September Massacres in 1792 and over 900 became official victims of the Terror. About 25,000 (a sixth of the clergy) emigrated or were deported. Many parishes were without a priest and, during the dechristianisation campaign of Year II, most churches were closed. Even the constitutional clergy were abandoned when the government refused to pay any clerical salaries in 1794.

In those areas where the majority of the clergy had taken the constitutional oath the result was a lowering of esteem for religion that lasted well into the nineteenth century. Many devout Catholics considered that constitutional clergymen were wrong to defy the Pope. The State was separated from the Church and was to remain so until Napoleon's **Concordat** with the Pope was agreed on 18 April 1802 (see page 198). Although the Concordat went some way to repairing and healing the divisions, in reality the relations between Church and State for most of the nineteenth century were embittered.

KEY TERM

Concordat An agreement between Napoleon and the Pope to try and end the divisions between the Church and State.

The nobility

Nobles were among the early leaders of the Revolution but withdrew from participation in public affairs after 1792. It has traditionally been viewed that as individuals they were among the greatest losers from the Revolution. They lost their feudal dues, which in some areas could amount to 60 per cent of their income. 'We never recovered,' wrote the Marquis de la Tour du Pin, 'from the blow to our fortune delivered on that night' (4 August 1789). They also lost their financial privileges and consequently paid more in taxation. The *vingtième* and capitation usually took about five per cent of their income; the new land tax on average took sixteen per cent. They lost their venal offices, their domination of high offices in the army, Church and State, and even their right to bequeath their estates undivided to their eldest son (inheritances had to be divided equally among sons).

On 19 June 1790 the nobility was abolished and the use of all titles was forbidden. From the beginning of the Revolution, nobles had been leaving France, and eventually at least 16,500 went abroad (seven to eight per cent of all nobles). The property of those who emigrated was confiscated and this affected between a quarter and a half of all noble land. About 1200 nobles were executed during the Terror and many were imprisoned for months as suspects. Nobles appear to have been the principal victims of the Revolution: many lost their lands and some lost their heads.

In recent years, the trend has been to revise and modify this traditional picture. It is now generally accepted that nobles who stayed in France were not extensively persecuted during the Terror. The majority retained their lands and did not lose their position of economic dominance. Napoleon's tax-lists show that nobles were still among the wealthiest people in France. For example, of the 30 biggest taxpayers on the Lozère in 1811, 26 were nobles. Under Napoleon many *émigré* nobles returned to France and began to buy back their lands. For example, in the Sarthe, nobles had lost 100,000 acres (about 40,500 hectares) but had recovered them all by 1830.

Although precise statistics are not available for the whole of France, nobles overall may have recovered a quarter of the land they had lost. Members of the ruling political elite in France both before and after the Revolution were large landowners and high officials, both noble (those with titles) and bourgeois (those without titles) who came to be called notables. Owing to the economic disruption caused by the Revolution, they continued to invest in land rather than industry, particularly when so much land came on to the market cheaply through the sale of *biens nationaux*. The Swiss economist and historian Francis d'Ivernois (1757–1842) asked what Frenchman was mad enough:

> To risk his fortune in a business enterprise, or in competition with foreign manufacturers? He would have to be satisfied with a profit of ten, or at most twelve per cent, while the State offers him the possibility of realising a return of thirty, forty or even fifty per cent, if he places his money in one of the confiscated estates.

This group of notables governed France up to 1880 at least, and in this sense the *ancien régime* continued well into the nineteenth century.

The bourgeoisie

Since 1900, the dominant interpretation of the French Revolution has been the Marxist interpretation, although this was challenged during the second half of the twentieth century. This was most clearly expressed in the period after the Second World War by Georges Lefebvre, and later by his disciple Albert Soboul. Lefebvre regarded the French Revolution as a bourgeois revolution. The commercial and industrial bourgeoisie had been growing in importance in the eighteenth century and had become stronger economically than the nobility. However, its economic strength was not reflected in its position in society. The bourgeoisie was kept out of positions of power by the privileged nobility and it resented the inferior position. Therefore, a class struggle developed between the rising bourgeoisie and the declining aristocracy, whose poorer members desperately clung to their privileges. The bourgeoisie were able to triumph in this struggle because the monarchy became bankrupt, and needed the financial support for which the price was a role in governing the country.

According to the Marxists, therefore, the French Revolution was a bourgeois revolution. Soboul maintained that 'The French Revolution constitutes the crowning achievement of a long economic and social evolution that made the bourgeoisie the master of the world.' He argued that businessmen and **entrepreneurs** assumed the dominant role hitherto occupied by inherited

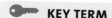 **KEY TERM**

Entrepreneurs Individuals prepared to take risks with their capital to support business schemes that will secure a profit.

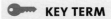
wealth, mainly landowners. These men, with their willingness to take risks and their spirit of initiative, invested their capital in business ventures. In this way they contributed to the emergence of **industrial capitalism** in France.

Responses to the Marxist interpretation

The Marxist interpretation has been challenged by a number of British and American historians. They point out that the bourgeoisie continued to invest in land rather than industry, just as they had done before the Revolution. There were few representatives of trade, finance or industry in the elected assemblies: 85 out of 648 deputies in the Constituent Assembly, 83 out of 749 in the Convention. Small in numbers, they did not take the lead in political affairs. There is no doubt that laws were passed which could eventually benefit the industrialist, for example:

- the abolition of internal customs barriers, guilds and price controls
- the prohibition of workers' associations
- the introduction of a uniform system of weights and measures.

Yet it was difficult to take advantage of these new laws until transport improved sufficiently to create a national market, and this had to wait for the expansion of the railways during the 1850s. Most merchants and manufacturers were worse off in 1799 than they had been in 1789. The French Revolution was not, therefore, either in its origins or its development, carried out by the mercantile and industrial bourgeoisie.

Gaining advantage from the Revolution

Over the course of the French Revolution (1789–c.1799), the bourgeoisie were its main beneficiaries and provided all its leaders after 1791 (Danton, Marat, Robespierre, Carnot). Many of the reforms of the Constituent Assembly were supposed to apply to all citizens equally but only the bourgeoisie could take full advantage of them. Workers and peasants benefited little when careers became open to talent, as they were not educated. When the *biens* were put up for sale they were sold in large lots and this, too, benefited the middle classes, as it was easier for them to raise the money than it was for the peasants. By 1799 they owned between 30 and 40 per cent of French land.

The voting system also favoured the bourgeoisie, as it was limited to property owners. Consequently, nearly all the members of the various assemblies were bourgeois, as were all the ministers. Most of the revolutionary bourgeoisie were lawyers. There were 166 of them in the Constituent Assembly, and another 278 members were public officials, most of whom had a legal training. In the Convention there were 241 lawyers and 227 officials.

Lawyers were among the most prominent beneficiaries from the Revolution, as they had the training to take advantage of careers open to talent. Many were elected to new local and national offices, which paid well. The central administration employed fewer than 700 officials in the 1780s but by 1794, owing to the war, this number had risen to 6000. Although the bourgeoisie had always filled the lower and middle ranks of the judiciary and the administration, with the Revolution they also took over the highest posts, which previously had all been held by nobles. Their dominance of the administration was to continue throughout the nineteenth century.

There were some among the bourgeoisie, however, who did not benefit from the Revolution, such as merchants of the Atlantic ports, manufacturers of luxury goods, and *rentiers*, who were paid in ultimately worthless *assignats*. In 1797 *rentiers* lost most of their investments in Ramel's 'bankruptcy of the two-thirds' (see page 146). Nevertheless, on balance most of the bourgeoisie did well out of the Revolution and would accept only those regimes which promised to maintain their gains.

The peasantry

It is impossible to divide peasants into separate categories, such as landowners, tenant farmers, sharecroppers and labourers. Although there were usually some of each category in the villages, most peasants did not fall into any one group. The majority held some of their land freehold, rented other parts and from time to time sold their labour. The impact of the Revolution on the peasantry was a mixture of gains and losses.

Losses

On the negative side:

- Income was lost when a depression in textile manufacturing damaged **cottage industry**.
- In many areas rents rose by as much as a quarter, when landlords were allowed to add the value of the abolished tithe to their rents.
- Conscription into military service, in 1793 and again in 1798, meant labour was lost on many holdings.
- Dechristianisation in 1793–4 resulted in the Catholic Church being persecuted in many parts of France. Many peasants were deeply attached to the Church.
- Peasants who produced for the market were badly affected by the Maximum on the price of grain in the Year II (see page 113) and by the grain requisitions to feed the towns and the army.

 **KEY TERM**

Cottage industry Small-scale textile production (spinning, weaving and iron work) carried out in a peasant's cottage or workshop and used to supplement income from farming.

The result of all these measures was a widespread, popular resistance movement, which in the Vendée flared into open revolt. In Brittany and Normandy, where the abolition of feudalism produced few benefits as most peasants rented their land, there were the pro-royalist rebels – the Chouans. In the south, too, there was widespread opposition, as the Revolution seemed to benefit the rich Protestants of towns like Nîmes rather than the local Catholics. In some areas this opposition was caught up in royalist counter-revolution but peasants generally did not wish to see a return to the *ancien régime,* which might bring with it a restoration of feudal dues.

The opposition of the peasantry was therefore anti-revolutionary rather than counter-revolutionary. They wanted stability, their old way of life and the exclusion of 'foreigners' (officials from Paris or from outside their own district) from their affairs, rather than a restoration of the Bourbon monarchy in all its glory. Resistance produced repression and executions – nearly 60 per cent of the official victims of the Terror were peasants or workers and many more were killed when the army devastated the Vendée.

Gains

Yet most peasants benefited in one way or another from the Revolution:

- All gained initially from the abolition of indirect taxes and their total tax burden was reduced.
- Those who owned land benefited from the abolition of feudal dues and the tithe.
- In the north and east, where the Church owned much land, peasants were able to buy some of the *biens,* although it was usually the richer peasants who were able to do this. In the south-west even sharecroppers bought *biens* and became supporters of the Revolution.
- Peasants also gained from inflation, which grew steadily between 1792 and 1797. They were able to pay off their debts with depreciating *assignats* and tenants were able to buy their land.
- Judicial and local government reforms were to the advantage of all the peasants. The abolition of seigneurial justice was a great benefit, as it was replaced by a much fairer system. The justice of the peace in each canton provided cheap and impartial justice.
- The right of self-government granted to local authorities favoured the peasants too, especially at the municipal level, where councils were elected and filled by peasants. Over a million people took part in these councils in 1790 and many more later. In the north and east most of these were rich peasants, whereas in Poitou poorer peasants, tenant farmers and sharecroppers took control. Peasants looked on municipal self-government as one of their greatest gains from the Revolution. Both the self-governing commune and Justices of the Peace survived to play important roles in the nineteenth century.

Wages

The poor peasants, the landless day-labourers and sharecroppers are usually regarded as among the greatest losers from the Revolution. They did not benefit from the abolition of feudal dues and they were hit hard by the inflation from 1792 to 1797, as wages failed to rise as quickly as prices. Many relied on cottage industry for survival and when the market for this collapsed, they became destitute. However, not everything was negative. They did gain from the abolition of indirect taxes. From 1797 to 1799 they gained from deflation, so that by 1799 their **real wages** were higher than they had been in 1789.

The Revolution, therefore, affected the peasants in different ways but for most (as for most bourgeoisie) their gains outweighed their losses, especially for those who owned land. Peter Jones, who has researched the peasantry, concludes that: 'Those who managed to survive the dearths of the Revolution and the terrible famine of 1795, experienced a real improvement in purchasing power; the first such improvement in several generations.'

Urban workers

The *sans-culottes* had welcomed the Revolution and had done a great deal to ensure that it was successful. They were to be bitterly disappointed by the first fruits of the Revolution. Many became unemployed as the *parlements* were closed and nobles emigrated. The Le Chapelier Law of 14 June 1791, while opening up many trades restricted by guilds, placed severe restrictions on workers' rights to organise in defence of their livelihoods.

In 1793 the Committee of Public Safety (CPS) gave in to many of their demands, such as a maximum price on bread. However, the bourgeois revolutionary leaders were not prepared in the long run to grant most of what they wanted. The urban workers disliked a free-market economy, yet this was imposed on them in 1794, with the result that prices rose dramatically. The bad harvest and harsh winter of 1794–5 reduced them to despair and contributed to the risings of Germinal and Prairial (see pages 135–6), which were crushed by the government.

Following the risings of Germinal and Prairial, workers played no further political role in the Revolution. Their economic fortunes continued to decline in 1797, owing to the inflation caused by the falling value of the *assignats*. Wages rose but much more slowly than prices. There was, however, a revival in the last years of the Directory from 1797 to 1799, when deflation ensured that real wages were higher than they had been for a very long time. These were also years of good harvests, when the price of bread dropped to two *sous* a pound (it had been fourteen *sous* in July 1789).

The poor

The poor suffered more than most during the Revolution. In normal times about a quarter of the population of large cities relied on poor relief. This number increased with the rise in unemployment, yet at the same time their means of obtaining relief were disappearing. The main source of help for the poor had been the Church, which had paid for this out of income from the tithe. When the tithe was abolished and Church lands were nationalised, the Church could no longer pay for aid to the poor.

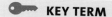

KEY TERM

Real wages The actual purchasing power of money.

Treatment for the poor when they were seriously ill had been provided in hospitals run by the Church. These were closed when the Church lost its sources of income. The constitution of 1793 said that all citizens had a right to public support but revolutionary governments were always short of money and nothing was done. As late as 1847 the number of hospitals in France was 42 per cent lower than in 1789, although the population was 7 million more.

The result of the decline in the Church's role in providing poor relief and hospitals was that the poor were unable to cope with the economic crisis of 1794–5, when a bad harvest was followed by a harsh winter. Many died, either from starvation or from diseases, which the undernourished were too weak to fight off. In Rouen the **mortality rate** doubled in 1795–6 and trebled the year after. There was also a marked rise in the number of suicides. The poor responded in the only ways they knew, by taking direct action. Some joined bands of brigands, which were to be found in many parts of France in the last years of the Directory.

KEY TERM

Mortality rate The death rate, which is measured per 1000 of the population.

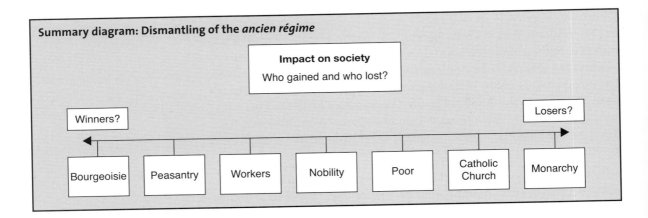

Summary diagram: Dismantling of the *ancien régime*

2 The economy

▶ *How did the war affect French trade?*

▶ *How did the Revolution affect the French economy?*

Marxist historians believed that by getting rid of feudalism, ending the monopolies of the guilds and unifying the national market, the Revolution, in Soboul's words, 'marked a decisive stage in the transition from feudalism to capitalism'. Not all historians agree with this interpretation. Alfred Cobban, in particular, rejects this view and contends that the Revolution was '… not for, but against, capitalism'. Non-Marxist historians opposed to the interpretation argue that the Revolution restricted, rather than promoted, the development of capitalism in France and that it was an economic disaster.

The most rapidly expanding sector of the French economy up to 1791 was overseas trade. On 14 August 1791 a slave revolt broke out on the West Indian island of Saint-Domingue, which provided three-quarters of France's colonial trade. This was followed in 1793 by war with Britain, and the blockade of the French coast by the Royal Navy. Prosperous Atlantic seaports such as Bordeaux and Nantes suffered severely from the naval blockade imposed by Britain, as did the industries in the hinterland – sugar refineries, linen and tobacco manufacturers – which had depended on imported raw materials. In 1797 France had only 200 ocean-going vessels, a tenth of the number of 1789. French exports fell by 50 per cent in the 1790s. Foreign trade had accounted for 25 per cent of France's **gross domestic product** in 1789; by 1796 it was down to nine per cent.

War had a varied effect on French industries. Some benefited and expanded while others declined. Among those industries and sectors which benefited were:

 **KEY TERM**

Gross domestic product
The total value of goods and services produced by an economy.

- Iron and coal industries expanded to meet the demand for military equipment – cannon and arms.
- The textile industry grew to meet the army's demand for uniforms and tents.
- The cotton industry gained most of all. It had been virtually ruined by English competition but with the war and French conquests it revived. English goods were kept out of territories under French control, so that French cotton production increased fourfold between the 1780s and 1810. This, however, was a short-term gain and could not be sustained. Once the war was over in 1815 cotton was hit again by British competition and some of the largest French manufacturers went bankrupt.
- During the war there was a shift in the location of industries from along the Atlantic coast, which was being blockaded by the British navy towards the Rhine. This favoured cities such as Strasbourg, which grew rich on the continental transit trade.

But other areas and industries did not do as well:

- Supplies of imported raw materials were disrupted by the war.
- Many foreign markets were lost because the Atlantic ports were blockaded by Britain.
- The linen industry in Brittany (which had exported to the West Indies and South America) saw production fall by a third, while industrial production at Marseille decreased by three-quarters.

By 1799 industrial production in France had fallen overall to two-thirds of its pre-war level. When paper money was withdrawn in 1797 industry faced other problems. There was a shortage of cash, interest rates were high and agricultural prices (and therefore the peasant market for industrial goods) collapsed.

Agriculture stagnated during the Revolution. Production kept pace with population growth but this was done by bringing more land into cultivation rather than by improving productivity, which did not rise until the 1840s. Yields remained low and old-fashioned techniques continued. Oxen were still used for pulling wooden (not metal) ploughs and the harvest was cut with sickles rather than scythes. Most peasants produced for subsistence only and plots remained small, especially when on his death, by law, a peasant's land was divided up equally among his sons.

Impact of the Revolution on the French economy

The Revolution held up the development of the French economy, which grew only slowly until the 1840s. **Per capita** agricultural production fell during the period with a veritable collapse occurring between 1792 and 1795. It was only by the end of the Napoleonic Empire in 1814 that French agriculture recovered to its 1789 levels, while industrial production in 1800 was still below its 1789 level.

Although, industrially, France had fallen behind Britain by 1789, the gap between them increased markedly during the Revolution. Wartime disruption and dislocation in France undoubtedly contributed towards this. The death of between 1.5 million and 2 million people also had a profound effect on the economy by reducing the market and the labour force. It was not until the coming of the railways, in the middle of the nineteenth century, that French industrialists could take advantage of a national market. Railways lowered the cost of transport and gave a great boost to the heavy industries of coal, iron and steel. Only then did factory production become the norm. These developments, which occurred largely between 1830 and 1870, brought the economic *ancien régime* to an end, something the Revolution had failed to do.

KEY TERM

Per capita An economic measure used to determine output, calculated by dividing the volume or value of production by the number of people in the population.

 # French army and warfare

▶ *What impact did the collapse of the* ancien régime *have on the army?*

It is possible to identify three areas where the impact of the Revolution was both obvious and significant in relation to the army and warfare.

Expansion and organisation of the army

In 1789 the royal army was very unrepresentative of the nation. Over 90 per cent of its officers were noblemen (who comprised between 0.5 and 1.5 per cent of the population). The majority of recruits were drawn from urban areas; only a quarter were peasants (as opposed to 80 per cent of the population). The army was also disproportionately young – over half were under 25 years of age.

As the Revolution progressed, the army's loyalty to the Crown declined, most notably following the flight to Varennes (see page 67). Alongside the regular army, there emerged a new force: the National Guard. It came to symbolise the Revolution and the growing power of the bourgeoisie. On 21 February 1793 these two forces – regular soldiers and volunteers – merged (the *amalgame*).

When revolutionary enthusiasm was married to professional military standards, a very powerful and effective force was created. Against the challenge of external enemies, the call to arms was answered by hundreds of thousands of young Frenchmen. Initially, numbers of volunteers greatly exceeded expectations. By the winter of 1792 France had over 450,000 men in arms, a figure that would rise to over 750,000 by the summer of 1794. Although these figures fluctuated, largely through desertions, the sheer size of the military force was both impressive and intimidating.

The army and French society

Not only did the army increase in size but its very nature changed as a result of the Revolution. The army came to symbolise the beliefs and values of the Revolution. In defending the Republic it was elevated in status and esteem in the eyes of the public, and assumed an influential role in society. It clearly adopted the principle of careers open to talent. Rapid and well-rewarded promotion for recruits from even the humblest of social backgrounds was an attractive possibility for ambitious career-orientated young men.

If class was no longer a barrier to promotion, then neither was age. Joubert, Jourdan and Soult were all generals by the age of 30. Many an ordinary soldier would aspire to hold a field-marshal's baton, even if few would ever attain it. Almost a quarter of the generals promoted during the Revolution had been **non-commissioned officers**. There was no better role model than Bonaparte himself, who rose rapidly up the ranks through talent and ability.

Successive waves of recruits, particularly the politically active *sans-culottes* from Paris and other cities, brought with them a passionate commitment to the cause and principles of 1789, and a willingness to die for *la patrie* (the fatherland). The representatives-on-mission had considerable powers to enforce the political beliefs of the Republic. A military force, enthused with revolutionary zeal, allied to a belief in the justice of its cause and bound together in the defence of its nation, had not been seen in Europe in almost two centuries. Within France the success and achievements of the army were genuinely popular with most people.

Military tactics, strategy and organisation

New methods were adopted to organise the army during the revolutionary war. In previous wars, French infantry marched into battle in line formation that enabled them to concentrate their fire on enemy positions. In 1791 new regulations were laid down on how the French army was to be deployed. Infantry could approach the battle in a column, then deploy into a line to fire, and then re-form back into a column without a great loss of time and momentum. These columns subsequently developed into attack columns whose key features were shock and mobility. The use of the numerically inferior attack columns did have one important limitation: although it gave commanders much greater mobility in the field, it lacked the concentrated firepower of the line. To

KEY TERM

Non-commissioned officers Soldiers with ranks such as corporal or sergeant.

try to compensate for this, horse artillery was introduced in 1791–2 to support the infantry.

A new tactic, which French armies developed to great effectiveness to support the attack columns, was the use of light infantry. Light infantry were highly mobile troops, deployed in patrolling and raiding; tactics known as **skirmishing**. These soldiers needed to be loyal, self-reliant and able to operate with a measure of independence. The high level of commitment and morale within the army, particularly among the infantry, allowed officers to disperse their soldiers for operational purposes into small groups. For organisational purposes the army was divided into *ordinaires*, small groups of fourteen to sixteen men who lived and fought together under the command of a corporal. These operated very effectively but the tactic was only possible because of good discipline and a high level of motivation and morale among the men.

KEY TERM

Skirmishers A small group of soldiers who operate independently, fighting minor engagements and living off the land.

4 Territorial impact of the Revolution

▶ *What impact did the Revolution have on European countries?*

The French Revolution and the Revolutionary War changed the map of Europe. During the Revolutionary War (1792–1801) France annexed large amounts of territory (see the map on page 150). With the exception of the former papal territory Avignon, all these territories were lost in 1815. Among the permanent changes resulting from the Revolutionary Wars were:

- In Italy, the city states of Genoa and Venice never recovered their independence.
- Austria lost Belgium (previously known as the Austrian Netherlands).
- The Holy Roman Empire was abolished.
- The process of redrawing the map of Germany was begun by amalgamating many small states.

Outside Europe, the Revolutionary Wars enabled Britain to consolidate its empire at the expense of countries that France coerced into alliances. The most notable example was the Netherlands, one of Britain's most important trading rivals. Britain seized the Dutch colonies of Ceylon (Sri Lanka) and the Cape of Good Hope (South Africa). Both territories were retained by Britain into the twentieth century. As well as being of strategic importance on the route to Australia, the Cape provided Britain with the base to expand its empire into southern Africa, while Ceylon became an important producer of tea and timber.

5 Ideological impact of the Revolution

▶ *What was the long-term political influence of Jacobinism?*
▶ *What did the French Revolution do to inspire national identity?*

The momentous and dramatic events of the period 1789–99 made an enormous impact on France in particular and Europe in general. One of the most influential legacies of the Revolution to future generations was in the field of ideas. The ideological impact of the Revolution long outlasted the structural and territorial changes created by the Republic. There are a number of areas where the ideological impact of the Revolution was significant.

Democratic republicanism

It is arguable that the most important ideological legacy of the Revolution was democratic republicanism. The French Revolution had a profound effect on the ideas people held and therefore on the policies they pursued. The veteran Welsh radical Dr Richard Price remarked that he was thankful to have lived through such an eventful and inspirational period. He hoped that British reformers would also take the initiative. Many British writers such as the poet William Wordsworth and the radical thinker Thomas Paine did react positively to the Revolution but they tended to be in a minority.

Wherever French armies went, French ideas and methods were spread as they created republics, established representative government, ended feudalism, seized Church lands and abolished privilege. These reforms and structures could be, and often were, reversed when the French withdrew. But ideas could not be eradicated so easily. Among the most influential, important and appealing of these ideas and concepts were:

- the sovereignty of the people
- equality before the law
- freedom from arbitrary arrest
- freedom of speech and association
- careers open to talent.

Conservatism

The violent and bloody birth of the First Republic did alienate many French people and a significant number of Europeans against democratic republicanism. In the eyes of many, republicanism became synonymous with Jacobinism and Terror. The changes that occurred in France were clearly not welcomed by everyone. When so many established institutions, beliefs and practices were attacked – monarchy, religion, privilege – some writers came to their defence and the ideology of conservatism evolved. One of the first writers to mount a sustained attack on the Revolution was Edmund Burke. In his book *Reflections on the Revolution in France*, published on 1 November 1790, Burke defended tradition, religious faith and slow change. He argued that violent revolutions produced chaos and ultimately tyranny: 'I do not know under what description to class the present ruling authority in France. It affects to be a pure democracy, though I think it in a direct train of becoming shortly a mischievous and ignoble oligarchy [rule by a minority].'

Burke's ideas inspired among others the Austrian statesman Metternich, who was a central figure in European affairs in the post-1815 period. Rulers who had supported reform in the 1780s now regarded it as dangerous and so there was a conservative reaction that lasted well into the nineteenth century.

Conservative ideas were not the only ones produced by the French Revolution. The definitive reply to Edmund Burke's attack on the Revolution was Thomas

SOURCE B

? Look at Source B. What do you think was the purpose behind the Republic's production and distribution of such boards throughout France?

A painted board publicising the unity and indivisibility of the Republic. This board is a good example of the importance the Republic placed on propaganda. Note the revolutionary symbols contained within the image: the *bonnet rouge*, the National Guard and the words liberty, equality and fraternity.

Paine's *The Rights of Man*, published in 1791. There were many revolutions during the first half of the nineteenth century, particularly in 1830 (France, Belgium, Italy, parts of Germany and Poland) and 1848 (France, Austria, Italy, Germany), largely because the French provided a model, which others sought to copy. Paine supported the principle of change when he commented: 'Every age and generation must be free to act for itself in all cases as the ages and generations which preceded it. The variety and presumptions of governing beyond the grave is the most ridiculous and insolent of all tyrannies.'

Liberalism

The revolutionaries, following their assault on privilege and absolutism, stressed the rights and liberties of individuals. These were clearly outlined in the Declaration of the Rights of Man and the Citizen (see page 42). A number of these principles would, in the mid-nineteenth century, be refined and recast as **liberalism**. Among the core values of liberalism are:

- Freedom of thought and conscience on all subjects (including religion), leading to freedom of expression and publication.
- Freedom of action and taste as long as it involves no harm to others.
- Freedom of individuals to unite as long as their union does not harm others.

Even within France, however, many of these ideas were ignored in practice during the Revolution – notably during the Terror. They nevertheless contributed to the **revolutionary myth**, which influenced so many people outside France, particularly middle-class liberals. Liberalism in the nineteenth century owed much to the French Revolution. The ethos of republicanism and the new networks of friendships and associations that it inspired was one way in which the Revolution left its mark on politics and political culture. In the longer term the legacy of the revolutionary struggle highlighted the possibilities for others confronted with oppression, particularly in Russia.

Jacobinism, Socialism and Marxism

Jacobinism during the Revolution is equated with revolutionary action in defence of the Republic and the rights of ordinary citizens. The debates in the Jacobin Club and the speeches and writings of its principal figures proved influential to future generations of left-wing idealists and revolutionaries.

Following the closure of the Jacobin Club in November 1794, disenchanted idealists who opposed the Thermidorian reaction planned an uprising. Babeuf's Conspiracy of Equals during March to May 1796 (see pages 143–4) clearly failed in its goals yet its core values – universal suffrage, liberating the oppressed, equality for all – helped to lay the foundations of one of the nineteenth century's most important political philosophies: socialism. Jacobinism also helped to sustain the revolutionary ideal of direct action – the *journées* manning the barricades – a tradition that resurfaced during the French Revolutions of 1830, 1848 and 1871.

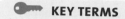

KEY TERMS

Liberalism A political belief that stresses the rights and liberties of the individual.

Revolutionary myth The frequently misguided belief that direct revolutionary action can bring about significant material improvement for the majority of society.

In 1848 Karl Marx published the *Communist Manifesto*. Marx owed a large debt to the Jacobin and later French socialists whose theoretical works and ideas revealed the possibilities that opened up when committed individuals challenged the *status quo*. Marx's ideas in turn influenced the Russian revolutionaries. Marx's analysis of economic and social change inspired a whole generation of French historians such as George Lefebvre and Albert Soboul to produce studies based on his ideas.

Marx interpreted history as a number of revolutionary phases leading ultimately to an **egalitarian society**. Feudalism would be replaced by bourgeois capitalism, which in turn would be replaced by socialism. For Marxist historians, the French Revolution witnessed the critical stage of the destruction of feudalism and the birth of capitalism in one of Europe's most powerful countries.

Nationalism

Nationalism was another powerful force that the French Revolution unleashed. Revolutionary leaders had deliberately set out to create a unified nation, by getting rid of all provincial privileges, internal customs duties and different systems of law. Sovereignty, said the Declaration of Rights, resides in the nation. Symbols such as the **tricolore** (the new national flag of France), the *Marseillaise* and huge national festivals (the first of which was the *Fête de la Fédération* on 14 July 1790 to celebrate the fall of the Bastille) were all used to rouse patriotic fervour. Army life also helped to create loyalty to the nation. Time served in the army was often the first occasion on which peasants had been outside their own locality or had come into contact with the French language (inhabitants of Brittany, for example, spoke Breton).

The success of revolutionary leaders in uniting the nation should not be exaggerated, however. As late as the Third Republic (1871), peasants in the south and west still had local rather than national loyalties and looked on people from outside their area as unwelcome 'foreigners'. Yet France's success in its wars was often attributed to nationalism and the *élan* of the French soldier. Many outside France were inspired by the right to **national self-determination** that the French proclaimed. In Italy national feeling was aroused, partly by the French example, and in Germany people also began to look to the formation of a united Germany.

One of the great legacies of the French Revolution was the principle of the right to resist oppression, which was enshrined in the constitution of 1793. In the early nineteenth century, Kolokotrones, a Greek bandit and patriot, said that according to his judgement:

> … *the French Revolution and the doings of Napoleon opened the eyes of the world. The nations knew nothing before and the people thought that kings were gods upon the earth and that they were bound to say that whatever they did was well done. Through this present change it is more difficult to rule the people.*

Summary diagram: The impact of the French Revolution

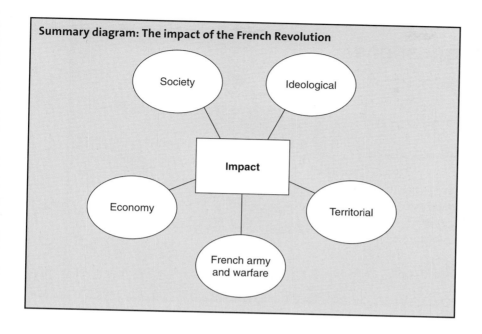

Chapter summary

The impact of the French Revolution was considerable and tangible. The changes first introduced by the National Assembly precipitated many others. France was transformed beyond recognition. The *ancien régime* was dismantled and replaced by a constitutional monarchy that in turn gave way to the First French Republic. Popular sovereignty flowered briefly. The ideals of liberty, equality and fraternity were spread during the Revolutionary War to many parts of Europe. A wide range of political ideas and beliefs emerged during the revolutionary period. While many gained from the Revolution others lost. From 1792 until 1815 (with one brief interlude of peace in 1802–3) Europe was plunged into the longest and most protracted war the continent had seen since the early seventeenth century. Under Napoleon new countries were created while old empires were dissolved.

Refresher questions

Use these questions to remind yourself of the key material covered in this chapter.

1 How radical were the changes created by the Revolution?

2 What was the impact of the Revolution on the Church?

3 How did the Revolution affect the French nobility?

4 How do Marxist historians view the role of the bourgeoisie in the French Revolution?

5 On what basis has the Marxist interpretation been challenged?

6 Why were the bourgeoisie able to prosper during the Revolution?

7 To what extent did the French peasantry benefit as a consequence of the Revolution?

8 Were workers better off as a result of the Revolution?

9 How did anti-Church policies affect the poor?

10 What developments in military organisation and tactics were introduced during the Revolution?

11 How did the Revolutionary War change the map of Europe?

12 What contribution did the Revolution make to political ideas?

 Question practice

1 To what extent did the Revolution fundamentally change the nature of French society in the years 1789–99?

2 Analyse the way that France was transformed as a result of the Revolution.

3 Discuss the view that Napoleon was nothing more than a military dictator.

4 Compare and contrast the approaches used by the Terror and the Directory to achieve stability.

5 Evaluate the contribution made by ideas to the French Revolution.

CHAPTER 8

Napoleon: Consulate and Empire

After the coup of Brumaire, Napoleon was appointed First Consul. The enormous ambition and belief Napoleon had that he was fulfilling the goals of the Revolution drove him to seize power for himself. His attempt to establish an empire plunged Europe into a long and protracted conflict.

This chapter will cover four broad themes:

★ The Napoleonic system in France

★ Establishment of the Napoleonic Empire

★ Creation of the Napoleonic Empire in Europe

★ Defeat and downfall of the Empire

The key debate on *page 213* of this chapter asks the question: Did Napoleon preserve or destroy the ideals of the Revolution?

Key dates

1799	Nov. 10	Coup of Brumaire	1804	May 18	Napoleon declared Emperor of the French
1801	July 15	Signing of the Concordat with the Pope	1805	Oct. 21	Battle of Trafalgar
1802	March 27	Peace of Amiens	1808	May 5	Forced abdication of the King of Spain
1803	May 18	Start of the Napoleonic War			Start of Peninsular War
1804	March 21	Civil Code issued	1812	June 22	Napoleon invaded Russia
	March 20	Murder of the Duc d'Enghien	1815	June 18	Battle of Waterloo

1 The Napoleonic system in France

▶ *What measures did Napoleon take to consolidate his power in France?*

The successful conclusion of the coup was only the beginning for Napoleon. He had gained political power, but needed to consolidate it if he were to make himself undisputed ruler of France. He began with the constitution.

The constitution of 1799

Late in the evening of 19 Brumaire, Year VIII (10 November 1799), the three newly elected provisional consuls (Napoleon, Sieyès and Ducos) swore an oath of allegiance to the Republic. From their base in the Luxembourg Palace in Paris, the consuls set to work on the new constitution, bypassing the two standing committees that were supposed to draw up the draft plans. In a series of long and often heated discussions:

- Sieyès proposed that Napoleon should occupy the role of a figurehead in the new constitution.
- Napoleon refused to accept the role of a figurehead. There must, he argued, be a First Consul as head of state with complete control, in peace and in war, at home and abroad; and *he* must be that consul. The roles of the second and third consuls also caused argument.
- Sieyès wanted them each to have *voix deliberative* (the right to one of three equal votes). Napoleon, however, insisted they should have only *voix consultative* (the right merely to express an opinion). In all matters his decision would be final.

Faced with Napoleon's domineering personality, Sieyès was eventually forced into the humiliating position of having to make the official nomination of Napoleon as First Consul. After six weeks of negotiations the government of France was transformed from one where political responsibility was spread as widely as possible to one where it was centralised in the hands of a single man. All three consuls would serve initially for ten years.

In a proclamation, Napoleon explained his reasons for seizing power: 'To make the Republic loved by its own citizens, respected abroad and feared by its enemies – such are the duties we have assumed in accepting the First Consulship' and he added reassuringly '… that the new constitution was based upon the true principles of representative government and on the sacred rights of property, equality and liberty. The powers it sets up will be strong and lasting'.

The new constitution provided for 'universal suffrage', unlike the property-based vote of the 1795 constitution, but this suffrage was so indirect as to be of little significance in relation to the idea of popular sovereignty. The references to a constitution based on representative government were merely words. Democratic involvement in the elections was minimal. While there was the appearance of adult male suffrage, there were no *elections*, only *presentations* of candidates suitable for appointment as deputies, and the choice of candidates was restricted to notables. The structure of the new constitution is shown in Figure 8.1 (opposite).

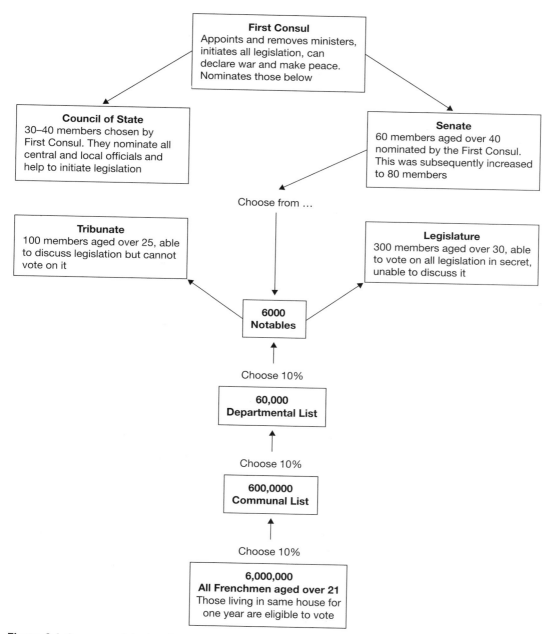

Figure 8.1 Summary of the key features of the constitution of Year VIII (1799).

The distribution of power during the Consulate

Power was firmly in the hands of the First Consul, who stood alone at the top of the political pyramid. The Senate had been intended by Sieyès as a brake on the executive, but under Napoleon it became an instrument of his personal power. It was intended to be the guardian of the existing constitution, but was also able

KEY TERM

Senatus-consultum
A procedure giving the Senate rights to preserve and amend the constitution and to agree major constitutional changes that Napoleon wished to introduce independently of the legislative body.

to amend it by a legal procedure known as ***senatus-consultum***. Napoleon used this procedure extensively from January 1801 onwards to block the wishes of the Tribunate and the Legislature.

Senators were appointed for life, with a substantial salary. They were rewarded with gifts of land and money, and enjoyed considerable prestige. Membership of the Senate increased from the original 80 to about 140 by 1814. Most of these additional members were directly nominated by Napoleon. As a result it developed into a largely consultative body anxious to please its benefactor and president, Napoleon.

The new constitution was submitted for approval in a plebiscite held in February 1800. Official results showed 3,011,007 voting in favour with 1562 against. A number of these plebiscites were held over the next fifteen years as an attempt to seek popular approval for significant changes, as shown in Table 8.1.

Table 8.1 Plebiscites held during the Consulate and Empire 1800–15

Year	Subject of plebiscite	Voting yes	Voting no
1800	Constitution of Year VIII	1,550,000*	1562
1802	Plebiscite on life consulate	3,653,000	8272
1804	Plebiscite on Empire	3,572,329	2569
1815	Plebiscite on *Acte Additionnel*†	1,552,942	5740

*Revised figure.
†Proposed significant amendment to the previous Napoleonic constitutions.

In a number of ways the constitution established a framework for consolidating the main social changes made by the Revolution. Among the most important of these was the vast transfer of land that had taken place largely at the expense of the Catholic Church, but also from the nobility. It was necessary to bind the beneficiaries of these transfers to the new regime. This was achieved by creating a political system which favoured the well-off propertied classes. Power in the new regime was far more centralised than it had been under the Directory; in a way it was a reversion back to the Jacobin phase of the Revolution (1793–4) when France was governed by a dictatorship (see pages 119–23). By cultivating the support of notables, Napoleon was seeking to incorporate and consolidate the new elite of talent and property that had emerged since 1789.

From Consul to Emperor

A group of former Breton Chouan tried to assassinate Napoleon in December 1800. They planned to explode a bomb placed in a barrel, concealed in a cart, as he rode past on his way to the opera. Napoleon was badly shaken by the blast but escaped unharmed. This made the Senate anxiously aware of the fragile nature of a regime dependent for its continuation on one man. Partly because of this, and partly as a demonstration of gratitude to the First Consul for his achievements at home and abroad, it was decided to offer him the consulship for life, with the right to nominate his successor. It was the first step towards the reintroduction of hereditary rule. Napoleon accepted and the decision was approved by plebiscite (see Table 8.1 above). While there is no evidence that the central government tampered directly with the figures, it is known that local officials often sent in results that they thought would be pleasing to their superiors, sometimes even recording a unanimous 'yes' vote when, in fact, no poll at all had been held.

Following the plebiscite, Napoleon's personal power increased immediately through his control of an enlarged Senate, which became responsible for everything not provided for by the constitution, and necessary to its working. This arrangement greatly reduced the power of the representative bodies, the Tribunate and the Legislature. They lost much of their importance, and met less frequently. The Tribunate was severely purged in 1802 for daring to criticise the proposed Civil Code (see page 195), and with a much reduced membership became little more than a rubber stamp for the remainder of its existence, while the Legislature's credibility was reduced by being 'packed' by Napoleon with 'safe' men who would not oppose his wishes.

Consolidating power

By 1803 Napoleon was riding in splendour around Paris and holding court in royal style. State ceremonies multiplied, etiquette was formalised, and official dress became more elaborate. The **Legion of Honour** (see page 193) had been introduced the previous year and there were hints that a nobility was to be re-established, the rumours fired by Napoleon's permission for a large number of *émigrés* to return to France.

In 1804 a series of disasters, royalist plots and counter-plots culminated in the affair of the Duc d'Enghien, a member of the Bourbon royal family alleged to be involved in a plot to overthrow Napoleon by murdering him and taking over the government. The Duke was kidnapped on Napoleon's orders while on neutral territory, tried and, on rather inadequate evidence, found guilty of conspiracy. On 20 March he was executed summarily in what amounted to judicial murder, justified by Napoleon on the grounds that he was entitled by the Corsican laws of vendetta to kill an enemy who threatened his personal safety.

In the wake of these events Napoleon began to prepare the people for his next step. There was widespread talk of making the consulship hereditary within the Bonaparte family, in the hope of providing for a smooth succession and the survival of the constitution should Napoleon meet an untimely death. Then, in May 1804, a formal motion was approved by the Senate that 'Napoleon Bonaparte at present First Consul be declared Emperor of the French, and that the imperial dignity be declared hereditary in his family.' A third plebiscite held in November 1804 approved the change. Remembering that 40 per cent of the army vote two years earlier had rejected the proposal, the government took no chances this time and did not actually poll the soldiers. They simply added in approximately half a million 'yes' votes on their behalf.

 KEY TERM

Legion of Honour A high-status organisation created by Napoleon to bind powerful men to his regime through granting them titles and rewards.

SOURCE A

What image is the artist trying to project in Source A?

Napoleon on the Imperial Throne by Jean-Auguste-Dominique Ingres, painted in 1806.

To seal the transformation of the consulship to that of a hereditary ruler, Napoleon planned a spectacular coronation to be held at Notre Dame Cathedral in Paris on 2 December 1804. In the presence of the Pope, Napoleon, as previously arranged, crowned himself Emperor then crowned his wife Joséphine as Empress. During the next two or three years the Tribunate and the Legislature were hardly consulted at all. The Tribunate was finally abolished in 1808 and, although the Legislature survived, it was able to do so only by maintaining its subservient attitude to Napoleon's demands. Government was increasingly conducted through the Senate and the Council of State, both of which were firmly under Napoleon's personal control.

All that remained to establish the Napoleonic dynasty securely was the production of a legitimate son and heir. In the years following his coronation it became increasingly obvious that an ageing Joséphine was unable to have children. Despite his continued fondness for her, Napoleon decided that a divorce was essential. He needed to persuade the Church to grant this but it was not easy. Although their original marriage had been a civil one, the Church had insisted on a second, Catholic ceremony as a necessary preliminary to the coronation in 1804.

In 1810, on the grounds of alleged irregularities in the conduct of the religious marriage, the Church unwillingly agreed to an annulment, leaving Napoleon free to remarry. A list of eighteen eligible princesses was drawn up for him and later that year, at the age of 40, he married Marie Louise of Austria, a niece of Marie Antoinette. In the following year the hoped-for son and heir, Napoleon, King of Rome, was born. The succession seemed assured, the dynasty secure.

Maintaining power

In order to maintain power, Napoleon was determined to prevent the political turbulence and economic chaos that had marred the Directory. He used a variety of methods to try and achieve this end. Bringing financial stability would restore the nation's prosperity and improve the lives of all social classes. **Patronage** was distributed, bribes were offered and supporters were appointed to government positions to bind them to the regime. Alongside these approaches, reforms and repression were also used.

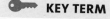

KEY TERM

Patronage The process of distributing gifts and favours in order to build up support.

Establishing financial stability

Of the many problems confronting the new government possibly the most pressing was the need to establish financial stability and secure an adequate revenue stream. There were only a few thousand francs available in the treasury in November 1799. Napoleon introduced a series of major financial reforms that went a considerable way to transforming the situation. As Napoleon lacked the technical skills to overhaul the financial system, he appointed a number of very able and efficient ministers to undertake this task. Among the key appointments were Gaudin as minister of finances in 1799 (a position he retained until 1814) and Barbé-Marbois at the treasury (1801–6). Both these appointments brought a measure of stability to state finances.

The early financial reforms introduced were:

- A much clearer division of roles between the ministry of finances (which oversaw collection of taxes and revenues) and the treasury (which dealt with government expenditure).
- The reorganisation of both direct and indirect tax collection.
- The first steps in establishing a public banking system.

One of Gaudin's most important reforms was to remove the assessment and collection of direct taxation from the control of local authorities and form a central organisation to undertake the task. The main source of government revenue continued to be the land tax. A much more detailed tax register indicating all those eligible to pay was drawn up. More efficient land registers listing ownership helped to ensure that the amount paid was spread more evenly. Although the system was reformed and stabilised the amount raised remained fairly steady at some 250 million francs a year until 1813, which represented 29 per cent of government revenue.

A more dramatic increase in revenue came from indirect taxes. Many of these had been abolished by the Constituent Assembly. However, faced with mounting deficits the Directory had reintroduced indirect taxes on certain goods. Napoleon centralised the collection of duties by creating a central excise office in 1804. Among the goods and services taxed were tobacco, alcohol, items made from gold and silver, playing cards and public transport. In 1806 salt was added to the list, which revived memories of the hated *gabelle* of the *ancien régime* (see page 5). Revenue from indirect taxes increased by over 400 per cent between 1806 and 1812 and was considered a much easier way of making up any shortfalls in government revenue from direct taxes. It is estimated that by 1813 revenue from all indirect taxes accounted for possibly 25 per cent of the government's revenue.

One of Napoleon's most important reforms (that still survives to this day) was the creation of the Bank of France in 1800. Although a private bank with its own shareholders, it was given a range of public functions such as the sole right to issue paper notes. A risky business venture in 1805 threatened the stability of the new bank. In order to boost state finances, a scheme aimed at importing silver from Mexico to Spain and then on to France was arranged. When the scheme ended in failure, Napoleon, in order to avert a more serious crisis, imposed stricter controls on the bank.

An important indicator of the financial health of a country is the stability of its currency. The inflation linked to the *assignat* was a clear reminder to Napoleon of the problems an unstable currency could pose. On 28 March 1803 he introduced the *franc de germinal*, which became the basis of his monetary system:

- The new gold and silver coins established a standard ratio of gold to silver at 1:15.5.
- Each one-franc coin would weigh five grams of silver.
- Other denominations would be minted in strict proportion to this (for example, a five-franc coin would contain 25 grams of silver and so on).

This reform gave France the soundest currency in Europe at that time. It would remain the basis of France's currency for the next 120 years.

Napoleon did achieve a measure of financial stability. When compared with the financial chaos of previous regimes, both the Consulate and the Empire were much more successful. The currency was stabilised, public debts were honoured and the wages of public officials and the army were paid.

While greater efficiency was brought to the government's finances, greater burdens were placed on it. State expenditure increased steadily as a result of increasing military expenditure from around 700 million francs in 1806 to over 1000 million in 1813. The widening gap between the government's income and its expenditure was made up by forcing defeated countries to pay a financial penalty. The military defeats of 1813–14 removed this source of income and marked a renewed period of instability.

Patronage and bribery

To secure his position Napoleon sought to attract and bind to his regime as many powerful political and military figures as possible. He adopted a number of strategies that appealed to people's self-interest, vanity and desire for status. He lavished gifts of money, land, titles, honours and government appointments in order to build up a strong group of powerful individuals with a clear motive for maintaining the regime in power. The main methods used were:

- The creation of the Legion of Honour by Napoleon in 1802. This was divided into fifteen cohorts (groups) each comprising 350 legionaries, 30 officers, twenty commandants and seven grand officers. Recipients received a distinctive decoration and a small annual award. In the twelve years following its establishment, 38,000 awards (only 4000 of which went to civilians) were made.
- Between 1804 and 1808, new titles were created for the officials of the new imperial court. These ranged from 'grand dignatories' such as the arch-chancellor, through 'grand officers', down to lesser dignatories such as the prefects of the palace.
- Some of these titles brought with them large estates, and were bestowed on court officials and statesmen, as well as on the eighteen outstanding generals who were created Marshals of France.
- In 1808 Napoleon began the creation of a new imperial nobility. All 'grand dignatories' became princes, archbishops became counts, mayors of large towns became barons, and members of the Legion of Honour were allowed to

call themselves Chevaliers. If the recipient possessed a large enough annual income – 200,000 francs in the case of a duke, for instance – the titles could be made hereditary. In all, about 3500 titles were granted between 1808 and 1814, many to military figures.

- Civilians benefited from the allocation of *senatoreries*. These were grants of large country estates to members of the Senate, together with a palatial residence and an annual income of 25,000 francs to support it. Included in the grant was appointment as *préfet* (prefect) not just of the usual department but of a whole region.
- Lesser individuals also benefited from Napoleon's personal gifts. For instance, more than 5000 presents of enough money to buy a house in Paris and to live there in comfort were made to army officers, government officials and minor members of the new nobility.

Napoleon realised early on that bribery as a means of control was unreliable, and was not in itself enough to maintain popular support even among the recipients. Therefore, compulsion, intimidation and indoctrination all became part of the Napoleonic system of government.

Reforms and repression

The restriction of individual liberty of thought, word and deed was an important element in Napoleon's autocratic government. By numerous measures, some more subtle than others, he built up over the years a system of supervision and control described by historian Richard Cobb as 'bureaucratic repression'.

Agents of control: police and prefects

A number of changes were made to the judiciary. Judges, instead of being elected as under the Directory, were appointed by the government for life and were kept subservient and loyal by a combination of close supervision and a system of purges. A new hierarchy of judicial tribunals was set up. The criminal, commercial and penal codes were updated in a similar way to the Civil Code. In 1810 a system of arbitrary imprisonment without trial (similar to the *lettres de cachet*, see page 32) was reintroduced, although it was never extensively used, a form of house arrest being more usual.

The two most important agents of control were the police and the prefects. For much of the Napoleonic era the minister of police was **Joseph Fouché**. Both police and prefects had very wide-ranging powers:

- They acted as trained spies, imposed censorship, set up surveillance of possible subversives, searched for army deserters and organised raids on areas believed to be sheltering **draft-dodgers** or enemy agents.
- They were assisted in the maintenance of law and order by a well-organised body of **gendarmes**. In 1810 there were 18,000 stationed throughout France. Reports were submitted to Napoleon daily by Fouché on the work of his department.

KEY FIGURE

Joseph Fouché (1759–1820)

A ruthless and feared figure involved in many plots and conspiracies, responsible for policing and internal security.

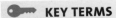

KEY TERMS

Draft-dodgers Men who avoided the call to serve in the army.

Gendarmes An organisation set up by the National Assembly in December 1790, which operated as an armed police force.

- They had a prefect (*préfet*) assisted by sub-prefects (*sous-préfets*) for each department. Other local officials such as mayors and all the municipal councils were nominated by the prefect. In addition to their official duties (tax collection, **conscription**, and so on) prefects were expected to spread propaganda, monitor public opinion in their areas and report on any suspicious political activity. Suspects could be placed under house arrest.

With such well-organised surveillance it is not surprising that the regime met with little serious political opposition, especially as its potential leaders, notables, intellectuals and members of the bourgeoisie, were increasingly tempted into allying themselves with the government in the hope of reward.

SOURCE B

From Lucien Bonaparte's explanation to the Prefects of their role, 1800.

The post demands of you a wide range of duties, but it offers you great rewards in the future. Your first task is to destroy irrevocably in your department, the influence of those events which for too long have dominated our minds. Do your utmost to bring hatred and passion to an end. In your public decisions, be always the first magistrate of your department, never a man of the Revolution. Do not tolerate any public reference to the labels which still cling to the diverse political parties of the Revolution. Apply yourself immediately to the conscription draft. Give special priority to the collection of taxes: the prompt payment is now a sacred duty. Agriculture, trade, the industries and professions must resume their honoured status. Respect and honour our farmers. Encourage the new generations; fix your attention on public education, and the formation of Men, Citizens and Frenchmen.

> Study Source B. What did Lucien Bonaparte consider to be the main function of the Prefects?

The Civil Code

The French legal system was extremely complex, with different systems operating in different parts of France. Although the Revolution had swept away many of the complexities, there remained scope for further reform. Napoleon took an active interest in the formulation of the new Civil Code which was issued on 21 March 1804 (in 1807 it was renamed the *Code Napoléon*). Among the most important sections of the code were those relating to individual rights and property rights. The code recognised the legal rights of those who had bought land confiscated from the Church and nobility. This was an attempt to bind them in to maintaining the regime. The system of inheritance of an estate introduced during the Revolution – *partage* – was confirmed. While the Civil Code maintained some of the most important gains of the Revolution – the abolition of feudalism, the removal of the privileged position of the Catholic Church within the State, freedom of conscience and equality before the law – it was also illiberal and restrictive. Napoleon took a personal part in preparing those sections that dealt with family law. He was intent on strengthening the authority of the father and the husband, who could send an adulterous wife or

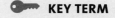 **KEY TERM**

Partage An estate is divided equally among all male heirs, unlike during the *ancien régime* when the eldest male heir inherited everything.

defiant child to prison. Divorce, although permitted in theory, was made very difficult and expensive to obtain.

Among the codes, the most illiberal measures were those relating to the treatment of black people and workers. Slavery was reintroduced in the French colonies 'in accordance with the laws current in 1789'. All workmen were made subject to close police supervision through use of the *livret*, without which it was legally impossible to obtain a job. Like a number of Napoleon's achievements there were two sides to the Civil Code. While it acknowledged many of the gains made during the Revolution it also confirmed the reaction against the achievements of the Republic through a return to a more authoritarian and restrictive legal system.

Censorship and propaganda

Napoleon had clear expectations that the French press would deliver all official propaganda. He was very aware of the press's power to undermine his regime so in 1800 he reduced the number of political journals published in Paris from 73 to nine, and forbade the production of any new ones. These survivors were kept short of reliable news and were forbidden to discuss controversial subjects. Their editors were forced to rely for news on articles published in *Le Moniteur*, which were written by Napoleon or his ministers. In 1809 censors were appointed to each newspaper and a year later provincial papers were reduced to one per department. In 1811 all except four of the Parisian papers were suppressed and those that remained were made subject to police supervision.

In the wider cultural field up to 1810, reports on all books, plays, lectures and posters that appeared in Paris were sent, often daily, to Napoleon. Publishers were required to forward two copies of every book, prior to publication, to police headquarters. In 1810 a regular system of censors was set up. More than half the printing presses in Paris were shut down, and publishers were forced to take out a licence and to swear an oath of loyalty to the government. Booksellers were strictly controlled and, if found to be selling material considered subversive, severely punished, even with death. Some authors were driven into exile for criticising the government, while dramatists were forbidden to mention any historical event that might, however indirectly, reflect adversely on the present regime. Many theatres were closed down. Others operated only under licence and were restricted to putting on a small repertory of officially sanctioned plays.

Sculptors, architects and artists got off more lightly, as Napoleon utilised their talents to project his image through paintings, monuments and pillars on a grand scale. Artists such as David and Ingres (see the illustration on page 190) were employed by Napoleon as State propagandists, depicting him as a romantic hero-figure, or the embodiment of supreme imperial authority in classical guise, often complete with toga and laurel wreath. David, as 'painter to the government', was given responsibility for supervising all paintings produced in France, with particular reference to the suitability of the subject matter.

KEY TERMS

Livret A combined work permit and record of employment.

Le Moniteur The official government journal.

Education

Napoleon believed that there were two main purposes for an education system:

- To provide the State with a ready supply of civilian officials and administrators and loyal and disciplined army officers. He intended to recruit these from among the sons of the property-owning classes.
- To bind the nation closer together: an aim that could only be fulfilled if the government took direct central control over the system.

Education for ordinary people was neglected by Napoleon as it had been during the *ancien régime* and the Revolution. All that was considered necessary was a simple 'moral education' and basic literacy and numeracy. This was provided in primary schools run by the Church, by the local community or by individuals. Napoleon often declared his belief in equal opportunities for all according to ability and irrespective of birth or wealth, what he called 'careers open to talents', but as far as education was concerned he generally failed to ensure that this was carried out in practice. He also did not consider the education of girls to be a priority. As Napoleon once said, 'marriage is their destiny', and therefore they did not need to think and should not be taught to do so.

It was in the field of secondary education that Napoleon sought to make an impact. In 1802 Napoleon replaced the ineffective system of schools set up during the Convention, the écoles centrales, with the more centrally controlled *lycées*. These new schools, there would eventually be 45 in total, were staffed by instructors chosen by Napoleon himself. The State provided 6400 scholarships to these schools, of which 2400 places were for the sons of soldiers and government officials. The remaining 4000 places were to be filled by competition from pupils from the best of the remaining secondary schools. In reality, the much sought-after places were almost entirely restricted to the sons of *notables*.

In this highly centralised system, the government-appointed teachers would deliver a common syllabus from identical textbooks. Conditions were strict with military discipline operating. So tightly controlled was the system that Napoleon boasted that he knew exactly what every pupil in France was studying from the time of day. The main aim of these schools was to train France's future civil servants and army officers.

In 1808 the Imperial University opened. It was not a university in the ordinary sense, where learning was freely carried out. Through its tightly controlled curricula its aim was to provide loyal teachers for the State secondary schools, which operated only by its permission and under its authority. Total obedience was demanded by the university from its member teachers, who had to take an oath of loyalty to their superiors. Lessons were standardised, and what was taught was dictated in accordance with the needs and demands of the government.

 **KEY TERM**

Lycées Selective schools introduced in 1802 for educating the sons of the privileged.

Religion

Since 1789 the Catholic Church and the French State had been in conflict (see pages 58–60). During the Directory there had been a revival of Catholic public worship that no government could safely have ignored or opposed. Napoleon's motives for seeking a *rapprochement* with the Pope were those of expediency. His own attitude to religion was ambivalent. Although the Napoleonic legend was to have him die in the Catholic faith, he paid it no more than lip service during his adult life. What he appreciated was the power of religion to act as the 'social bond' cementing together a divided people. Napoleon saw the importance and benefits in bringing an end to the schism between clergy who had sworn allegiance to the Revolution and those who had not (see page 60). Religious peace would help to bring political and social peace to France, as Catholicism had become identified with the royalist cause and needed instead to be identified with the people as a whole.

Discussions with the papacy lasted many months before the Concordat was finally signed on 15 July 1801. Under the agreement:

- The separation of Church and State, which had been one of the main policies of the Revolution, was to end.
- The Catholic Church recognised the Revolution and agreed that no attempt would be made to recover Church lands.
- A State-controlled Church was established, and its clergy became paid civil servants, appointed by the government and bound to it by oath.
- While it was agreed that Catholic worship should be 'freely exercised in France', it was also agreed that there would be toleration for other religions.

The Concordat was published by Napoleon in April 1802 as part of a wide-ranging ecclesiastical law on to which he tacked the so-called 'Organic Articles'. These were a series of articles limiting in every possible way papal control over the French bishops, while at the same time increasing State control over the activities of the clergy.

Tensions between Church and State remained, however. Napoleon angered Pope Pius VII by ordering, without reference to him, that the Church throughout the Empire should celebrate 16 August (the day after his own birthday) as St Napoleon's Day, unceremoniously removing from the calendar of saints the existing occupant of that date. The cult of the Emperor had reached its peak. It was clear that the Church was no longer the privileged First Estate it had been under the *ancien régime* with its tax exemptions and vast, landed estates. There appeared to be very little prospect that either would ever be restored.

KEY TERM

Rapprochement The restoration of friendly relations between countries or people previously hostile.

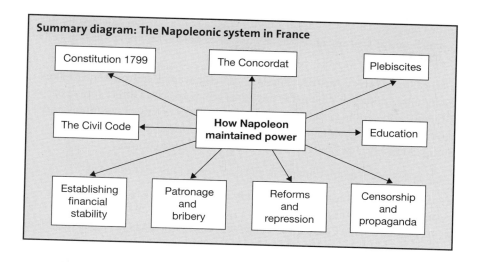

Summary diagram: The Napoleonic system in France

- Constitution 1799
- The Concordat
- Plebiscites
- The Civil Code
- **How Napoleon maintained power**
- Education
- Establishing financial stability
- Patronage and bribery
- Reforms and repression
- Censorship and propaganda

2 Establishment of the Napoleonic Empire

▶ *What constituted the Napoleonic Empire and why was it created?*

Although the official birth of the Empire was on 18 May 1804, when Napoleon proclaimed himself hereditary Emperor of the French, in reality it had started its unofficial life long before then, with the Revolutionary conquests and those of the Consulate (see pages 155–7). Both of these had pushed the frontiers of 'old France' (the France of 1790) out towards its '**natural frontiers**' – and beyond.

The 'empire' is often referred to as if it were a single entity embracing all French-controlled Europe. In reality it was a more complicated arrangement than that. The French Empire, properly speaking, was the following:

- France of the natural frontiers (Rhine, Alps, Pyrenees).
- The annexed territories (*pays réunis*, ruled from Paris) of Piedmont, Parma, Tuscany, the Papal States, the Illyrian Provinces and, after 1810, the Netherlands.
- A semicircle of nominally independent **satellite states** (*pays conquis*) ruled by Frenchmen, usually Bonaparte relatives, which formed a buffer zone protecting the borders of the French Empire from attack. These states, combined with the French Empire proper, formed the Grand Empire. At various times these included Switzerland, the kingdoms of Spain, Naples and Italy, the Confederation of the Rhine (which included the kingdom of Westphalia) and until 1810, the Netherlands and the Grand Duchy of Warsaw (created out of conquered Polish lands and acting as a barrier to Russian expansion into central Europe; see the map on page 205). In northern Europe,

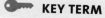

KEY TERM

Satellite state A state that is subservient to another, and cannot act independently.

Sweden came under French influence when it was compelled to operate the **continental system**, and to accept one of Napoleon's marshals as heir to its throne.

Of the Great Powers, Austria, Prussia and Russia were each from time to time brought by military or diplomatic pressures into Napoleon's direct sphere of influence and each in turn became his ally, although not always willingly and only for a limited period. Only the Ottoman Empire and Britain, among the European powers, remained always outside Napoleon's control.

Napoleon's own explanation for the need to expand his territories was:

- to protect the territory of revolutionary France from attack by the 'old monarchies' of Europe
- to export the Civil Code, the Concordat and other benefits of Napoleonic rule to the oppressed peoples of neighbouring states
- to provide oppressed peoples with liberty, equality and prosperity
- to ensure the end of the old regimes in Europe
- to provide guarantees to citizens everywhere in the Empire against arbitrary government action.

Historians have argued at length over what really drove Napoleon to create the Empire. Some believe that his conquests offered him opportunities to exploit the territories not only to secure his military domination, but also to reorganise the civil life of the annexed lands, and that his imperial vision was a natural extension of his personal dynastic ambition. He was also determined to place as many of his close family and allies either on the thrones of newly conquered countries or to administer them (see page 217). Napoleon hoped that this would ensure complete loyalty to him. In the case of Spain this policy proved disastrous (see pages 204–7).

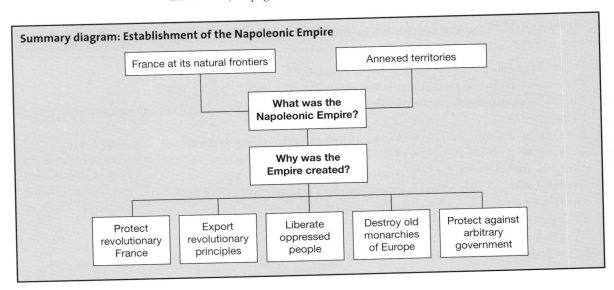

Summary diagram: Establishment of the Napoleonic Empire

Creation of the Napoleonic Empire in Europe

▶ *What methods did Napoleon use to create his European empire?*

For many, the most memorable of Napoleon's achievements were his military conquests, which laid the basis of his empire in Europe. His early military successes in Italy have been noted in Chapter 6 (see page 149). Following these he had taken an army to Egypt to try to disrupt British power in the eastern Mediterranean. The campaign was a failure and he returned to France and joined in the plot to overthrow the Directory (pages 154–6).

The need for an early victory and a quick peace after the *coup d'état* of November 1799, in order to strengthen his own position as First Consul, led Napoleon back to Italy. There, in June 1800, after a march across the Alps, he inflicted a decisive defeat on the Austrians at Marengo. A further French victory at Hohenlinden in Bavaria six months later brought about the peace of Luneville. It recognised French possession of the Austrian Netherlands (Belgium) as well as the left bank of the Rhine and the gains in Italy. Austria lost control of all northern Italy, except Venetia, and its influence in Germany was reduced.

With the collapse of the Second Coalition, Britain agreed to the Peace of Amiens (27 March 1802), by which France withdrew from the Papal States and Naples, and Britain returned most of its conquests including Egypt, which was restored to the Ottoman Empire.

The continuation of the Napoleonic War

The peace settlement proved to be unstable, in effect nothing more than a truce in a war that had already been going on for almost a decade. After a period of increasingly acrimonious relations between France and Britain the war resumed once again on 18 May 1803.

War of the Third Coalition 1803–5

The Third Coalition of 1803–5 saw Britain ally with Austria, Russia and a number of smaller powers to try and counter Napoleon. While France was the dominant power on land, Britain was in clear control of the sea. Neither in itself was sufficient for victory. Napoleon tried to remedy this by planning an invasion of Britain. A large army was to be transported across the English Channel by a combined Franco-Spanish fleet. The plan failed when the Royal Navy under Nelson won a great sea battle off Trafalgar on 21 October 1805. Even before this disaster, Napoleon had gathered up his army of England and marched south to the Danube to confront Austria, who had declared war on France during the summer.

On the continent, Napoleon's armies won a series of spectacular victories in a rapid campaign. The Austrians was defeated at Ulm in October 1805, where they were outmanoeuvred by Napoleon and forced to surrender. The decisive battle in the war of the third coalition was Austerlitz (December 1805), where an Austro-Russian army was beaten. This caused Russia to retreat rapidly out of Napoleon's reach and Austria to agree to the Treaty of Pressburg. According to the treaty:

- Austria recognised French supremacy in northern Italy.
- Austria gave up various German territories to Napoleon's allies and lost its authority in Germany.
- Austria was forced to pay France a large war indemnity.

War of the Fourth Coalition 1806–7

Concern over the domination of France in the German-speaking territories formerly controlled by Austria and creation of the Confederation of the Rhine drew Prussia into a coalition with Britain and Russia. The breakdown of complicated negotiations between Napoleon and Prussia, involving Prussia's acquisition of Hanover in return for adherence to Napoleon's continental system, was also a factor which led to the war.

In a remarkable one-week campaign, Napoleon destroyed Prussia at the twin battles of Jena and Auerstadt (October 1806). In February 1807 Napoleon marched through Poland to attack Russia, his remaining continental enemy, winning an inconclusive victory over the Russians in the bitter Battle of Eylau. A major defeat at Friedland in June convinced the Russians of the need to make peace. This was done in July 1807 at Tilsit, in a personal meeting between Napoleon and Tsar Alexander I that took place initially on a raft in the middle of the River Niemen, which marked the Russian frontier.

In a series of short campaigns over two years (1805–7), Napoleon had in turn defeated three of his four major opponents. In November 1806 he established the continental blockade to deal with the remaining one, Britain, which had taken no active part in the war, restricting itself to supplying allies with subsidies. Napoleon's achievements were:

- French domination in Germany by defeating Austria and abolishing the Holy Roman Empire.
- The creation of the Confederation of the Rhine as a French satellite state.
- The destruction of Prussian power in Poland, which was converted into the Grand Duchy of Warsaw.
- Prussia's lands in the west created into the new satellite kingdom of Westphalia.
- Napoleon crowning himself King of Italy, and adding Parma and Tuscany to the existing French possessions of Piedmont and Lombardy.
- Naples becoming a French satellite.

- Russia being forced to concede peace in 1807, and Tsar Alexander being compelled to make a formal alliance with France.

By the end of 1807 Napoleon controlled, directly or indirectly, the greater part of Europe. The 'Grand Empire' had come into being.

Military and strategic developments

During the years 1805–7 Napoleon created what became the Grand Empire. On the battlefields of Europe his forces were triumphant. His victories were gained as the consequence of a number of interrelated factors. Among these were circumstances that related to him personally and those concerned with the changing nature of warfare and the opponents he faced. The most important were:

- Napoleon's leadership qualities. He was a great general who achieved important conquests in a relatively short space of time, but also knew how to exploit his victories, to extract the maximum advantage from those he defeated. French domination therefore relied on diplomatic success as well as military achievements, and the great achievement of French diplomacy was to keep the coalition powers divided.
- Through the issue of daily bulletins, Napoleon formed a special bond between himself and the army. He played on the ideas of military glory, of patriotism and of comradeship, while giving at the same time the impression that he had a deep paternal concern for his men.
- Napoleon's forces were a product of the Revolution which had brought into existence a mass army forged in the belief that they were spreading revolutionary ideals. His army was based on the strength of the whole nation.
- Between 1801 and 1805 Napoleon created what became the ***Grande Armée***. The whole army was divided into corps of about 25,000–30,000 men, each composed of two or three divisions, infantry and cavalry; some of the cavalry were kept separate, as were the reserve artillery and several elite groups, the most important of which was the Imperial Guard. He controlled the army directly, which allowed unity of command and flexibility in action. Each corps was given a particular role on a campaign march, but this role could, if necessary, be changed quickly.
- New tactics were developed which emphasised troop mobility (infantrymen were required to march 20–25 km a day) and living off the land instead of relying on military food supplies.
- From 1805 onwards he developed the use of war as *une bonne affaire* ('a good thing') financially. Peace treaties imposed on defeated countries not only provided for maintaining Napoleon's troops on their territory (food and shelter), but included the payment of massive indemnities: Prussia was forced to find 311 million francs after being defeated at Jena in 1806. War had become self-financing.

 **KEY TERM**

Grande Armée Napoleon's renamed army after 1805. At its largest in 1812 it numbered over 600,000 men, among them Poles, Italians, Swiss and Bavarians.

- The only consistent theme running through the years from 1800 to 1815 was his hatred for Britain. Following the defeat of his invasion plan in 1805, Napoleon adopted another strategy to try to defeat Britain. He planned to destabilise the British economy by means of the continental system. This system envisaged blockading British trade by denying it access to European markets. The continental system had an important consequence for the war since it meant the need for further conquests to try to close mainland Europe to British exports.
- The weakness of Napoleon's enemies. Britain, Russia, Austria and later Prussia – formed a series of anti-French alliances with each other, but these were continually undermined by their mutual suspicions and jealousy. Only Britain remained opposed to France for the whole period. The other three powers were tempted away from time to time by Napoleon's offers of territory.

4 Defeat and downfall of the Empire

▶ *How did the Peninsular War and the retreat from Moscow contribute in bringing about Napoleon's downfall?*

From the height of his power in Europe in early 1810, Napoleon and his Empire collapsed in spectacular fashion by 1815. Two events in particular played a crucial role in Napoleon's downfall: the Peninsular War (1808–14) and the invasion of Russia in 1812.

The Peninsular War

To try to secure the defeat of Britain, Napoleon decided to enforce the continental system (see page 200) much more rigorously. In 1808 he invaded and occupied the Papal States in an attempt to force the Pope to impose this strategy. However, British goods were continuing to enter Europe via its long-standing ally, Portugal. The value of British exports entering Europe through Portuguese ports actually doubled between 1808 and 1809 to nearly £1 million, and by 1811 the annual total had increased to more than £6 million. Portugal's more powerful neighbour, Spain, was a country very much in decline and whose government and vast overseas empire in the Americas were ruled very inefficiently.

To ensure that the continental system was fully enforced, and to stop British imports entering the **Iberian peninsula**, Napoleon on 5 May 1808 deposed the Spanish king and his heir, and placed his own brother Joseph on the throne.

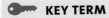

KEY TERM

Iberian peninsula Spain and Portugal combined.

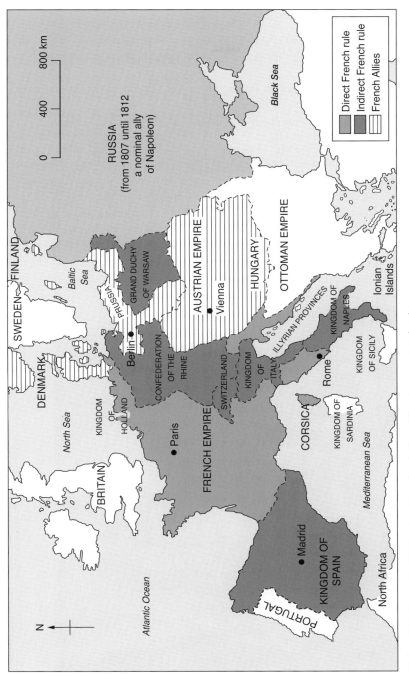

Figure 8.2 Europe in 1810, when Napoleon's Grand Empire was at its height.

There were a number of consequences:

- Large numbers of ordinary Spanish people rose in revolt against French rule.
- Maintaining garrisons in Spain proved to be a significant drain on French military resources.
- The Franco-Spanish attack on Portugal prompted Britain to commit military forces to defend its ally.
- Napoleon's inability to resolve the situation cast doubts on his military and political judgement.

As soon as Joseph arrived in Spain in May 1808 he was confronted by a revolt in Madrid which French forces put down with great ferocity. A hundred Spaniards were executed in retaliation for the killing of 31 Frenchmen. The artist Goya's horrific images helped to rouse the whole population to patriotic anger against the French occupying forces (see below). Local resistance committees (*juntas*) were set up, co-ordinated by the clergy and members of the nobility, to raise guerrilla fighters and regular soldiers.

? What do you think was the intention behind producing the image in Source C?

SOURCE C

The Disasters of War: Heroic feat! Against the dead! created by Francisco Goya in the period 1810–14. Goya was the first modern artist to use the power of visual images to depict the horrific reality of war and to bring this to a large audience.

A small and comparatively inexperienced French army was defeated at Baylen by a force of Spanish regular troops. The sensation created by this defeat brought Napoleon himself to Spain with 100,000 veterans of the *Grande Armée*. A British expeditionary force was dispatched to the peninsula in answer to a Spanish request for help and quickly drove the French out of Portugal.

The campaign fought in the Iberian peninsula over the next six years was a brutal guerrilla war. In 1812 it was estimated that there were between 33,000 and 50,000 Spanish irregular forces engaged in the campaign against Napoleon. The arrival of the Duke of Wellington in Portugal in 1808 provided a substantial boost to the anti-French campaign. Wellington's army numbered some 35,000 men and, because they lacked both artillery and cavalry, they relied heavily on guerrilla forces. In an attempt to stabilise the military situation, Napoleon went to Spain at the head of an army of 160,000 men in October 1808. Within two months, however, he had moved north to counter another threat.

SOURCE D

From Étienne-Denis Pasquier, *Memoirs*, quoted in Jean Tulard, *Napoleon*, Methuen, 1986, pp. 264–5.

Napoleon could not long remain ignorant of the fact that Austria was arming so actively as to indicate some very serious plans. Finally he had been informed that, giving way to pressure from England, she was preparing to take advantage of his absence in order to cross the frontiers, invade Bavaria, wage war in the Rhine and thus bring about the deliverance of Germany. It was a fine occasion to attempt so considerable an undertaking. This was one of the moments in his life when his very soul must have been prey to the keenest agitations. There were also intrigues rife in the heart of his own government.

> Study Source D. Why, according to Pasquier, did Napoleon leave Spain? **?**

Wellington proved to be a formidable opponent, and although a cautious commander he was able to exploit French weaknesses regarding lack of supplies while at the same time fully utilising British naval supremacy to resupply and reinforce his own forces. In 1810–11 Marshal Massena attacked Lisbon, failed in his objective and suffered 25,000 casualties in the process. As Wellington shrewdly observed in 1811, there were 353,000 French troops in Spain and yet they had no authority beyond the spot where they stood.

Britain was unable to prevent the defeat of Austria in 1809 or the invasion of Russia in 1812. In the wake of France's military commitment and disasters in Russia, however, Wellington moved on the offensive. In 1812 he captured Ciudad Rodrigo and Badajoz. Following the defeat of Marmont at Salamanca he entered Madrid. Northern Spain was liberated in 1813 following his victory at Vittoria. French forces were driven back across the Pyrenees and finally defeated at Toulouse in 1814. The war in Spain was never popular in France. French military prestige was eroded during the long, drawn-out campaign against guerrillas, which was both expensive and demoralising. It is aptly called the **Spanish ulcer**.

 KEY TERM

Spanish ulcer Used by Napoleon as a term for a wound that weakens the victim without ever being fatal.

The invasion of Russia 1812

The improved relations between France and Russia that the treaty of Tilsit in 1807 brought about proved to be difficult to maintain, and both sides felt uncomfortable about the relationship. A number of issues caused friction between the two countries and led to a resumption of hostilities. The main factors that led to conflict were:

- Each had a mutual distrust of the other's hostile expansionist aims in the Baltic, central Europe and the Balkans.
- Napoleon refused to support the Tsar's ambitions to seize Constantinople.
- Alexander attacked Sweden with French encouragement, but without French agreement seized and annexed Swedish Finland.
- There were arguments over the future of the Grand Duchy of Warsaw.
- The main disagreement arose over the Tsar's virtual withdrawal from the continental blockade. On the last day of 1810 he introduced a new trade tariff that discriminated against France and in favour of Britain.

Enforcing the continental blockade was a priority. The army Napoleon gathered to invade Russia was the largest he had ever assembled. The *Grande Armée* of 600,000 consisted of Germans, Swiss, Spanish, Portuguese, Italians, Poles and Lithuanians. Only about 270,000 of the total were Frenchmen. Napoleon had never before commanded such a large force, over such a vast area. During the course of the campaign he was inexplicably indecisive and lethargic at critical moments.

On 22 June 1812, without any declaration of war, Napoleon crossed the River Niemen. He was unable to use his usual strategy of luring the enemy towards him and forcing a decisive battle early in the campaign. The much smaller Russian armies continually retreated before him, destroying food supplies as they went. Napoleon was therefore drawn ever deeper into Russia, extending his supply lines and increasing the difficulties for his large, slow-moving force of catching up with the enemy.

KEY TERM

Scorched earth A policy of destroying all food and shelter in front of an invading army to deny them essential supplies.

The Russian army's **scorched earth** tactic meant that Napoleon found it difficult to feed his men and horses. By the time Napoleon reached the outskirts of Moscow on 7 September the Russians decided to stand and fight. In a day-long battle of enormous ferocity, Napoleon won a victory of sorts, after a prolonged artillery duel, but at great cost in men and guns. The French lost 30,000 men, and the Russians 50,000. On 14 September Napoleon's advance guard rode into a largely deserted and burning Moscow. The Tsar refused to negotiate despite the loss of Moscow.

The retreat from Moscow

The unusually mild autumn tempted Napoleon to linger in Moscow for over a month. He ignored the warnings of bad weather to come, and only the eventual realisation that the *Grande Armée* would starve to death if he stayed longer in the ruined and empty city caused him to order a return home. Laden with loot and slowed down by their wounded, the army began the retreat on 19 October. The retreat was one of the greatest military disasters of Napoleon's career. Sickness and skirmishes, famine and exhaustion took their toll, and the onset of the severe Russian winter made any problems significantly worse. The *Grande Armée* was effectively destroyed. Only 25,000 survived to reach Germany by the end of 1812. The fragility of the imperial government was exposed by the Malet affair (2–3 October 1812), when a plot by a former general almost succeeded in persuading some key officials that the Emperor was dead and a provisional government needed to be formed. But the ruse failed to convince everyone and the plotters were arrested and quickly executed.

SOURCE E

From the memoirs of a French *émigré*, General Comte de Rochechouart, serving with the Russian imperial guard, 1812.

Nothing in the world more saddening, more distressing. One saw heaped bodies of men, women and children: soldiers of all arms, and nations, choked by the fugitives or hit by Russian grapeshot; horses, carriages, guns, ammunition wagons, abandoned carts. One cannot imagine a more terrifying sight than the appearance of the two broken bridges and the river frozen right to the bottom. Immense riches lay scattered on this shore of death. Peasants and Cossacks prowled around these piles of dead, removing whatever was most valuable. Both sides of the road were piled with the dead in all positions, or with men dying of cold, hunger, exhaustion, their uniforms in tatters, and beseeching us to take them prisoner. However much we wished to help, unfortunately we could do nothing.

Read Source E. What image of the retreat does Rochechouart provide in his memoirs?

There were a number of factors which help to explain Napoleon's defeat in Russia. The *Grande Armée* was lost through a combination of bad management, poor supply arrangements, lack of local knowledge and over-confidence. Napoleon had allowed himself nine weeks to defeat Russia and return in triumph to Germany. His army had only summer clothing and enough food for three weeks (he intended to be comfortably ensconced in Moscow as Emperor of the East by then). Many supplies proved inadequate or non-existent. There was no fodder for the horses nor frost nails for their shoes, no maps covering more than a few miles inside the Russian border, and no bandages for the wounded. There was unusual confusion in the French army command as well. General Caulincourt wrote after leaving Moscow, 'Never was a retreat worse planned, or carried out with less discipline; never did convoys march so badly … To lack of forethought we owed a great part of our disaster.'

The final campaigns 1813–15

The Russian disaster encouraged Napoleon's enemies to construct a new anti-French coalition. Although this was not a formal alliance, by late summer 1813, for the first time *all* the Great Powers, Britain, Russia, Prussia and

Austria, were at war with Napoleon. In October the numerical superiority of the combined armies of Austria, Prussia and Russia enabled them to win a decisive but expensive victory at Leipzig in the three-day 'Battle of the Nations'. Outnumbered, and heavily defeated, Napoleon was forced back to the Rhine. His influence in Germany gone, the Grand Empire was starting to unravel. The members of the fourth coalition agreed a formal alliance through the Treaty of Chaumont in March 1814. This treaty, which converted the coalition into a Quadruple Alliance, committed each of the four powers not to conclude a separate peace but to fight on until Napoleon was defeated.

In France there was discontent and opposition to the war as preparations began in bitter winter weather for a new campaign. Napoleon set to work to raise yet another army and to find the money to equip it. The financial situation was desperate, and the burden of conscription had become intolerable in a country that had been at war for 20 years. Despite the fact that for the first time since 1792 France was facing invasion by the 'kings' of old Europe, the country was war weary and there was no real enthusiasm for continuing the struggle. Although Napoleon won a series of small victories he was unable to prevent his enemies from entering Paris in March 1814. He abdicated in favour of his young son, but the allies restored the Bourbons, with Louis XVIII becoming the new king. The terms of Napoleon's future were settled by the Treaty of Fontainebleau. Napoleon was granted the sovereignty of the Island of Elba and a pension.

The Hundred Days

Following Napoleon's abdication, the future of France and its Empire was decided at Vienna. Differences between the victorious allies emerged regarding the post-war settlement. Napoleon, sensing an opportunity to split the allies and recover his throne, left Elba and landed in France to launch a new campaign which lasted 100 days. He immediately gathered together an army of former soldiers. His immediate targets were the two allied armies in Belgium under Wellington and the Prussian general, Blucher. Napoleon hoped to defeat them before they could combine with significant numbers of Austrian and Russian forces heading towards France.

On 18 June 1815 one of the decisive battles in European history was fought near the Belgian village of Waterloo. Napoleon had a slight numerical advantage over Wellington: 72,000 men to 68,000. The outcome of this evenly balanced struggle was ultimately determined in favour of the allies by the arrival of the Prussians. As Wellington said the next day, 'it was a damned close thing – the nearest run thing you ever saw in your life'. Napoleon's hopes of continuing the campaign were dashed when he failed to secure further support. Without political or popular support he had no option but to agree to demands for his second abdication.

Louis XVIII entered Paris for the second time on 8 July. After Napoleon's final abdication and exile in June, the second Treaty of Paris (November 1815) reduced the frontiers of France beyond the proposals of the previous year, to those of 1790. The First Empire was finally at an end.

Assessing Napoleon's impact on France

There is a measure of agreement that France changed less in the Napoleonic period than during the shorter revolutionary one. In many ways aspects of his regime resembled the *ancien régime*:

- Governmental and administrative reforms replaced the popular sovereignty of the Revolution (loosely controlled, devolved government based on a system of elections) with a centralised autocratic rule not unlike that of the *ancien régime*, especially after the establishment of the Empire in 1804.
- Legal and judicial reforms were based on the authoritarianism of Roman law.
- The suppression of freedom of expression and his extension of police powers were more like those of the Bourbon monarchy than of the Revolution (with the exception of the Jacobin dictatorship).
- Opposition was vigorously rooted out. Life was geared to the service of the State and its ruler in a way never previously seen in France, even in the time of Louis XIV.
- By the Concordat the Catholic Church was restored to a position of power and influence in the State with few exceptions as it had been during the *ancien régime*.
- Although, for administrative purposes, the departments of the Revolution were retained, he reintroduced the 40,000 pre-1789 communes as the basic territorial and 'electoral' unit.
- A central role in local government during the Napoleonic era was the prefect, who, although he resembled the *intendent* of the *ancien régime*, in reality had far more power.
- During the Revolution, the nobility and all ranks and status had been abolished. Under Napoleon a new imperial nobility was formed and the Legion of Honour recreated a hierarchy of ranks.

Despite the authoritarian nature of his regime, Napoleon *did* maintain the great gains of the Revolution. He confirmed in the constitution and the Civil Code, the end of feudalism in France and the equality of Frenchmen before the law, and in the Concordat the irrevocability of the sale of the *biens nationaux* (see page 195).

In a number of areas the Napoleonic era did not significantly transform France, although the country did change. The most notable feature of Napoleon's rule was the almost continuous period of war: unbroken after 1803 until his overthrow in 1815. This had a profound impact on the country in a number of areas:

- *Society.* The wars had a dramatic effect on French population. The 916,000 killed (out of 2 million in the army) between 1800 and 1814 represented about seven per cent of the total population of France. They were, however, mostly young men of marriageable age – a devastating 38 per cent of men born in the years 1790–5 were killed, the majority of them between 1812 and 1814. To the extent that this must have left many young women without husbands, and have reduced further the already declining birth rate, Napoleon's wars must accept some responsibility for the slow growth of the population in nineteenth-century France.

- *The economy.* Behind the protection of the continental system, French industry did expand slowly during Napoleon's rule, albeit from a rather low base. Textile production increased, as did the iron and coal industry. Trade with continental Europe certainly expanded. Across industry as a whole there is little evidence that by 1815 France was on the verge of an industrial revolution of the kind experienced in Britain.

- *Culture.* Even allowing for the stifling effect of his policies of propaganda and indoctrination, Napoleon was not much concerned with the arts, literature, sculpture, painting or drama, except in so far as they glorified himself. He closed down most of the theatres in Paris. Paris itself changed little under Napoleon, apart from the addition of a number of triumphal monuments in classical style: the Arc de Triomphe and the column in the Place Vendôme that bears a statue of Napoleon in a toga. The style of the years 1800–15 was known as 'Empire' (perhaps to emphasise the importance of official art), and is seen at its most distinctive in the context of interior decoration, where it directly reflects Napoleon's own interests, inspired by the classical world of Greece and Rome or by Egypt.

- *The frontiers of France.* At the height of the Empire in 1811 Napoleon controlled, either directly or through his allies and satellites, most of mainland Europe. The prestige of having the largest European empire since that of Rome counted for little when the first Treaty of Paris (1814) pushed the frontiers of France back to those of 1792 and the second Treaty of Paris pushed them back to 1790. There was nothing left of the imperial possessions. Even the 'natural frontiers' were lost. In territorial terms no trace of the Empire survived.

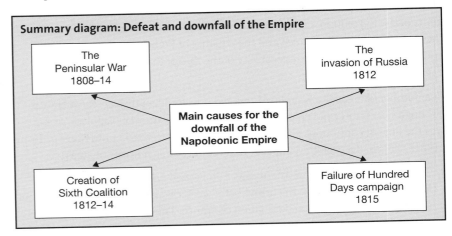

Summary diagram: Defeat and downfall of the Empire

The Peninsular War 1808–14

The invasion of Russia 1812

Main causes for the downfall of the Napoleonic Empire

Creation of Sixth Coalition 1812–14

Failure of Hundred Days campaign 1815

Key debate

▶ *Did Napoleon preserve or destroy the ideals of the Revolution?*

Napoleon is one of the most famous men in history. His rule impacted in one way or another on most of the population of Europe in his day. The dramatic events of his rise and fall have sometimes overshadowed his relationship with the Revolution which brought him to the fore and gave him the opportunity to progress, shine and ultimately seize power. An area of debate is whether Napoleon preserved or destroyed the ideals of the Revolution.

The Marxist interpretation

For most Marxist historians the Napoleonic period is viewed through the prism of betrayal and treachery. They saw the popular ideals of 1789 being gradually eroded, then abandoned and a version of the *ancien régime* re-emerge. Georges Lefebvre, one of the most influential Marxist historians, explored the Emperor's complex relationship with the Revolution in his book *Napoleon*.

EXTRACT 1

From Georges Lefebvre, *Napoleon*, 1935, quoted in Pieter Geyl, editor, *Napoleon: For and Against*, Peregrine Books, 1976, p. 379.

There has remained in him something of the uprooted person. Also of the man torn from his class: he is not entirely a noblemen nor entirely of the people. He has served the King and the Revolution without attaching himself to either. Neither in the old nor in the new order did he find principles which might have provided him with a norm or a limit. A successful soldier, a pupil of the philosophes*, he detested feudalism, civil inequality, religious intolerance. In enlightened despotism he saw the way to reconcile authority and social and political reform. He became its last and most illustrious representative, and this is the sense in which he was the man of the Revolution. But his impetuous individuality never accepted democracy, so that he rejected the great expectation of the eighteenth century which inspired revolutionary idealism.*

The revisionist view

François Furet, as a leading revisionist historian of the French Revolution, argues that Napoleon did want to preserve many of the gains made since 1789 but within the context of his own overwhelming and grandiose ambitions. These ambitions ultimately lay outside of France.

EXTRACT 2

From François Furet, *The French Revolution 1770–1814*, Blackwell, 1988, p. 217.

National reconciliation – one of Bonaparte's great ideas – was not the rehabilitation of the past, or even the search for a balance between the ancien régime *and the Revolution. On the contrary, it assumed an acceptance of what had happened since 1789, and the desire to defend revolutionary attainments, both at home and abroad. The First Consul was more keenly aware than anyone during that first winter when he needed to keep an eye on everything, that his destiny was being decided outside France, on the battlefields where he was awaited by the European coalition which had been repulsed – but not vanquished – that autumn. For the fundamental contract between Bonaparte and public opinion was the guarantee of revolutionary conquests and therefore of a victorious peace. The rest was subordinate to this suspensive condition – victory.*

Modernising the State

One of the central themes explored by Martin Lyons is whether or not Napoleon modernised the French State in any way and how his policies tied in with the ideals of the Revolution. As a ruler, Napoleon spent a great deal of time away from France on his many military campaigns.

EXTRACT 3

From Martyn Lyons, *Napoleon Bonaparte and the Legacy of the French Revolution*, Palgrave, 1994, p. 295.

Napoleon's regime was the fulfilment of the bourgeois Revolution of 1789–99. The new state which emerged from the Revolution and was shaped by Napoleon, was a secular state, without a trace of the divine sanction which had been one of the ideological props of the old regime monarchy. It was a state based on a conscripted army and staffed by a professional bureaucracy. Administration was rationalised in the sense that corruption and favouritism were officially outlawed. The affairs of all citizens were dealt with in principle on the basis of equality and according to fixed regulations, instead of being at the mercy of a monarch's whims. Above all the modern state was a well-informed state which used its own machinery to collect data on the lives and activities of its subjects. As it knew them better, it policed them more closely and it taxed them more efficiently.

An updated overview

Michel Broers has provided a detailed account of Napoleon's military achievements while seeking at the same time to set these within the broader picture of the revolutionary period from which he came to prominence and ultimately power.

EXTRACT 4

From Michael Broers, *Napoleon: Soldier of Destiny*, Faber & Faber, 2014, p. 322.

Napoleon truly did return the Revolution to its original principles, as the first pronouncement of the Consulate had sworn to do. The Estates General had been called in 1789 to help solve the crisis of the French state by setting its finances on a permanently sound footing. This the Revolutionaries had spectacularly failed to do ... Napoleon managed to fulfil the Revolution's promises by taking full advantage of the peaceful circumstances of these years [the late 1790s to 1803]. He would begin to squander it as the wars accelerated, but the institutions and administrative practices he fostered, together with the land register he initiated, survived his own excesses to become the basis for a modern system of management. These characteristics were the hallmarks of the best Napoleonic reforms: clarity of purpose; institutional solidity; and an ability to build for the future as well as cope with a current crisis.

> How far do the historians quoted in Extracts 1, 2, 3 and 4 agree or differ in their interpretation of whether Napoleon maintained the ideals of the French Revolution?

Chapter summary

Napoleon Bonaparte was one of the most remarkable figures in history. He rose to power through opportunities provided by the Revolution, his own brilliance as a military commander and his determination and belief in his own abilities. Whether Napoleon preserved or destroyed the ideals of the Revolution is a matter of historical debate. He used various methods to maintain power. Supporters were bound to the regime by patronage and reward while opponents were rooted out. He skilfully used propaganda and image to create among the population a sense of pride in the Empires achievements: *la gloire*.

The Napoleonic War which spanned his entire reign was the defining feature of his period in power. As his continental enemies were defeated in turn he created new states as part of a universal empire. From the zenith of his power in 1808 a series of blunders and misjudgements in Spain and Russia created military and economic crises which inspired his enemies to once again combine to try and defeat him, to which end they were ultimately successful.

 ## Refresher questions

Use these questions to remind yourself of the key material covered in this chapter.

1 What were the main features of the new constitution?

2 How was power distributed during the Consulate?

3 What measures were taken to establish financial stability?

4 How did Napoleon ensure support for his regime?

5 What were the main changes Napoleon made to the judicial system?

6 How did prefects and the police control opposition?

7 How did Napoleon enforce censorship and propaganda?

8 What did Napoleon consider to be the purpose of education?

9 Why did Napoleon agree the Concordat?

10 Why did the war resume in 1803 and what was the outcome of Napoleon's plan to invade Britain?

11 What factors contributed to Napoleon's military success between 1803 and 1807?

12 Why and with what consequences did Napoleon become involved in the Peninsular War?

13 What were the consequences of the retreat from Moscow?

14 How was Napoleon finally defeated?

15 To what extent did Napoleon preserve the Revolution?

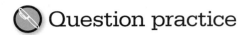

Question practice

ESSAY QUESTIONS

1 'The Spanish ulcer was entirely responsible for Napoleon's downfall.' How far do you agree?
2 To what extent was Napoleon's rule dependent on the support of the army?
3 How successful was Napoleon in preserving the gains of the Revolution?
4 How important a role did Britain play in the defeat of Napoleon?
5 Which of the following had the greater impact on the course of the Napoleonic Wars? i) The battle of Trafalgar. ii) The battle of Austerlitz. Explain your answer with reference to both i) and ii).

INTERPRETATION QUESTION

1 Read the interpretation and then answer the question that follows. 'Napoleon truly did return the Revolution to its original principles.' (From Michael Broers, *Napoleon Soldier of Destiny*, 2014.) Evaluate the strengths and limitations of this interpretation, making reference to other interpretations that you have studied.

SOURCE QUESTION

1 With reference to Sources B (page 195), D (page 207) and E (page 209), and your understanding of the historical context, assess the value of these sources to a historian studying the impact of Napoleon's rule.

Appendix: The Napoleonic family tree

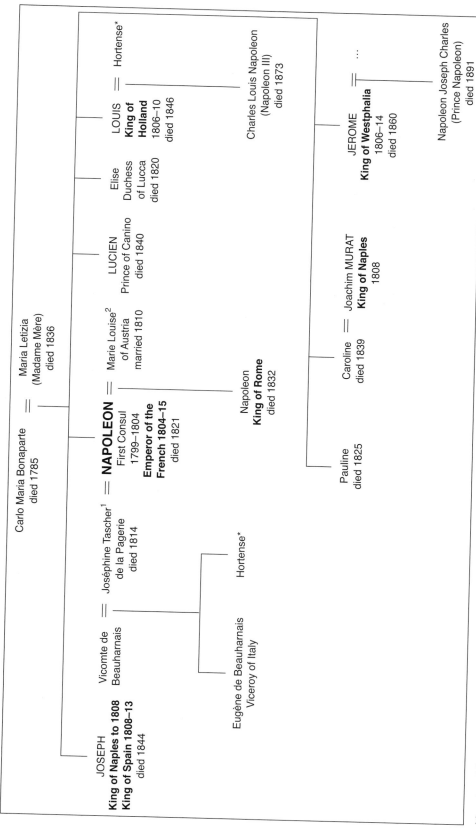

Note how Napoleon sought to place close members of his family on the thrones of countries he was seeking to control.

[1] Joséphine was Napoleon's first wife.

[2] Marie Louise was Napoleon's second wife.

*Hortense was Joséphine's daughter from her first marriage, and married Napoleon's brother, Louis.

OCR A level History

Essay guidance

The assessment of OCR Units Y213 and Y243: The French Revolution and the rule of Napoleon 1774–1815 depends on whether you are studying it for AS or A level:

- for the AS exam, you will answer one essay question from a choice of two, and one interpretation question, for which there is no choice
- for the A level exam you will answer one essay question from a choice of two and one shorter essay question, also from a choice of two.

The guidance below is for answering both AS and A level essay questions. Guidance for the shorter essay question is at the end of this section. Guidance on answering interpretation questions is on page 223.

For both OCR AS and A level History, the types of essay questions set and the skills required to achieve a high grade for Unit Group 2 are the same. The skills are made very clear by both mark schemes, which emphasise that the answer must:

- focus on the demands of the question
- be supported by accurate and relevant factual knowledge
- be analytical and logical
- reach a supported judgement about the issue in the question.

There are a number of skills that you will need to develop to reach the higher levels in the marking bands:

- understand the wording of the question
- plan an answer to the question set
- write a focused opening paragraph
- avoid irrelevance and description
- write analytically

- write a conclusion which reaches a supported judgement based on the argument in the main body of the essay.

These skills will be developed in the section below, but are further developed in the 'Period Study' chapters of the *OCR A level History* series (British Period Studies and Enquiries).

Understanding the wording of the question

To stay focused on the question set, it is important to read the question carefully and focus on the key words and phrases. Unless you directly address the demands of the question you will not score highly. Remember that in questions where there is a named factor you must write a good analytical paragraph about the given factor, even if you argue that it was not the most important.

Types of AS and A level questions you might find in the exams	The factors and issues you would need to consider in answering them
1 Assess the reasons why the French Revolution broke out in 1789.	Weigh up the relative importance of a range of factors as to why the French Revolution broke out in 1789.
2 To what extent were the actions of Louis XVI the most important reason for the failure to establish a constitutional monarchy?	Weigh up the relative importance of a range of factors, including the actions of Louis XVI, with other factors in the failure to establish a constitutional monarchy.
3 'The outbreak of the war in 1792 was the most important reason for the overthrow of the monarchy.' How far do you agree?	Weigh up the relative importance of a range of factors, including the outbreak of the war in 1792, to reach a balanced judgement.

Types of AS and A level questions you might find in the exams	The factors and issues you would need to consider in answering them
4 How successful was the Terror?	This question requires you make a judgement about the success of the Terror. Instead of thinking about factors, you would need to think about issues such as: • What might constitute success, given the circumstances of 1793. • The problems confronting the republic. • The aims of the CPS. • How the Terror impacted on the areas of Federal Revolt. • Robespierre's beliefs. • The extent to which the security of the republic was established by 1794.

Planning an answer

Many plans simply list dates and events – this should be avoided as it encourages a descriptive or narrative answer, rather than an analytical answer. The plan should be an outline of your argument; this means you need to think carefully about the issues you intend to discuss and their relative importance before you start writing your answer. It should therefore be a list of the factors or issues you are going to discuss and a comment on their relative importance.

For question 1 in the table, your plan might look something like this:

- A consideration of the structure of the *ancien régime* – link to problems.
- Finance – the problems of shortage of government revenue.
- Finance – the inequality of the taxation system.
- Role of the royal family – problems of weak leadership.
- Failure of the reform process.
- Ideas of the *philosophes* and their impact on the bourgeoisie and liberal nobility.

The opening paragraph

Many students spend time 'setting the scene'; the opening paragraph becomes little more than an introduction to the topic – this should be avoided. Instead, make it clear what your argument is going to be. Offer your view about the issue in the question – what do you consider was the most important reason for the outbreak of the revolution? – and then introduce the other issues you intend to discuss. In the plan it is suggested that the structure of the *ancien régime* was an important factor. This should be made clear in the opening paragraph, with a brief comment as to why – perhaps the way in which it excluded the majority of the population from a role in government. This will give the examiner a clear overview of your essay, rather than it being a 'mystery tour' where the argument becomes clear only at the end. You should also refer to any important issues that the question raises. For example:

There were a number of reasons why the French Revolution broke out in 1789 including problems relating to the structure of the ancien régime[1]. However, the most important reason was the problem of finance[2]. This was particularly important as it undermined the whole fabric of royal government, rendering it impotent[3].

1 The student is aware that there were a number of important reasons.
2 The student offers a clear view as to what he or she considers to be the most important reason – a thesis is offered.
3 There is a brief justification to support the thesis.

Avoid irrelevance and description

Hopefully the plan will stop you simply writing all you know about why the revolution broke out and force you to weigh up the role of a range of factors. Similarly, it should also help prevent you from simply writing about the issue of finance. You will not lose marks if you do that, but neither will you gain any credit, and you will waste valuable time.

Write analytically

This is perhaps the hardest, but most important skill you need to develop. An analytical approach can be helped by ensuring that the opening sentence of each paragraph introduces an idea, which directly answers the question and is not just a piece of factual information. In a very strong answer it should be possible to simply read the opening sentences of all the paragraphs and know what argument is being put forward.

If we look at the second question, on the failure of the constitutional monarchy (see page 218), the following are possible sentences with which to start paragraphs:

- The actions of Louis XVI were important in the failure to establish a constitutional monarchy as they created distrust among many and lost him the support he had retained.
- The revolutionary clubs, such as the Jacobins, which grew in popularity, rejected the concept of monarchy.
- The peasantry were disillusioned by the lack of changes and this led to the outbreak of rural revolution.
- The flight of Louis to Varennes undermined credibility in the new constitution before it had even been implemented.
- The urban discontent caused by rising prices and unemployment was exploited by the political societies who linked the economic protests to the demand for a republic and removal of the monarchy.

You would then go on to discuss both sides of the argument raised by the opening sentence, using relevant knowledge about the issue to support each side of the argument. The final sentence of the paragraph would reach a judgement on the role played by the factor you are discussing in considering the failure to establish a constitutional monarchy. This approach would ensure that the final sentence of each paragraph links back to the actual question you are answering. If you can do this for each paragraph you will have a series of mini-essays,

which discuss a factor and reach a conclusion or judgement about the importance of that factor or issue. For example:

The flight to Varennes was important[1], particularly in the short term, in bringing about the failure to establish a constitutional monarchy. Before his departure, Louis had drawn up a proclamation to the French people in which he rejected the changes of the revolution, which caused many to question whether he could remain as head of state. His flight also caused many who had previously supported him to question the extent to which he could be trusted, as he hoped to be able to renegotiate the parts of the constitution he disliked, whereas his popularity had depended on him being willing to support the revolution. The flight was a clear indication that Louis was willing to go back on agreements he had accepted, such as the Constitution of the Clergy, and this caused many to doubt his sincerity and encouraged talk of replacing the monarchy with a republic[2]. It was the flight that encouraged the Assembly to suspend the king, and in the short term, further encouraged Republicanism and therefore the failure of the attempts to establish a constitutional monarchy[3].

1 The sentence puts forward a clear view that the flight to Varennes was an important factor.
2 The importance of the flight to Varennes in bringing about the failure of the constitutional monarchy is fully explained.
3 The importance of the flight is discussed.

The conclusion

The conclusion provides the opportunity to bring together all the interim judgements to reach an overall judgement about the question. Using the interim judgements will ensure that your conclusion is based on the argument in the main body of the essay and does not offer a different view. For the essay answering question 1 (see page 218), you can decide what was the most important reason in explaining why the French Revolution broke out, but for questions 2 and 3 you will need to comment on the importance of the named factor – the actions of Louis XVI or the outbreak of the war in 1792 – as well as explain why you think a different factor is more important, if that has been your line of argument. Or, if you think the named factor is the most important, you would need to explain why that was more important than the other factors or issues you have discussed.

Consider the following conclusion to question 2: To what extent were the actions of Louis XVI the most important reason for the failure to establish a constitutional monarchy?

The failure to establish a constitutional monarchy was, at least in part, due to the growing support for a republic in the revolutionary clubs, such as the Jacobins, and among the urban workers who were suffering from falling wages and rising grain prices[1]. This urban discontent was used by the clubs to increase the demand for a republic, where representatives were directly elected, making the revolution more radical and less willing to accept a constitutional monarchy. Similarly, in the countryside the growing unrest caused by the failure to abolish feudal dues also resulted in greater radicalism and distrust in the concept of a constitutional monarchy. However, in the short term, it was the king's flight to Varennes that brought about the failure to establish a constitutional monarchy as it reinforced the distrust many had of him and further encouraged support for a republic[2]. He had shown that he was not committed to the revolution and would not accept the measures he disliked, an issue which the republicans were able to exploit[3].

1 This is a strong conclusion because the answer reaches a judgement and suggests that growing support for republicanism was important in the failure.
2 The relative importance of the named factor is discussed – the actions of Louis – but is weighed up against other factors to reach an overall judgement.
3 The student has also been able to show links between the other factors to reach a balanced judgement, which brings in a range of issues, showing the interplay between them.

How to write a good essay for the A level short answer questions

This question will require you to weigh up the importance of two factors or issues in relation to an event or a development. For example:

Which was more important as a cause of the French Revolution?

(i) The ideas of the Enlightenment.

(ii) The financial crisis.

Explain your answer with reference to both (i) and (ii).

As with the long essays, the skills required are made very clear by the mark scheme, which emphasises that the answer must:

- analyse the two issues
- evaluate the two issues
- support your analysis and evaluation with detailed and accurate knowledge
- reach a supported judgement as to which factor was more important in relation to the issue in the question.

The skills required are very similar to those for the longer essays. However, there is no need for an introduction, nor are you required to compare the two factors or issues in the main body of the essay, although either approach can still score full marks.

The Enlightenment resulted in the emergence in France of a group known as the philosophes who challenged many ideas, particularly that of absolute monarchy[1]. They were critical of much of the ancien régime and the ideas on which it was based. Their challenge helped to undermine one of the pillars of the regime, namely the Church and the role of the king as God's servant[2]. They were also in favour of liberty, which was also a challenge to the ancien régime. However, their ideas were not revolutionary, but they did influence many who would become revolutionaries[3].

1 The answer explains one of the ways the Enlightenment was important.
2 The implications of this development are considered.

3 The wider implications and limits to their role are hinted at, and this could be developed and contrasted with the financial problems.

The answer could go on to argue how, although they were critical of some aspects of the *ancien régime*, they did not oppose it and were in themselves not revolutionaries.

Most importantly, the conclusion must reach a supported judgement as to the relative importance of the factors in relation to the issue in the question. For example:

Both of these issues had an impact on the outbreak of the revolution, but the financial crisis was more important in the outbreak of the revolution[1]. The Enlightenment was less important, not only was it a long-term cause and only provided the preconditions for the revolution, but the men who were influenced by its ideas were not revolutionaries, although they did inspire others who were. In contrast, the financial crisis and the bankruptcy was a cause of the political crisis of 1787–8, and ultimately led to the summoning of the Estates-General, which helped to bring to a head the long-term problems that France had faced, which triggered the outbreak of revolution[2].

1 The response explains the relative importance of the two factors and offers a clear view.
2 The response supports the view offered in the opening sentence and therefore reaches a supported judgement.

Interpretation guidance

How to write a good essay

The guidance below is for answering the AS interpretation question OCR Unit Y243 The French Revolution and the rule of Napoleon 1774–1815. Guidance on answering essay questions is on page 218.

The OCR specification outlines the two key topics from which the interpretation question will be drawn. For this book these are:

- The causes of the French Revolution from 1774 and the events of 1789.
- Napoleon Bonaparte to 1807.

The specification also lists the main debates to consider.

It is also worth remembering that this is an AS unit and not an A level historiography paper. The aim of this element of the unit is to develop an awareness that the past can be interpreted in different ways.

The question will require you to assess the strengths and limitations of a historian's interpretation of an issue related to one of the specified key topics.

You should be able to place the interpretation within the context of the wider historical debate on the key topic. However, you will *not* be required to know the names of individual historians associated with the debate or to have studied the specific books of any historians. It may even be counter-productive to be aware of particular historians' views, as this may lead you to simply describe their view, rather than analyse the given interpretation.

There are a number of skills you need to develop if you are to reach the higher levels in the mark bands:

- To be able to understand the wording of the question.
- To be able to explain the interpretation and how it fits into the debate about the issue or topic.

- To be able to consider both the strengths and weaknesses of the interpretation by using your own knowledge of the topic.

Here is an example of a question you will face in the exam:

> 'Napoleon truly did return the revolution to its original principles.'
>
> From Michael Broers, *Napoleon: Soldier of Destiny*, 2014.

Evaluate the strengths and limitations of this interpretation, making reference to other interpretations that you have studied.

Approaching the question

There are several steps to take to answer this question:

1 Explain the interpretation and put it into the context

In the first paragraph you should explain the interpretation and the view it is putting forward. This paragraph places the interpretation in the context of the historical debate and explains any key words or phrases relating to the given interpretation. A suggested opening might be as follows:

The interpretation puts forward the view that the revolution had in some way strayed from its original principles. The author suggests that Napoleon through his efforts was able to bring it back to its original ideals[1]. In raising the issue of 'original principles', Broers is referring to the ideals which the early revolutionaries espoused – liberty equality, fraternity – and others enshrined in the Declaration of the Rights of Man. The concept of original principles is important because many argue that these had become lost as the revolution evolved[2]. For many, the revolution had been greeted with so much optimism but had lurched to the left and then to the right, and in the process had seemingly abandoned its original principles and high ideals. The interpretation suggests that Napoleon was 'truly' reversing this process[3].

1 The opening two sentences are clearly focused on the given interpretation. They clearly explain that there was a view that the revolution had strayed from its original principles and that Napoleon returned it to these, but there is no detailed own knowledge added at this point.
2 The second sentence explains what is meant by 'original principles' and this is developed in the following sentence.
3 The last sentence begins to place Napoleon's policies within the wider historical debate and suggests that this historian's emphasis on it might challenge those of other writers.

In order to place Broers' view in the context of the debate about whether Napoleon did truly return the revolution to its original principles, you could go on to suggest that there are a wide range of views to be considered and that if he did anything it was to revert to aspects of the *ancien régime*: restoration of the nobility, accommodation with the papacy, a monarchy.

2 Consider the strengths of the interpretation

In the second paragraph consider the strengths of the interpretation by bringing in your own knowledge that supports the given view. A suggested response might start as follows when considering the strengths of the view:

There is some merit in Broers' interpretation as Napoleon did set out to preserve the interests of the bourgeoisie in line with many of the clauses of the Declaration of the Rights of Man[1]. Many French people were disillusioned with the chaos and anarchy which they considered to be features of the early years of the republic and the political instability many associated with the Directory[2]. These factors contribute to the way in which the rule of Napoleon can be interpreted as essentially positive[3].

1 The answer clearly focuses on the strength of the given interpretation.
2 The response provides some support for the view in the interpretation from the candidate's own knowledge, this is not particularly detailed or precise,

but this could be developed in the remainder of the paragraph.
3 The final sentence links together the factors.

In the remainder of the paragraph you could show how these factors were linked and how, when Napoleon seized power in 1799 through the coup of Brumaire, he set about consolidating his position by binding support to his regime.

3 Consider the weaknesses of the interpretation

In the third paragraph consider the weaknesses of the given interpretation by bringing in knowledge that can challenge the given interpretation and explains what is missing from the interpretation. A suggested response might start as follows when considering the weaknesses of the view:

However there are a number of possible weaknesses to Broers' interpretation[1]. Most importantly, it does not deal clearly with the way in which Napoleon overturned a number of key reforms introduced during the revolution. The nobility had been abolished but a form of imperial nobility re-emerged during the Empire. The role of the Catholic Church was restored by the Concordat[2]. The interpretation does not consider other ways in which Napoleon drew on features associated with the ancien régime[3].

1 The opening makes it very clear that this paragraph will deal with the weaknesses of the interpretation.
2 It explains clearly the first weakness and provides evidence to support the claim, the evidence is not detailed and could be developed, but the answer focuses on explaining the weakness, rather than providing lots of detail.
3 Although more detail could have been provided about the changing nature of economic factors, the answer goes on to explain a second weakness, that there were other ways in which Napoleon drew from the *ancien régime*, and this could be developed in the remainder of the paragraph.

Answers might go on to argue that Napoleon although he made great use of the opportunities for personal advancement offered by the revolution, was very much his own man and was determined to create a system based around himself and his family. That the talented should advance irrespective of their social background was a feature he was keen to promote, yet many of the changes he made were restrictive. The freedom of the press, which flourished during the revolution, gave way to censorship and state propaganda. The paragraph might therefore suggest that the interpretation provides a partial answer which needs further development.

There is no requirement for you to reach a judgement as to which view you find more convincing or valid.

Assessing the interpretation

In assessing the interpretation you should consider the following:

- Identify and explain the issue being discussed in the interpretation: whether Napoleon returned the revolution to its original principles.
- Explain the view being put forward in the interpretation: the interpretation is arguing that the revolution in the 1790s had been blown off course and that Napoleon was returning it to its original principles.
- Explain how the interpretation fits into the wider debate about the issue: although it is possible to present Napoleon as a son of the revolution

and that he was keen to ensure that certain of the gains of 1789 were preserved, the way his rule evolved, particularly after he made himself emperor in 1804, suggests that a number of features bore more resemblance to the Bourbon monarchy than the revolution.

In other interpretations you might need to:

- Consider whether there is any particular emphasis within the interpretation that needs explaining or commenting on, for example, if the interpretation says that something is 'the only reason' or 'the single most important reason'.
- Comment on any concepts that the interpretation raises, such as 'total war', 'authoritarian system', 'liberalisation'.
- Consider the focus of the interpretation, for example, if an interpretation focuses on an urban viewpoint, what was the rural viewpoint? Is the viewpoint given in the interpretation the same for all areas of society?

In summary: this is what is important for answering interpretation questions:

- Explaining the interpretation.
- Placing the interpretation in the context of the wider historical debate about the issue it considers.
- Explaining the strengths *and* weaknesses of the view in the extract.

AQA A level History

Essay guidance

At both AS and A level for AQA Component 2: Depth Study: France in Revolution 1774–1815 you will need to answer an essay question in the exam. Each essay question is marked out of 25:

- for the AS exam, Section B: Answer **one** essay question from a choice of two
- for the A level exam, Section B: answer **two** essay questions from a choice of three.

There are several question stems which all have the same basic requirement: to analyse and reach a conclusion, based on the evidence you provide.

The AS questions often give a quotation and then ask whether you agree or disagree with this view. Almost inevitably, your answer will be a mixture of both. It is the same task as for A level – just phrased differently in the question. Detailed essays are more likely to do well than vague or generalised essays, especially in the Depth Studies of Paper 2.

The AQA mark scheme is essentially the same for AS and the full A level (see the AQA website, www.aqa.org.uk). Both emphasise the need to analyse and evaluate the key features related to the periods studied. The key feature of the highest level is sustained analysis: analysis that unites the whole of the essay.

Writing an essay: general skills

- *Focus and structure.* Be sure what the question is asking and plan what the paragraphs should be about.
- *Focused introduction to the essay.* Be sure that the introductory sentence relates directly to the focus of the question and that each paragraph highlights the structure of the answer.
- *Use detail.* Make sure that you show detailed knowledge, but only as part of an explanation being made in relation to the question. No knowledge should be standalone; it should be used in context.
- *Explanatory analysis and evaluation.* Consider what words and phrases to use in an answer to strengthen the explanation.
- *Argument and counter-argument.* Think of how arguments can be balanced so as to give contrasting views.
- *Resolution.* Think how best to 'resolve' contradictory arguments.
- *Relative significance and evaluation.* Think how best to reach a judgement when trying to assess the relative importance of various factors, and their possible interrelationship.

Planning an essay

Practice question 1

'The civil war in the Vendée was the only significant crisis faced by the republican government during 1793.' Explain why you agree or disagree with this view.

This question requires you to analyse the extent to which the civil war in the Vendée was the only significant crisis faced by the republican government during 1793. You must discuss the following:

- How the civil war in the Vendée was a significant threat to the authority of the republican government in 1793 (your primary focus).
- Other potentially significant threats to government authority in 1793 suggesting that you disagree with the view (your secondary focus).

A clear structure makes for a much more effective essay and is crucial for achieving the highest marks. You need three or four paragraphs to structure this question effectively. In each paragraph you will deal with one factor. One of these *must* be the factor in the question.

A very basic plan for this question might look like this:

- Paragraph 1: the way in which the civil war in the Vendée was a significant crisis for the republican government.
- Paragraph 2: consideration of whether or not the civil war was the only significant crisis faced by the republican government – hint at others.
- Paragraph 3: suggest that there were other crises in addition to the one in the Vendée: the war, economic collapse, the federal revolt. Focus on whether you agree or disagree with the view.

It is a good idea to cover the factor named in the question first, so that you don't run out of time and forget to do it. Then cover the others in what you think is their order of importance, or in the order that appears logical in terms of the sequence of paragraphs.

The introduction

Maintaining focus is vital. One way to do this from the beginning of your essay is to use the words in the question to help write your argument. The first sentence of question 1, for example, could look like this:

The civil war in the Vendée had a profound impact on the republican government and was undoubtedly a significant crisis for it, but there were a number of other crises it also had to deal with which were equally challenging.

This opening sentence provides a clear focus on the demands of the question, although it could, of course, be written in a more exciting style.

Focus throughout the essay

Structuring your essay well will help with keeping the focus of your essay on the question. To maintain a focus on the wording in question 1, you could begin your first main paragraph with 'weakness'.

The civil war in the Vendée posed an enormous threat to the authority of the republican government, although it is arguable as to whether it was the only significant crisis it faced in 1793.

- This sentence begins with a clear point that refers to the primary focus of the question – the civil war in the Vendée – while questioning the validity of the view.
- You could then have a paragraph for each of your other factors.
- It will be important to make sure that each paragraph focuses on analysis and includes relevant details that are used as part of the argument and that you indicate whether or not you agree or disagree with the view.
- You may wish to number your factors. This helps to make your structure clear and helps you to maintain focus.

Deploying detail

As well as focus and structure, your essay will be judged on the extent to which it includes accurate detail. There are several different kinds of evidence you could use that might be described as detailed. These include correct dates, names of relevant people, statistics and events. For example, for question 1 you could use terms such as federal revolt and collapsing value of the *assignat*. You can also make your essay more detailed by using the correct technical vocabulary.

Analysis and explanation

'Analysis' covers a variety of high-level skills including explanation and evaluation; in essence, it means breaking down something complex into smaller parts. A clear structure which breaks down a complex question into a series of paragraphs is the first step towards writing an analytical essay. The purpose of explanation is to provide evidence for why something happened, or why something is true or false. An explanatory statement requires two parts: a *claim* and a *justification*.

For example, for question 1, you might want to argue that one important reason for disagreeing with the view was that the collapsing value of the *assignat* and the economic crisis posed a very serious threat to the stability of the republic. Once you have made your point, and supported it with relevant detail, you can then explain how this answers the question. For example, you could conclude your paragraph like this:

So it is possible to argue that the collapse of the economy and the falling value of the assignat had a much wider impact[1] because[2] it affected the entire population of France, whereas the civil war was confined to the rather narrowly defined area of the Vendée and its neighbouring departments[3].

1 The first part of this sentence is the claim while the second part justifies the claim.
2 'Because' is a very important word to use when writing an explanation, as it shows the relationship between the claim and the justification.
3 The justification.

Evaluation

Evaluation means considering the importance of two or more different factors, weighing them against each other and reaching a judgement. This is a good skill to use at the end of an essay because the conclusion should reach a judgement which answers the question. For example, your conclusion to question 1 might read as follows:

Clearly, the civil war in the Vendée had a great impact on the government and was a significant crisis. It forced the movement to deal with rebels while it was also at war with many powerful countries. However, it is possible to disagree with the view as the government was confronted by a range of other crises which threatened to destabilise it. The economic crisis potentially had a much greater and wider impact as it affected more people. Therefore, the civil war in the Vendée was not the only significant crisis faced by the republican government in 1793.

Words like 'clearly', 'however' and 'therefore' are helpful to contrast the importance of the different factors.

Complex essay writing: argument and counter-argument

Essays that develop a good argument are more likely to reach the highest levels. This is because argumentative essays are much more likely to develop sustained analysis. As you know, your essays are judged on the extent to which they analyse.

After setting up an argument in your introduction, you should develop it throughout the essay. One way of doing this is to adopt an argument–counter-argument structure. A counter-argument is one that disagrees with the main argument of the essay. This is a good way of evaluating the importance of the different factors that you discuss. Essays of this type will develop an argument in one paragraph and then set out an opposing argument in another paragraph. Sometimes this will include juxtaposing the differing views of historians on a topic.

Good essays will analyse the key issues. They will probably have a clear piece of analysis at the end of each paragraph. While this analysis might be good, it will generally relate only to the issue discussed in that paragraph.

Excellent essays will be analytical throughout. As well as the analysis of each factor discussed above, there will be an overall analysis. This will run throughout the essay and can be achieved through developing a clear, relevant and coherent argument.

A good way of achieving sustained analysis is to consider which factor is most important. Here is an example of an introduction that sets out an argument for question 1:

The civil war in the Vendée was a significant crisis faced by the republican government but it is debatable if it was the only one[1]. Over the course of 1793 the authority of the government was significantly challenged on a number of diverse fronts[2]. While it is possible to see the events in the Vendée as posing a significant threat the other crises should not in any way be minimised. The economic instability and the falling value of the assignat were causing far greater hardship to more of the population than the events in the Vendée. Moreover, the military threat from France's external enemies was a real cause of concern and a potential threat to the survival of the republic[3].

1 The introduction begins with a claim.
2 The introduction continues with another reason.
3 Concludes with an outline of an argument of the most important reason.

- This introduction focuses on the question and sets out the key factors that the essay will develop.
- It introduces an argument about which factor was most significant.
- However, it also sets out an argument that can then be developed throughout each paragraph, and is rounded off with an overall judgement in the conclusion.

Complex essay writing: resolution and relative significance

Having written an essay that explains the argument and counter-arguments, you should then resolve the tension between the argument and the counter-argument in your conclusion. It is important that the writing is precise and summarises the arguments made in the main body of the essay. You need to reach a supported overall judgement. One very appropriate way to do this is by evaluating the relative significance of different factors, in the light of valid criteria. Relative significance means how important one factor is compared to another.

The best essays will always make a judgement about which was most important based on valid criteria. These can be very simple – and will depend on the topic and the exact question.

The following criteria are often useful:

- Duration: which factor was important for the longest amount of time?
- Scope: which factor affected the most people?
- Effectiveness: which factor achieved most?
- Impact: which factor led to the most fundamental change?

As an example, you could compare the factors in terms of their duration and their impact. A conclusion that follows this advice should be capable of reaching a high level (if written, in full, with appropriate details) because it reaches an overall judgement that is supported through evaluating the relative significance of different factors in the light of valid criteria.

Having written an introduction and the main body of an essay for question 1, a concluding paragraph that aims to meet the exacting criteria for reaching a complex judgement could look like this:

The immediate necessity in the spring of 1793 to dispatch military forces to the Vendée to deal with the civil war that had broken out must be viewed within the context of a range of other crises that the Committee of Public Safety had to deal with. Events in the Vendée cannot be taken in isolation and were part of a wider set of challenges confronting the government. On the economic front the value of the assignat was falling and there were food shortages in many cities. The federal revolt which broke out in June also required military force to restore order. These internal challenges were in addition to the war which was raging along France's northern frontier. What confronted the republic was a perfect storm of opposition, both internal and external, leading to the conclusion that events in the Vendée were not the only significant threat to the republic in 1793.

Sources guidance

Whether you are taking the AS exam or the full A level exam for AQA Component 2: Depth Study: France in Revolution 1774–1815, Section A presents you with sources and a question which involves evaluation of their utility or value.

AS exam	A level exam
Section A: answer question 1, based on two primary sources. (25 marks)	Section A: answer question 1, based on three primary sources. (30 marks)
Question focus: with reference to these sources and your understanding of the historical context, which of these two sources is more valuable in explaining … ?	Question focus: with reference to these sources and your understanding of the historical context, assess the value of these three sources to a historian studying …

Sources and sample questions

Study the sources. They are all concerned with events relating to the war of 1792.

SOURCE 1

From the Declaration of Pillnitz, which was issued jointly by Emperor Leopold II of Austria and Frederick William II, King of Prussia on 27 August 1791.

His Majesty the Emperor and His Majesty the King of Prussia … jointly declare that they regard the present position of his Majesty the King of France as a matter of common concern to all the sovereigns of Europe. They trust that the powers whose aid is supplied will not fail to recognise this fact: and that, accordingly, they will not refuse to co-operate with their said Majesties in employing, in proportion to their forces, the most effective means for enabling the King of France to consolidate with complete freedom the foundations of a monarchical government … In which case their said Majesties are resolved to act promptly, in mutual accord, with the forces necessary to attain the proposed objective. In the meantime, they will give their troops such orders as are necessary to have them ready for active service.

SOURCE 2

From the decree 'The country in danger', passed by the Legislative Assembly 11 July 1792.

Large numbers of troops are marching on our frontiers. All those who hate liberty are taking up arms against our constitution. Citizens, the country is in danger. May those who have the honour of being the first to march to the defence of that which is dearest to them never forget that they are Frenchmen and free, that their fellow citizens in their homes are upholding the security of the individual and of property, that the magistrates of the people are ever watchful, that with the calm courage of true strength everyone is waiting for the signal from the law to act, and the country will be saved.

SOURCE 3

From a letter written by the leading Girondin supporter Madame Roland, 9 September 1792.

My friend Danton controls everything: Robespierre is his puppet. Marat holds his torch and his dagger: this would-be tribune reigns – at the moment we are merely oppressed, but waiting for the time when we become his victims. If you knew the awful details of the killing expeditions! Women brutally raped before being torn to pieces by these tigers, guts cut out and worn as ribbons, human flesh eaten dripping with blood. You know my enthusiasm for the Revolution: well I am ashamed of it! Its reputation is tarnished by these scoundrels, it is becoming hideous. It is degrading to stay here, but it is forbidden to leave Paris. Goodbye, if it is too late for us, save the rest of France from the crimes of these madmen.

AS style question

With reference to Sources 2 and 3, and your understanding of the historical context, which of these two sources is more valuable in explaining why France was facing such a serious crisis in 1792?

The mark schemes

AS mark scheme

See the AQA website (www.aqa.org.uk) for the full mark schemes. This summary of the AS mark scheme shows how it rewards analysis and evaluation of the source material within the historical context.

Level 1	Describing the source content or offering generic phrases.
Level 2	Some relevant but limited comments on the value of one source *or* some limited comment on both.
Level 3	Some relevant comments on the value of the sources and some explicit reference to the issue identified in the question.
Level 4	Relevant well-supported comments on the value and a supported conclusion, but with limited judgement.
Level 5	Very good understanding of the value in relation to the issue identified. Sources evaluated thoroughly and with a well-substantiated conclusion related to which is more valuable.

A level style question

With reference to Sources 1, 2 and 3, and your understanding of the historical context, assess the value of these sources to a historian studying the revolutionary war in 1792.

A level mark scheme

This summary of the A level mark scheme shows how it is similar to the AS one, but covers three sources, not two. Also the wording of the question means that there is no explicit requirement to decide which of the three sources is the most valuable. Concentrate instead on a very thorough analysis of the content and evaluation of the provenance of each source, using contextual knowledge.

Level 1	Some limited comment on the value of at least one source.
Level 2	Some limited comments on the value of the sources *or* on content or provenance *or* comments on all three sources but no reference to the value of the sources.
Level 3	Some understanding of all three sources in relation to both content and provenance, with some historical context; but analysis limited.
Level 4	Good understanding of all three sources in relation to content, provenance and historical context to give a balanced argument on their value for the purpose specified in the question.
Level 5	As Level 4, but with a substantiated judgement.

Working towards an answer

It is important that knowledge is used to show an understanding of the relationship between the sources and the issue raised in the question. Answers should be concerned with the following:

- provenance
- arguments used (and you can agree/disagree)
- tone and emphasis of the sources.

The sources

The two or three sources used each time will be contemporary – probably of varying types (for example, diaries, newspaper accounts, government reports). The sources will all be on the same broad topic area. Each source will have value. Your task is to evaluate how much – in terms of its content and its provenance.

You will need to assess the *value of the content* by using your own knowledge. Is the information accurate? Is it giving only part of the evidence and ignoring other aspects? Is the tone of the writing significant?

You will need to evaluate the *provenance* of the source by considering who wrote it, and when, where and why. What was its purpose? Was it produced to express an opinion; to record facts; to influence the opinion of others? Even if it was intended to be accurate, the writer may have been biased – either deliberately or unconsciously. The writer, for example, might have only known part of the situation and reached a judgement solely based on that.

Here is a guide to analysing the provenance, content and tone for Sources 1, 2 and 3.

Analysing the sources

To answer the question effectively, you need to read the sources carefully and pull out the relevant points as well as add your own knowledge. You must remember to keep the focus on the question at all times.

Source 1 (page 230)

Provenance:

- The source is from the Declaration of Pillnitz, which was issued jointly by the Austrian emperors and the King of Prussia. They had very grave concerns about the danger posed by the revolution in France.
- It is taken from a jointly issued declaration – as an open document it was meant to reach as wide an audience as possible.

Content and argument:

- The source argues that the plight of the French king is a cause of grave concern.
- They hope that Louis will be able to establish monarchical government.
- If this does not occur then they will intervene.

Tone and emphasis:

- The entire tone of the declaration is threatening. Unless they achieve their demands there will be grave consequences. These will be of a military nature.

Own knowledge:

- Use your knowledge to agree/disagree with the source, for example: details about how the revolution in France posed a significant threat to the other great monarchies of Europe – especially the absolute ones. Liberty, equality and fraternity would undermine the very fabric of their social and political structures.

Source 2 (page 230)

Provenance:

- The source is taken from a decree passed by the Legislative Assembly.
- It offers a clear indication of what the government wished to do in a crisis.

Content and argument:

- The source argues that large numbers of foreign troops are marching on the French frontier.

- All citizens who wish to uphold individual security and property are urged to make themselves available to defend the country.

Tone and emphasis:

- The tone of the decree leaves no doubt as to the gravity of the situation facing the nation.

Own knowledge:

- Use your knowledge to agree/disagree with the source, for example: evidence is offered as to the gravity of the crisis, this is understandable given the state of the French army, from which substantial number of officers of noble background had given up their posts and joined the ranks of the *émigrés* – and in many cases the counter-revolution.

Source 3 (page 231)

Provenance:

- The source is from a high-profile figure in the Girondin group who was present in Paris at the time.
- It is written by Madame Roland, a leading figure among those supporting the revolution. Her salon was an important meeting place for those on the political left.

Content and argument:

- The source sees the revolution descending into the most brutal anarchy.
- Madame Roland singles out Danton as the orchestrator of this butchery.

Tone and emphasis:

- The tone is one of shock and indignation about the way events are unfolding – this is evident from the language she uses.

Own knowledge:

- Use your knowledge to agree/disagree with the source, for example: the events being described are the September massacres, which can be considered the first example of the Terror. Fear and suspicion of betrayal by a fifth column lay behind these brutal events.

Answering AS questions

You have 45 minutes to answer the question. It is important that you spend at least one-quarter of the time reading and planning your answer. Generally, when writing an answer, you need to check that you are remaining focused on the issue identified in the question and are relating this to the sources and your knowledge.

- You might decide to write a paragraph on each 'strand' (that is, provenance, content and tone), comparing the two sources, and then write a short concluding paragraph with an explained judgement on which source is more valuable.
- For writing about content, you may find it helpful to adopt a comparative approach, for example when the evidence in one source is contradicted or questioned by the evidence in another source.

At AS level you are asked to provide a judgement on which is more valuable. Make sure that this is based on clear arguments with strong evidence, and not on general assertions.

Planning and writing your answer

- Think how you can best plan an answer.
- Plan in terms of the headings above, perhaps combining 'provenance' with 'tone and emphasis', and compare the two sources.

As an example, here is a comparison of Sources 2 and 3 in terms of provenance, and tone and emphasis:

The two sources have different viewpoints. In terms of their provenance, Source 2 is an emotional decree passed by the Legislative Assembly. The viewpoint is based on the urgent desire to protect the revolution and its gains. Source 3 is the view of a private individual – albeit one with a political connection who has produced an emotional response to the horrific events unfolding in Paris – the September massacres.

Then compare the *content and argument* of each source, by using your knowledge. For example:

Source 2 is arguing for large numbers of patriotic citizens to march to the defence of their country which is in 'danger', and to prolong the gains they have benefited from as a consequence of their revolution. The enemy is those who 'hate liberty', and the constitution.

Source 3, however, focuses on the brutal massacres which were taking place in the prisons of Paris. During these events between 1100 and 1400 people were brutally killed by the sans-culottes with no attempt to restrain them by the authorities. The source does not explain why there was a crisis but does emphasise a consequence of it.

Which is *more valuable*? This can be judged in terms of which is likely to be more valuable in terms of where the source came from; or in terms of the accuracy of its content. However, remember the focus of the question – in this case, why France was facing such a serious crisis in 1792.

With these sources, you could argue that Source 2 is the more valuable because in summoning the population to defend the country which is in danger it emphasises the real sense of crisis faced by the government, whereas Source 3 is more limited to the panic that unfolded in the city without explaining the context in which the massacres took place.

Then check the following:

- Have you covered the 'provenance' and 'content' strands?
- Have you included sufficient knowledge to show understanding of the historical context?

Answering A level questions

The same general points for answering AS questions (see 'Answering AS questions') apply to A level questions, although of course here there are three sources and you need to assess the value of each of the three, rather than choose which is most valuable. Make sure that you remain focused on the question and that when you use your knowledge it is used to substantiate (add to) an argument relating to the content or provenance of the source.

If you are answering the A level question with Sources 1, 2 and 3 above:

- Keep the different 'strands' explained above in your mind when working out how best to plan an answer.
- Follow the guidance about 'provenance' and 'content' (see the AS guidance).
- Here you are *not* asked to explain which is the most valuable of the three sources. You can deal with each of the three sources in turn if you wish.
- However, you can build in comparisons if it is helpful – but it is not essential. It will depend to some extent on the three sources.
- You need to include sufficient knowledge to show understanding of the historical context. This might encourage cross-referencing of the content of the three sources, mixed with your own knowledge.
- Each paragraph needs to show clarity of argument in terms of the issue identified by the question.

Edexcel A level History

Essay guidance

Edexcel's Paper 2, Unit 2C.1: France in Revolution, 1774–99 is assessed by an exam comprising two sections:

- Section A tests the depth of your historical knowledge through source analysis (see page 239 for guidance on this).
- Section B requires you to write one essay from a choice of two from your own knowledge.

The following advice relates to Paper 2, Section B. It is relevant to A level and AS level questions. Generally, the AS exam is similar to the A level exam. Both examine the same content and require similar skills; nonetheless, there are differences, which are discussed below.

Essay skills

In order to get a high grade in Section B of Paper 2 your essay must contain four essential qualities:

- focused analysis
- relevant detail
- supported judgement
- organisation, coherence and clarity.

This section focuses on the following aspects of exam technique:

- understanding the nature of the question
- planning an answer to the question set
- writing a focused introduction
- deploying relevant detail
- writing analytically
- reaching a supported judgement.

The nature of the question

Section B questions are designed to test the depth of your historical knowledge. Therefore, they can focus on relatively short periods, or single events, or indeed on the whole period from 1774 to 1799. Moreover,

they can focus on different historical processes or 'concepts'. These include:

- cause
- consequence
- change/continuity
- similarity/difference
- significance.

These different question focuses require slightly different approaches:

Cause	1	To what extent were the financial problems of the government primarily responsible for the French Revolution?
Consequence	2	To what extent was the reform of the legal system the most significant consequence of the establishment of the National Assembly in 1789?
Continuity and change	3	"The government of the Directory in the years 1795–9 represented a return to stable government from the chaos of 1789–94.' How far do you agree with this statement?
Similarities and differences	4	'Supporters of the Terror were overwhelmingly motivated by a desire to secure the survival of the Republic.' How far do you agree with this statement in the years 1793–4?
Significance	5	'The National Assembly's reforms of the Catholic Church changed the course of the French Revolution.' How far do you agree with this statement?

Some questions include a 'stated factor'. The most common type of stated factor question would ask how far one factor caused something. For example, for the first question in the table: 'To what extent were the financial problems of the government primarily responsible for the French Revolution?' In this type of question you would be expected to evaluate the importance of financial problems – the 'stated factor' – compared to other factors.

AS and A level questions

AS level questions are generally similar to A level questions but the wording will be slightly less complex.

A level question	AS level question	
To what extent did the outbreak of civil war in the Vendée lead to the emergence of government by Terror in 1793?	To what extent did the outbreak of civil war in the Vendée cause the Terror from 1793?	The A level question focuses on the complex notion of 'emergence' whereas the AS question focuses on the relatively simple issue of 'cause'
'The reforms passed by the National Assembly radically altered France in the years 1789–91'. How far do you agree with this statement?	How far did the reforms of the National Assembly change France in the years 1789–91?	The AS question asks you how far the reforms of the National Assembly changed France. The A level question asks you to make a more complex judgement: how far did the reforms of the National Assembly radically alter France?

To achieve the highest level at A level, you will have to deal with the full complexity of the question. For example, if you were dealing with question 5, about the reform of the Catholic Church, you would have to deal with the question of how far it 'changed the course' of the Revolution, not merely the extent to which it constituted a change. 'Changing the course' of the Revolution implies a dramatic turning point of immense significance, rather than a mere change.

Planning your answer

It is crucial that you understand the focus of the question. Therefore, read the question carefully before you start planning. Check the following:

- The chronological focus: which years should your essay deal with?
- The topic focus: what aspect of your course does the question deal with?
- The conceptual focus: is this a causes, consequences, change/continuity, similarity/difference or significance question?

For example, for question 3 you could point these out as follows:

'The government of the Directory[1] in the years 1795–9[2] represented a return to stable government[3] from the chaos of 1789–94.'[2] How far do you agree with this statement?

1 Topic focus: the period of the Directory.
2 Chronological focus: 1789–99.
3 Conceptual focus: continuity/change.

Your plan should reflect the task that you have been set. Section B asks you to write an analytical, coherent and well-structured essay from your own knowledge, which reaches a supported conclusion in around 40 minutes.

- To ensure that your essay is coherent and well structured, your essay should comprise a series of paragraphs, each focusing on a different point.
- Your paragraphs should come in a logical order. For example, you could write your paragraphs in order of importance, so you begin with the most important issues and end with the least important.
- In essays where there is a 'stated factor', it is a good idea to start with the stated factor before moving on to the other points.
- To make sure you keep to time, you should aim to write three or four paragraphs plus an introduction and a conclusion.

The opening paragraph

The opening paragraph should do four main things:

- answer the question directly
- set out your essential argument
- outline the factors or issues that you will discuss
- define key terms used in the question – where necessary.

Different questions require you to define different terms, for example:

A level question	Key terms
'The National Assembly's reforms of the Catholic Church changed the course of the French Revolution.' How far do you agree with this statement?	Here it is worth explaining how you would define something that 'changed the course' of the Revolution
'Supporters of the Terror were overwhelmingly motivated by a desire to secure the survival of the Republic.' How far do you agree with this statement in the years 1793–4?	In this example, it is worth defining 'overwhelmingly motivated'

Here's an example introduction in answer to question 2 in the table on page 235: 'To what extent was the reform of the legal system the most significant consequence of the establishment of the National Assembly in 1789?'

The reform of the legal system was one greatly significant consequence of the establishment of the National Assembly in 1789, but it was not the most significant consequence[1]. The reform of the legal system did lead to a more humane penal code, a standardised system of law and tried to ensure that judges were accountable and appropriately qualified. The changes made to the Church were much more significant, however, affecting the entire position of the Church in relation to the State, dividing the clergy and leading to a rise in support of movements opposed to the Revolution. The economic changes made by the Assembly were a significant consequence of its establishment but their impact was not as wide-ranging or seismic as the reforms of the Catholic Church[2]. The reforms of the Church were the most significant consequence of the establishment of the National Assembly because of the far-reaching implications of the changes and the severity of the reactions to them[3].

1 The essay starts with a clear answer to the question.
2 This section explains the significance of the main factor before going on to outline the other factors to be discussed in the essay.
3 Finally, the essential argument is stated.

The opening paragraph: advice

- Don't write more than a couple of sentences on general background knowledge. This is unlikely to focus explicitly on the question.
- After defining key terms, refer back to these definitions when justifying your conclusion.
- The introduction should reflect the rest of the essay. Don't make one argument in your introduction, then make a different argument in the essay.

Deploying relevant detail

Paper 2 tests the depth of your historical knowledge. Therefore, you will need to deploy historical detail. In the main body of your essay your paragraphs should begin with a clear point, be full of relevant detail and end with explanation or evaluation. A detailed answer might include statistics, proper names, dates and technical terms. For example, if you were writing a paragraph about the reforms of the National Assembly between 1789 and 1791, you would be expected to provide details of any measures used in support of your answer – names and any relevant terms of legislation.

Writing analytically

The quality of your analysis is one of the key factors that determines the mark you achieve. Writing analytically means clearly showing the relationships between the ideas in your essay. Analysis includes two key skills: explanation and evaluation.

Explanation

Explanation means giving reasons. An explanatory sentence has three parts:

- a claim: a statement that something is true or false
- a reason: a statement that justifies the claim
- a relationship: a word or phrase that shows the relationship between the claim and the reason.

Imagine you are answering question 1 in the table on page 235: 'To what extent were the financial problems of the government primarily responsible for the French Revolution?' Your paragraph on finance should start with a clear point, which would then be supported by a number of examples. Finally, you would round off the paragraph with some explanation:

The financial problems which beset the Bourbon monarchy were a very important factor in bringing about the French Revolution[1] because[2] government bankruptcy ultimately forced Louis XVI to summon the Estates-General for 1789[3].

1 Claim.
2 Relationship.
3 Reason.

Make sure of the following:

- the reason you give genuinely justifies the claim you have made
- your explanation is focused on the question.

Reaching a supported judgement

Finally, your essay should reach a supported judgement. The obvious place to do this is in the conclusion of your essay. Even so, the judgement should reflect the findings of your essay. The conclusion should present:

- a clear judgement that answers the question
- an evaluation of the evidence that supports the judgement
- finally, the evaluation should reflect a valid criterion.

Evaluation and criteria

Evaluation means weighing up to reach a judgement. Therefore, evaluation requires you to:

- summarise both sides of the issue
- reach a conclusion that reflects the proper weight of both sides.

So, for question 2 in the table on page 235: 'To what extent was the reform of the legal system the most significant consequence of the establishment of the National Assembly in 1789?', the conclusion might look like this:

In conclusion, the reforms of legal system were indeed a significant consequence of the establishment of the National Assembly in 1789[1]. The legal reforms created a standardised judicial system that employed better qualified judges and whose punishments became more humane and proportionate. This would have changed the way that a proportion of French people experienced justice[2]. Despite this, however, the reforms of the legal system were not the most significant consequence of the establishment of the National Assembly. The reforms to the Catholic Church were much more significant. The reforms changed the very way that the State and Church operated in relation to each other, created a divided Church, and made the divisions within the wider French nation greater as they brought mass support to the counter-revolutionary movement[3]. So while the legal reforms were a significant consequence for those working within, or experiencing, the justice system, the changes to the Catholic Church had a much more wide-ranging and profound impact on the people and institutions of France[4].

1 The conclusion starts with a clear judgement in relation to the named factor.
2 This sentence then considers the ways in which the named factor was significant.
3 The conclusion next explores the most significant factor and justifies its argument.
4 The essay ends with a final judgment that is supported by the evidence of the essay.

The judgement is supported in part by evaluating the evidence, and in part by linking it to valid criteria. In this case, the criterion is the definition of modernisation set out in the introduction. Significantly, this criterion is specific to this essay, and different essays will require you to think of different criteria to help you make your judgement.

Sources guidance

Edexcel's Paper 2, Option 2C.1: France in Revolution, 1774–99 is assessed by an exam comprising two sections:

- Section A tests the depth of your historical knowledge through source analysis.
- Section B requires you to write one essay from a choice of two from your own knowledge (see page 235 for guidance on this).

The following advice relates to Paper 2, Section A. It is relevant to A level and AS level questions. Generally, the AS exam is similar to the A level exam. Both examine the same content and require similar skills; nonetheless, there are differences, which are discussed below.

The questions in Paper 2, Section A, are structured differently in the A level and AS exams.

AS exam	Full A level exam
Section A: contains one compulsory question divided into two parts.	Section A: contains a single compulsory question worth 20 marks. The question asks you to evaluate the usefulness of two sources for a specific historical enquiry.
Part a) is worth 8 marks. It focuses on the value of a single source for a specific enquiry.	
Part b) is worth 12 marks. It asks you to weigh the value of a single source for a specific enquiry.	Together the two sources will comprise about 400 words.
Together the two sources will comprise about 350 words.	
Questions will start with the following stems: a) Why is Source 1 valuable to the historian for an enquiry about … b) How much weight do you give the evidence of Source 2 for an enquiry into …	Questions will start with the following stem: How far could the historian make use of Sources 1 and 2 together to investigate …

Edexcel style questions

AS style question

a) Study Sources 1 and 2 before you answer this question.

Why is Source 1 valuable to the historian for an enquiry into the changing attitudes to the French monarchy at the end of the *ancien régime* in the years 1774–89?

Explain your answer using the source, the information given about it and your own knowledge of the historical context.

b) How much weight do you give the evidence in Source 2 for an enquiry into the causes of the outbreak of the French Revolution in 1789? Explain your answer using the source, the information given about it and your own knowledge of the historical context.

A level style question

Study Sources 1 and 2 before you answer this question.

How far could the historian make use of Sources 1 and 2 together to investigate the difficulties facing Louis XVI and his ministers in the 1780s?

Explain your answer, using both sources, the information given about them and your own knowledge of the historical context.

Sources 1 and 2

SOURCE I

From secret correspondence sent to the Empress Maria Theresa by the Austrian ambassador and leading diplomat in Paris, Florimond Claude, Comte de Mercy-Argenteau (c.1787).

Among the rumours which circulate contrary to the prestige and reputation essential to a Queen of France, there is one which appears more dangerous and unpleasant than the rest. It is complained quite openly that the queen is extravagant and encourages extravagances. The public at first viewed with pleasure the king's gift of the Trianon[1] to the queen; but it began to be disturbed and alarmed by Her Majesty's expenditure there. By her order the gardens have been completely changed into an English garden, which cost at least

150,000 livres. The queen has had a theatre built at the Trianon; she has only presented one play there, followed by a supper which was very expensive. The queen's allowance has been doubled, and yet she has contracted debts. The chief cause of the queen's debts is known. She has bought many diamonds and her card playing has become very costly.

[1] Trianon – a large detached mansion built in the grounds of the royal palace at Versailles.

SOURCE 2

From the Marquis de Bouille's *Memoirs of the French Revolution*, which was published in 1797. When the revolution broke out in 1789 Bouille was a staunch supporter of the monarchy. As a military commander he was responsible for suppressing a number of army mutinies. From 1790 he was active in attempting to help Louis and his family escape out of France.

The most striking of the country's troubles was the chaos in its finances, the result of years of extravagance intensified by the expense of the American War of Independence, which had cost the state over twelve hundred million livres. No one could think of any remedy but a search for fresh funds, as the old ones were exhausted. M. de Calonne the Minister of Finance conceived a bold and wide-reaching plan. Without either threatening the basis of the French monarchy, this

plan changed the previous system of financial administration and attacked the vices at their root. The worst of these problems was the arbitrary system of allocation, the oppressive costs of collection, and the abuses of privilege by the richest section of taxpayers. The whole weight of public expenditure was borne by the most numerous but least wealthy part of the nation which was crushed by the burden.

Understanding the questions

- To answer the question successfully you must understand how the question works.
- The question is written precisely in order to make sure that you understand the task. Each part of the question has a specific meaning.
- You must use the source, the information given about the source, and your own knowledge of the historical context when answering the question.

Understanding the AS question

a) Why is Source 1 valuable to the historian for an enquiry[1] into the changing attitudes to the French monarchy at the end of the *ancien régime* in the years 1774–89[2]?

1 You must focus on the reasons why the source could be helpful to a historian. Indeed, you can get maximum marks without considering the source's limitations.

2 The final part of the question focuses on a specific topic that a historian might investigate. In this case: 'changing attitudes to the French monarchy at the end of the *ancien régime*'.

b) How much weight do you give the evidence in Source 2[1] for an enquiry[2] into the causes of the outbreak of the French Revolution in 1789[3]?

1 This question focuses on evaluating the extent to which the source contains evidence. Therefore, you must consider the ways in which the source is valuable and the limitations of the source.
2 This is the essence of the task: you must focus on what a historian could legitimately conclude from studying this source.
3 This is the specific topic that you are considering the source for: 'the outbreak of the French Revolution in 1789'.

Understanding the A level question

How far[1] could the historian make use of Sources 1 and 2[2] together[3] to investigate the difficulties facing Louis XVI and his ministers in the 1780s[4]? Explain your answer, using both sources, the information given about them and your own knowledge of the historical context [5].

1 You must evaluate the extent of something, rather than giving a simple 'yes' or 'no' answer.
2 This is the essence of the task: you must focus on what a historian could legitimately conclude from studying these sources.
3 You must examine the sources as a pair and make a judgement about both sources, rather than simply making separate judgements about each source.
4 The final part of the question focuses on a specific topic that a historian might investigate. In this case: 'the difficulties facing Louis XVI and his ministers in the 1780s'.
5 This instruction lists the resources you should use: the sources, the information given about the sources and your own knowledge of the historical context that you have learnt during the course.

Source skills

Generally, Section A of Paper 2 tests your ability to evaluated source material. More specifically, the sources presented in Section A will be taken from the period that you have studied: 1774–99, or be written by people who witnessed these events. Your job is to analyse the sources by reading them in the context of the values and assumptions of the society and the period that produced them.

Examiners will mark your work by focusing on the extent to which you are able to:

- Interpret and analyse source material:
  - At a basic level, this means you can understand the sources and select, copy, paraphrase and summarise the source or sources to help answer the question.
  - At a higher level, your interpretation of the sources includes the ability to explain, analyse and make inferences based on the sources.
  - At the highest levels, you will be expected to analyse the source in a sophisticated way. This includes the ability to distinguish between information, opinions and arguments contained in the sources.
- Deploy knowledge of historical context in relation to the sources:
  - At a basic level, this means the ability to link the sources to your knowledge of the context in which the source was written, using this knowledge to expand or support the information contained in the sources.
  - At a higher level, you will be able to use your contextual knowledge to make inferences, and to expand, support or challenge the details mentioned in the sources.
  - At the highest levels, you will be able to examine the value and limits of the material contained in the sources by interpreting the sources in the context of the values and assumptions of the society that produced them.
- Evaluate the usefulness and weight of the source material:
  - At a basic level, evaluation of the source will based on simplistic criteria about reliability and bias.
  - At a higher level, evaluation of the source will based on the nature and purpose of the source.
  - At the highest levels, evaluation of the source will based on a valid criterion that is justified in the course of the essay. You will also be able to distinguish between the value of different aspects of the sources.

Make sure your source evaluation is sophisticated. Avoid crude statements about bias, and avoid simplistic assumptions such as a source written immediately after an event is reliable, whereas a source written years later is unreliable.

Try to see things through the eyes of the writer:

- how does the writer understand the world?
- what assumptions does the writer have?
- who is the writer trying to influence?
- what views is the writer trying to challenge?

Basic skill: comprehension

The most basic source skill is comprehension: understanding what the sources mean. There are a variety of techniques that you can use to aid comprehension. For example, you could read the sources included in this book and in past papers:

- read the sources out loud
- look up any words that you don't understand and make a glossary
- make flash cards containing brief biographies of the writers of the sources.

You can demonstrate comprehension by copying, paraphrasing and summarising the sources. However, keep this to the minimum as comprehension is a low-level skill and you need to leave room for higher-level skills.

Advanced skill: contextualising the sources

First, to analyse the sources correctly you need to understand them in the context in which they were written. People in France in the final years of the *ancien régime* – the 1780s – viewed the world rather differently to people in early twenty-first century Britain. The sources reflect this. Your job is to understand the values and assumptions behind the sources:

- One way of contextualising the sources is to consider the nature, origins and purpose of the sources. However, this can lead to formulaic responses.

- An alternative is to consider two levels of context. First, you should establish the general context. In this case, Sources 1 and 2 refer to a period in which France was facing enormous financial pressures and was tottering on the edge of bankruptcy.

Second, you can look for specific references to contemporary events or debates in the sources. For example:

Sources 1 and 2 both refer to finance. They reflect the very serious concern in the government with the dire position that it was in. The government was unable to meet its financial obligations and was weighed down by crushing interest payments. Its expenditure was significantly greater than its income. In Source 1 there is a clear implication that royal extravagance – by Marie Antoinette – is a very real concern as it is likely to impact on the standing of the monarchy. The reference to diamonds allows you to infer that the source is referring to the affair of the diamond necklace (1785–6). Source 2 offers insight into the chaotic structure of royal finances against a context of tax exemptions and abuses linked to the way the ancien régime was organised.

Use context to make judgements

- Start by establishing the general context of the source:
  - Ask yourself, what was going on at the time when the source was written, or the time of the events described in the source?
  - What are the key debates that the source might be contributing to?
- Next, look for key words and phrases that establish the specific context. Does the source refer to specific people, events, or books that might be important?
- Make sure your contextualisation focuses on the question.
- Use the context when evaluating the usefulness and limitations of the source.

For example:

Source 1 is valuable to a historian investigating the problems facing Louis XVI and his ministers in the years immediately prior to the French Revolution. It shows how concerned the Austrian ambassador was about the way perceptions of the queen were being damaged, possibly irreparably, as a consequence of a series of financial scandals. Source 2 is valuable because it clearly indicates the nature of the financial problems facing the monarchy. According to Source 2, years of extravagance – which Source 1 appears to confirm – and the expenses incurred during the American War of Independence, had brought France to a state of bankruptcy. A central factor in the crisis was the widespread abuses noted in the source, which were prevalent during the ancien régime and which Bouille firmly emphasises. These were to a degree accentuated by royal extravagance. It is possible to infer that financial issues, coupled with perceptions of the queen, were significant and difficult problems facing the government of France prior to 1789.

Glossary of terms

Active citizens   Citizens who, depending on the amount of taxes paid, could vote and stand as deputies.

Agents nationaux   National agents appointed by, and responsible to, the central government. Their role was to monitor the enforcement of all revolutionary laws.

Altar of the fatherland   A large memorial to commemorate the Revolution.

Ancien régime   French society and government before the Revolution of 1789.

Annates   Payments made by the French Church to the Pope.

Annex   To incorporate foreign territory into a state, usually forcibly and against the will of the local people.

Anti-clericalism   Opposition to the Catholic Church.

Anti-republican opposition   Forces opposed to the Republic, mainly former members of the nobility, refractory priests and monarchists.

Appel nominal   Each deputy was required to declare publicly his decision on the guilt or innocence of Louis XVI.

Armée révolutionnaire   *Sans-culottes* sent to the provinces to confront counter-revolutionary forces and ensure the movement of food supplies.

Armistice   An agreement between two countries to end hostilities. This would precede a peace settlement that would formally mark the end of a war.

Artisan   A skilled worker or craftsman.

Assignat   Bonds backed up by the sale of Church land that circulated as a form of paper currency.

Austrian Committee   Influential politicians and close confidants of Marie Antoinette who kept in close secret contact with Vienna, capital of the Habsburg Empire.

Avignon   Territory controlled by the Pope in southern France.

Balance the budget   To create a situation in which the government's expenditure is equal to its income.

Bankruptcy of the two-thirds   The government wrote off two-thirds of the debt it owed its creditors.

Biens nationaux   The nationalised property of the Church as ordered by the decree of 2 November 1789.

Bonnet rouge   The red cap popularly known as the cap of liberty, which became an important symbol of the Revolution.

Bourgeoisie   Middle-class urban dwellers who made a living through their intellectual skills or business practices.

Brigandage   Outbreaks of lawlessness and violence by groups of bandits.

Brissotins   Supporters of Jacques Brissot who later merged with the Girondins.

Cahiers   Lists of grievances and suggestions for reform drawn up by representatives of each estate and each community and presented to the Estates-General for consideration.

Canton   An administrative subdivision of a department.

Centralisation   Direct central control of the various parts of government, with less power to the regions.

Centre   Those who sat facing the speaker of the Legislative Assembly favouring neither left nor right.

Certificates of citizenship   Proof of good citizenship and support for the Republic, without which no one could be employed.

Checks and balances   Ensuring that the power given to the executive was balanced by the power granted to the legislature.

Chouan   Guerrilla groups operating in the Vendée between 1794 and 1796.

Citizens' militia   A bourgeois defence force set up to protect the interests of property owners in Paris. After the storming of the Bastille it became the National Guard.

Collective bargaining   Where a trade union negotiates with employers on behalf of workers who are members.

Comités de surveillance   Surveillance or watch committees, sometimes known simply as revolutionary committees.

Committee of General Security   Had overall responsibility for police security, surveillance and spying.

Committee of Public Safety   Effectively, the government of France during 1793–4 and one of the twin pillars of the Terror along with the Committee of General Security.

Commune   The smallest administrative unit in France.

Communist   A follower of the political belief that centres on social and economic equality as outlined by Karl Marx.

Concordat   An agreement between Napoleon and the Pope to try and end the divisions between the Church and State.

Conscription   Compulsory military service.

Conservatives   Those who did not want any reforms. They were deeply suspicious and sceptical of the need for any social or political change.

Conspiracy of Equals   Babeuf's theory of how to organise a revolution, using a small group of committed revolutionaries rather than a mass movement.

Constitution   A written document detailing how a country is to be governed, laws made, powers apportioned and elections conducted.

Constitutional monarchists   Supporters of Louis who welcomed the granting of limited democratic rights to the French people.

Constitutional monarchy   Where the powers of the Crown are limited by a constitution. Also known as a limited monarchy.

Consulate   The system of government that replaced the Directory. It took its name from the three consuls, of whom Napoleon was the most important as first consul. They formed the executive in the new constitution of 1799.

Continental system   The attempt by Napoleon to bring economic chaos to Britain by preventing its exports entering Europe.

Conventionnels   Members of the Convention between 1792 and 1795.

Corvée   Unpaid labour service to maintain roads. In many places money replaced the service.

Cottage industry   Small-scale textile production (spinning, weaving and iron work) carried out in a peasant's cottage or workshop and used to supplement income from farming.

Counter-revolutionaries   Groups and individuals hostile to the Revolution, who wished to reverse any changes it made at the earliest opportunity.

Coup of Thermidor   The overthrow of Robespierre and his closest supporters, which marked the end of the Terror.

Cult of the Supreme Being   Robespierre's alternative civic religion to the Catholic faith.

Decentralised   Decision-making devolved from the centre to the regions of a country.

Dechristianisation   Ruthless anti-religious policies conducted by some Jacobin supporters against the Church, aimed at destroying its influence.

Decree of Fraternity   The Convention offered support to those in any state wishing to overthrow their rulers and establish democratic political systems.

Deficit   When expenditure is greater than income it results in a deficit.

Deflation   A fall in prices and in money value as demand for goods and services falls.

Departments   On 26 February 1790, 83 new divisions for local administration in France were created to replace the old divisions of the *ancien régime*.

Diocese   An area served by a bishop. It is made up of a large number of parishes.

Disenfranchised   Stripped of the right to vote.

Draft-dodgers   Men who avoided the call to serve in the army.

Egalitarian society   Where citizens enjoy equal rights and are not discriminated against on the basis of gender or social class. This is neatly summed up by the phrase most frequently linked with the Revolution: liberty, equality and fraternity.

Egalitarianism   Derived from 'equality' – the aim to have all citizens equal, with no disparities in wealth, status or opportunity.

Élan   Patriotic enthusiasm, commitment and identity with the revolutionary cause within the army.

Émigrés   People, mainly aristocrats, who fled France during the Revolution. Many *émigrés* joined foreign opponents of the Revolution.

Enragés   An extreme revolutionary group led by Jacques Roux which had considerable influence on the Parisian *sans-culottes*.

Entrepreneurs   Individuals prepared to take risks with their capital to support business schemes that will secure a profit.

Estates-General   Elected representatives of all three estates of the realm. This body was only summoned in times of extreme national crisis, and had last met in 1614.

Executive power   The power to make decisions relating to the government of a country.

Federalism   A rejection of the central authority of the State in favour of regional authority.

Fédérés   National guardsmen from the provinces who arrived in Paris to display during the *Fête de la Fédération* commemorating the fall of the Bastille, 14 July 1792.

Feudal dues   Financial or work obligations imposed on the peasantry by landowners.

Feuillants   Constitutional monarchists, among them Lafayette, who split from the Jacobin Club following the flight to Varennes.

First Coalition   A loose anti-French alliance created by Britain and consisting of the Netherlands, Spain, Piedmont, Naples, Prussia, Russia, Austria and Portugal. Russia refused to commit soldiers to the coalition when Britain did not send money to support Russia's armies.

Forced loan   A measure compelling the wealthy to loan money to the government.

Francs   On 7 April 1795 the Convention introduced the silver franc as the official unit of currency replacing the *livre*.

Free market   A trading system with no artificial price controls. Prices are determined solely by supply and demand.

Free trade   Trade without the imposition of taxes and duties on the goods.

Gardes-françaises   An elite royal infantry regiment, many of whom deserted to join opponents of the King in July 1789.

Gendarmes   An organisation set up by the National Assembly in December 1790, which operated as an armed police force.

General Maximum   Tables that fix the prices of a wide range of foods and commodities.

Généralités   The 34 areas into which France was divided for the purpose of collecting taxes and other administrative functions; each area was under the control of an *intendant*.

Germinal   Popular demonstration on 1 April 1795 in Paris. Named after a month in the new revolutionary calendar.

Girondins   A small group of deputies from the Gironde and their associates, notably Brissot.

Grande Armée   Napoleon's renamed army after 1805. At its largest in 1812 it numbered over 600,000 men, among them Poles, Italians, Swiss and Bavarians.

Great Powers   Countries that were more powerful than others on the basis of their military, economic and territorial strength – the major ones were Austria, France, Prussia, Russia and Britain.

Gross domestic product   The total value of goods and services produced by an economy.

Guerrilla warfare   Military action by irregular bands avoiding direct confrontation with the larger opposing forces. They did not wear uniforms in order to blend in with civilians.

Guild   An organisation that tightly controls entry into a trade.

Guillotine   A machine introduced in 1792 for decapitating victims in a relatively painless way. It became synonymous with the Terror.

Habsburg Empire   Territory that roughly corresponds to modern-day Austria, Hungary, the Czech Republic and Slovakia. The empire also considered itself to be the leading German state.

Hoarders   Those who bought up supplies of food, keeping them until prices rose and then selling them at a large profit.

Iberian peninsula   Spain and Portugal combined.

Indulgents   Supporters of Danton and Desmoulins who wished to see a relaxation of the Terror.

Industrial capitalism   An economic system where money (capital) is invested in industry for the purpose of making a profit.

Inflation   A decline in the value of money, which leads to an increase in the price of goods.

Insurrection   An uprising of ordinary people, predominantly *sans-culottes*.

Intendants   Officials directly appointed by and answerable to the Crown who were mainly responsible for police, justice, finance, public works, and trade and industry.

Irish Nationalists   Irish who were staunchly anti-British and wished to be free from what they considered foreign rule. During the Revolution they approached the republicans for support.

Jeunesse dorée   'Gilded youth': young men who dressed extravagantly as a reaction to the restrictions of the Terror. They were also known as Muscadins.

Journée   Day of popular action and disturbance linked to great political change.

La Marseillaise   The rousing song composed by Rouget de l'Isle in 1792 and adopted as the anthem of the Republic on 14 July 1795.

La patrie en danger   'The fatherland is in danger' became a rallying cry to ordinary people to help save the country.

Laboureurs   The upper level of the peasantry who owned a plough and hired labour to work their land.

Laissez-faire   Non-interference in economic matters, so that trade and industry should be free from state interference.

Law of Hostages   Relatives of any French citizens opposing the Republic would be imprisoned at their own expense and their property seized to pay for damage done by anti-government rebels.

Law of Prairial   The most severe of the laws passed by the revolutionary government. The purpose of the law was to reform the Revolutionary Tribunal to secure more convictions. The law paved the way for the Great Terror.

Law of Suspects   Anyone suspected of counter-revolutionary activity and undermining the Republic could be arrested and held without trial indefinitely.

Laws of Ventose   Property of those recognised as enemies of the Revolution could be seized and distributed among the poor.

Le Moniteur   The official government journal.

Left   Those seated on the left of the speaker of the Legislative Assembly favouring extreme policies such as removing the King and having a republic.

Legion of Honour   A high-status organisation created by Napoleon to bind powerful men to his regime through granting them titles and rewards.

Legislative Assembly   Came into existence in October 1791 and was the second elected Assembly to rule during the Revolution. It differed from the National/Constituent Assembly in that all members were directly elected.

Legislative power   The power to make laws. In an absolute system this power belongs to the Crown, while in a democracy it rests with elected representatives.

Lettres de cachet   Sealed instructions from the Crown allowing detention without trial of a named individual.

Levée en masse   All the resources of the State – people, buildings and resources – put at its disposal for military use.

Levy   An assessment to raise an agreed number of conscripts.

Liberalism   A political belief that stresses the rights and liberties of the individual.

Liberals   Deputies who were far more tolerant of differing political views and who supported a measure of cautious reform.

Livres   France's currency during the *ancien régime*. In 1789, 1 *livre* was roughly 8p in today's money.

Livret   A combined work permit and record of employment.

Lycées   Selective schools introduced in 1802 for educating the sons of the privileged.

Mandats territoriaux   The new paper currency issued by the Directory in March 1796 and withdrawn in February 1797, when worth only one per cent of face value.

Martial law   The suspension of civil liberties by the State in an attempt to restore public order when there is severe rioting and mass disobedience.

Marxist historians   Those who interpret the Revolution as part of Marx's analysis of history as a series of class-based struggles, resulting ultimately in the triumph of the proletariat.

Menu peuple   Used to describe ordinary people living in towns.

Militants   Those who differed from ordinary *sans-culottes* in that they adopted an extreme political position such as arguing for a republic, greater democracy and the destruction of privilege.

Mobilising   Calling up part-time soldiers or national guardsmen for military service.

Monarchist   Active supporter of the Bourbon monarchy.

Montagnards   The Mountain – the name given to Jacobin deputies who occupied the upper seats to the left of the speaker in the tiered chamber of the National Assembly.

Mortality rate   The death rate, which is measured per 1000 of the population.

National debt   Money borrowed by the government from its own people in the form of bonds and loans, on which it has to pay interest. This debt increased during the Revolution and the war.

National self-determination   The right of national groups such as Italians, Poles and Germans to govern themselves.

National synod   An assembly of representatives of the entire Church.

Nationalised   Taken in to state control.

Natural frontiers   Barriers, such as rivers, mountain ranges and the sea, that separate countries.

Non-commissioned officers   Soldiers with ranks such as corporal or sergeant.

Non-jurors   Those members of the clergy who refused to take the new oath of allegiance to the Civil Constitution.

Notables   Rich, powerful individuals; the elite who controlled the political and economic life of France.

Paris Sections   Paris was divided into 48 Sections to replace the 60 electoral districts of 1789; the Section became the power base of the *sans-culottes*.

Parlementaire   Judges who held hereditary positions on one of the thirteen *parlements*.

Parlements   The 13 high courts of appeal. All edicts handed down by the Crown had to be registered by the *parlements* before they could be enforced as law.

Partage   An estate is divided equally among all male heirs, unlike during the *ancien régime* when the eldest male heir inherited everything.

Passive citizens   Approximately 2.7 million citizens who enjoyed the civic rights provided by the Declaration of the Rights of Man, but paid insufficient taxes to qualify for a vote.

Patriot party   A loose group of progressive reformers, mainly nobles and bourgeoisie, who wanted changes to the political structure – a reduction in royal power in order to enhance their own positions.

Patronage   The process of distributing gifts and favours in order to build up support.

Pays d'états   Areas that had local representative assemblies of the three estates that contributed to the assessment and collection of royal taxes.

Penal code   A list of the laws of France and the punishments for breaking those laws.

Per capita   An economic measure used to determine output, calculated by dividing the volume or value of production by the number of people in the population.

Philosophes   A group of writers and thinkers who formed the core of the French Enlightenment.

Physiocrats   A group of French intellectuals who believed that land was the only source of wealth and that landowners should therefore pay the bulk of taxes.

Picketing   The practice of strikers trying to persuade others to join in.

The Plain   The majority of deputies in the Convention who sat on the lower seats of the tiered assembly hall.

Plebiscite   A popular vote on a single issue.

Plurality   The holding of more than one bishopric or parish by an individual.

Politicisation   A process in which people who were previously unconcerned with politics take an active interest in political issues which affect their daily lives.

Popular movement   Crowds of politically active Parisians who periodically took to the streets to protest.

Popular sovereignty   The idea that the people should exercise control over their government, usually by directly electing a representative assembly.

Prairial   A large popular uprising in Paris on 20–1 May 1795. It was named after a month in the new revolutionary calendar.

Prefect   A centrally appointed government official whose task was to administer a department and ensure that government policy was carried out.

Primary assemblies   Meeting places for voters.

Purge   Forced removal of political opponents.

Rapprochement   The restoration of friendly relations between countries or people previously hostile.

Real wages   The actual purchasing power of money.

Refractory priests   Those priests who refused to take the oath.

Regicides   Those involved in the trial and execution of Louis XVI.

Regular army   Full-time professional soldiers. As events unfolded the white uniforms of the *ancien régime* were replaced by ones that reflected the colours of the Revolution: red, white and blue.

Representatives-on-mission   Mainly Jacobin deputies from the Convention sent to various parts of France to reassert government authority.

Republic   A political system which does not have a hereditary head of state and where the supremacy of the people is recognised through mass democracy.

Requisitioning   Compulsory purchase by the government of supplies of food and horses paid for in *assignats* – the new paper currency.

Revisionist historians   Those who reject Marxist analysis and provide a revised interpretation.

Revolutionary myth   The frequently misguided belief that direct revolutionary action can bring about significant material improvement for the majority of society.

Revolutionary Tribunal   A court specialising in trying those accused of counter-revolutionary activities.

Revolutionary War   Fought by France against other European powers between 1792 and 1802.

Right   Those seated on the right of the speaker of the Legislative Assembly and supporting a limited monarchy.

Saint-Cloud   A former royal palace in the suburbs of Paris away from the influence of Paris, where the plotters believed that Jacobinism was still a powerful force.

Sans-culottes   Literally 'those without knee-breeches': those who wore trousers and were classed as workers. It was later used as a label to identify the more extreme urban revolutionaries of 1792–5.

Satellite republics   States that had the appearance of being independent but were in reality under French control. Also known as 'sister republics'.

Satellite state   A state that is subservient to another, and cannot act independently.

Scorched earth   A policy of destroying all food and shelter in front of an invading army to deny them essential supplies.

Séance royale   Session of the Estates-General in the presence of the monarch.

Second Coalition   Formed in 1799 and consisting of Britain, Russia, Austria, Turkey, Portugal and Naples.

Self-denying ordinance   Members of the National Assembly were not permitted to stand for election to the new Legislative Assembly.

Senatus-consultum   A procedure giving the Senate rights to preserve and amend the constitution and to agree major constitutional changes that Napoleon wished to introduce independently of the legislative body.

Separation of Church and State   The Republic was legally committed to religious neutrality. In order to serve their parishioners, priests were required to follow French law as opposed to Church law.

Separation of powers   The division of executive and legislative powers so that the government could not make laws without the support of the legislature.

Serfdom   A system in which people were the property of the landowner.

Skirmishers   A small group of soldiers who operate independently, fighting minor engagements and living off the land.

Social interpretation   An emphasis on changes in society – population trends, social class – as having a significant impact on the Revolution.

Spanish ulcer   Used by Napoleon as a term for a wound that weakens the victim without ever being fatal.

State monopoly   A system whereby the State exercises total control over an industry and can set whatever price it wishes.

Summary execution decree   From 19 March 1793 any rebels captured with arms were to be executed immediately.

Suspensive veto   The right to delay a measure proposed by the Assembly.

Tax farming   A system where the government agrees a tax assessment figure for an area, which is then collected by a company that bids for the right to collect it.

Tax rolls   Lists of citizens who had to pay taxes to the State.

The Terror   The period roughly covering March 1793 to August 1794 when extreme policies were used by the Jacobin government to ensure the survival of the Republic.

Terrorist   An active supporter of the policies of the Terror.

Thermidor   A month in the new revolutionary calendar, equivalent to 19 July to 17 August.

Thermidorians   Those individuals and groups who had helped to overthrow Robespierre.

Total war   All aspects of the State – population, economy and buildings – were used by the government to try and ensure victory.

Tricolore   The symbol of the Revolution. It combined the red and blue colours of Paris with the white of the Bourbons.

United Provinces   Present-day Netherlands, ruled at the time by the House of Orange.

Universal male suffrage   A vote for every man over a certain age.

Venality   The sale and purchase of certain jobs which could be inherited by descendants.

Verona Declaration   A reactionary statement issued by the new heir to the throne promising to reverse many of the gains made during the Revolution.

Versailles   The royal palace of the Bourbons and the seat of royal government built outside Paris by Louis XIV.

Vertu   Virtue – meaning moral excellence.

Voting by head   Decisions taken by the Estates-General would be agreed by a simple vote with a majority sufficient to agree any policy. This favoured the Third Estate, which had the most deputies.

Voting by order   Each estate votes separately on any issue. Any two estates together would outvote the third.

Further reading

Books relevant to the whole period

Richard Cobb and Colin Jones, *The French Revolution: Voices from a Momentous Epoch, 1789–1795* (Simon & Schuster, 1988)

Large format and well-illustrated survey of the Revolution containing many source extracts

William Doyle, *The Oxford History of the French Revolution*, second edition (Oxford University Press, 2002)

One of the best studies of the period up to 1802, informed, scholarly and very readable

François Furet, *Interpreting the French Revolution* (Cambridge University Press, 1981)

Revisionist interpretation of the Revolution by a leading French academic

John Hardman, *The French Revolution Sourcebook* (Arnold, 1999)

A comprehensive and broad selection of sources with useful commentaries, covering the period 1776–95

Colin Jones, *The Longman Companion to the French Revolution* (Longman, 1988)

The indispensable single-volume guide to most matters of factual content, events, statistics, structures, people and so on, covering the period 1774–1800

George Rudé, *The French Revolution* (Weidenfeld & Nicholson, 1988)

An authoritative work that takes in the Napoleonic period and considers the wider legacy of the Revolution post-1815

Simon Schama, *Citizens* (Viking, 1989)

Hugely popular and entertaining narrative survey of the Revolution, crammed with anecdotes and detail

Albert Soboul, *The French Revolution 1787–1799* (Unwin, 1989)

The classic Marxist textbook of the Revolution by one of its greatest scholars

Chapter 1

John Hardman, *French Politics 1774–1789* (Longman, 1995)

Informed study of the origins of the Revolution with a clear emphasis on the political machinations

John Hardman, *Louis XVI* (Arnold, 2000)

An attempt to reassess Louis' reputation in the light of new sources

Georges Lefebvre, *The Coming of the French Revolution* (Vintage Books, 1995)

The origins of the Revolution from a Marxist perspective

J.H. Shennan, *France before the Revolution* (Methuen, 1983)

A short synthesis of the key problems that led to the Revolution

Chapter 2

Jacques Godechot, *The Taking of the Bastille, July 14th 1789* (Faber & Faber, 1970)

An important study of the events leading up to 14 July 1789

Munro Price, *The Fall of the French Monarchy* (Pan, 2002)

A gripping account of the fall of the French monarchy drawn from a wide range of contemporary sources

Chapter 3

Nigel Aston, *Religion and Revolution in France, 1780–1804* (Macmillan, 2000)

A very thorough and detailed examination of the impact of the Revolution on the Catholic Church and other religious groups

P.M. Jones, *The Peasantry and the French Revolution* (Cambridge University Press, 1988)

Excellent and unique study on one of the largest groups in eighteenth-century French society

Michael L. Kennedy, *The Jacobin Clubs in the French Revolution, 1793–1795* (Berghahn Books, 2000)

Detailed and informative assessment of the rise of the Jacobin clubs

John McManners, *The French Revolution and the Church* (SPCK, 1969)

One of the best concise academic studies of the impact of the Revolution on the Catholic Church

Chapter 4

T.C.W. Blanning, *The Origins of The French Revolutionary Wars* (Longman, 1986)

A very useful and detailed guide to these wars

Andrew Freeman, editor, *The Compromising of Louis XVI. The Armoire de Fer and the French Revolution* (University of Liverpool Press, 1989)

A dispassionate survey of the contents of the *armoire de fer*. Contains many source extracts

Michel Vovelle, *The Fall of the French Monarchy 1787–1792* (Cambridge University Press, 1984)

A clear and effective analysis of the events leading up to the overthrow of the monarchy

Michael Walzer, *Regicide and Revolution* (Cambridge University Press, 1974)

Detailed focus on Louis' trial, contains many of the speeches delivered by the leading protagonists

Chapter 5

David Andress, *The Terror: Civil War in the French Revolution* (Little Brown, 2005)

An illuminating overview of the Terror

Josh Brooman, *The Reign of Terror in France. Jean-Baptiste Carrier and the Drownings at Nantes* (Longman, 1986)

Brief account of one of the most violent episode of the Terror, contains many unique source extracts

Hugh Gough, *The Terror in the French Revolution* (Palgrave, 1998)

An excellent introduction to the Terror, contains a very detailed bibliographical guide

Peter McPhee, *Robespierre: A Revolutionary Life* (Yale University Press, 2012)

Convincing and powerful examination of one of the most controversial figures of the Revolution

Ruth Scurr, *Fatal Purity: Robespierre and the French Revolution* (Chatto & Windus, 2006)

A thought-provoking and stimulating account of Robespierre and the Terror, particularly compelling when considering his idealism

Albert Soboul, *The Parisian* Sans-Culottes *and the French Revolution* (Oxford University Press, 1964)

Classic Marxist account of the impact of this revolutionary group

Charles Tilly, *The Vendée* (Edward Arnold, 1964)

One of the best accounts of the civil war in western France

Sophie Wahnich, *In Defence of the Terror* (Verso, 2012)

Thought-provoking account which seeks to justify the Terror

Chapter 6

Georges Lefebvre, *The Directory* (Routledge & Kegan Paul, 1965)

A somewhat dated but still valuable Marxist account of the Directory from one of the Revolution's greatest historians

M.J. Sydenham, *The First French Republic 1792–1804* (Batsford, 1974)

Well-presented and clear analysis of the strengths and weaknesses of the First Republic

Denis Woronoff, *The Thermidorian Regime and the Directory 1794–1799* (Cambridge University Press, 1984)

Clear and comprehensive introduction to five years of infighting that paved the way for Napoleon

Chapter 7

Florin Aftalion, *The French Revolution: An Economic Interpretation* (Cambridge University Press, 1990)

Offers a detailed insight into the impact of the Revolution on the French economy

Alfred Cobban, *The Social Interpretation of the French Revolution* **(Cambridge University Press, 1964)**

The first work to challenge the dominance of the Marxist interpretation and offer an alternative view

Peter Davies, *The Debate on the French Revolution* **(Manchester University Press, 2006)**

Thought-provoking and stimulating survey of interpretations of the French Revolution

Gary Kates, editor, *The French Revolution: Recent Debates and New Controversies* **(Routledge, 1998)**

A wide-ranging collection of essays from some of the leading lights in their fields

Gwynne Lewis, *French Revolution: Rethinking the Debate* **(Routledge & Kegan Paul, 1993)**

Balanced and stimulating summation of the debate surrounding the French Revolution

Chapter 8

Michael Broers, *Napoleon: Soldier of Destiny* **(Faber & Faber, 2014)**

A powerful and evocative biography which offers both a critical overview of Napoleon's life and an empathetic insight into the society which propelled his career

Philip Dwyer, *Napoleon: The Path to Power 1769–1799*, **Vol. 1 (Bloomsbury, 2007);** *Citizen Emperor: Napoleon in Power 1799–1815*, **Vol. 2 (Bloomsbury, 2014)**

The most detailed and authoritative account of the Emperor's career in two volumes

Geoffrey Ellis, *Napoleon* **(Longman, 1997)**

Though-provoking survey of Napoleon in power

Charles Esdaile, *Napoleon's Wars* **(Penguin, 2007)**

Detailed and important analysis of Napoleon's wars by a leading expert in the field

Pieter Geyl, *Napoleon: For and Against* **(Peregrine Books, 1965)**

Classic synthesis of a wide range of studies on Napoleon, compiled by a leading Dutch academic between 1940 and 1945 while under the yoke of Nazi occupation

Robert B. Holtman, *The Napoleonic Revolution* **(Louisiana State University Press, 1995)**

An informative account of the changes made by Napoleon in both France and Europe

Martyn Lyons, *Napoleon Bonaparte and the Legacy of the French Revolution* **(Palgrave, 1994)**

Accessible and effective coverage of the entire Napoleonic period

Andrew Roberts, *Napoleon the Great* **(Allen Lane, 2014)**

Detailed and sympathetic biography of Napoleon, as one of history's 'great men'

Film

Andrzej Wajda, *Danton* **(1983)**

A critically acclaimed and powerful French-language film about the deteriorating relations between Robespierre and Danton. One of the best films about the French Revolution

Index